HARLEM: NEGRO METROPOLIS

Books by Claude McKay

SONGS OF JAMAICA

SPRING IN NEW HAMPSHIRE

HARLEM SHADOWS

HOME TO HARLEM

BANJO

GINGERTOWN

BANANA BOTTOM

A LONG WAY FROM HOME

HARLEM: NEGRO METROPOLIS

SELECTED POEMS

Photo by Lewis

HARLEM:
NEGRO METROPOLIS

By

CLAUDE McKAY

Illustrated with Photographs

A HARVEST BOOK

HARCOURT BRACE JOVANOVICH, INC.

NEW YORK

Acknowledgments

Communist Negro pamphlets published prior to the time of the Popular Front graciously were placed at the disposal of the author by Harlem's pioneer Communist, Miss Grace Campbell.

The details of Marcus Garvey's latter days on the island of Jamaica are largely from the personal report of an eyewitness, Simon Williamson of Kansas City, Mo., who was a student delegate to the Jamaica Convention of 1929. Mr. Williamson remained in Jamaica as a student of the Philosophy of Marcus Garvey. He has also generously made available his considerable collection of Negro material, consisting of pamphlets, excerpts from various articles and newspaper cuttings.

Mr. Collis H. Crocker furnished a batch of broadsides of Harlem's recent political campaigns.

Mrs. Catherine Latimer, Reference Librarian in the Negro Division of the 135th Street Branch Library, was very helpful with enlightening information and items from her collection of cuttings from Negro newspapers.

Mr. Francis O. Minor provided invaluable material from his collection of newspapers, magazine articles and broadsides of the Sufi movement, supplemented by intimate personal experience of his late chief, Sufi Abdul Hamid.

To check up on and verify leads and facts there were informal conversations with the following persons:

Columbus Austin
Mrs. Dorothy Bayen
Kenneth Bright
W. A. Domingo
Count Gary

Rufus Gibson,
   135th St. Library assistant
Y. Hikida
Dr. Willis N. Huggins
Ben Mandel

Dr. Peter Marshall Murray   Madame Dorothy Fu Futtam
Dr. C. B. Powell   Arnold P. Johnson
A. Phillip Randolph   Attorney Arthur Madison
Arthur Reid   Henry Lee Moon
Floyd G. Snelson   Rev. A. C. Powell, Jr.
Justice James S. Watson   Theodore Poston
Charles White   Realtor John W. Walker
Wilfred R. Bain   Edward K. Welsh
Romare Bearden   Harold Williams
Frank Crosswaith

Also the Democratic leaders of the 21st and 19th Assembly Districts respectively, Herbert P. Bruce and Assemblyman Daniel L. Burrows; former Alderman and President of the Harlem Association of Trade and Commerce, George W. Harris; Matthew Eder, Secretary, Uptown Chamber of Commerce; Caspar Holstein, Proprietor of the Turf Club; Captain A. L. King, President New York Division (Marcus Garvey's) U. N. I. A.; Thomas W. Tilghman, Proprietor, The Hollywood Bar and Grill; Edna Thomas, Secretary, Negro Actors Guild; Mabel Keaton Staupers, R. N., Executive Secretary, National Association of Colored Graduate Nurses; Wayman A. Evans, President New York City Branch of National Alliance of Postal Employees and James M. Kinloch of the Board of Directors; Rev. John H. Johnson, Rector, St. Martin's Episcopal Church; Mr. John Lamb, Secretary to Father Divine.

And in the Puerto Rican Colony, Assemblyman Oscar Garcia Rivera; Library Assistants Pura Bellpré and Rose Montero; Vincent Medina, Manager Teatro Hispano; Guillermo Martinez and Benigno de Jesus of the Puerto Rican Employees Association and Gumersindo Plano.

The author wishes to thank *The American Mercury* for giving him permission to use small portions of material which appear in this book in modified form.

Contents

List of Illustrations

HARLEM: NEGRO METROPOLIS

Harlem Vista

Harlem: Negro Capital of the Nation is the title of a column which appears in a large bloc of the nation's Aframerican weeklies. But critics in other cities have challenged the claim with facetious taunts and jabs at Harlem. Some jeer at Harlem as the capital of clowns whose fame rests upon cults and cabarets. They say that Harlem is a vast circus in which the people seem satisfied with an army of noise makers who swing in the dance halls and sing wildly in peace kingdoms; that they love spectacular parades of drums and uniforms, and prancing on the pavements by day and jiving in the honkey-tonks by night.

These critics do not regard Harlem as a typical American Negro community, such as exists in Chicago, New Orleans, Atlanta and Durham. Such communities are more sober and balanced than Harlem, which is hectic and fluid. Harlem *is* lacking in group solidarity and the high seriousness of other Aframerican communities. Even intellectually, Harlem is backward, some contend, although it has more well-paid teachers and excellent schools, libraries and librarians than any other black belt. For the widely circulated national Negro weeklies are not located in Harlem. They are published in Pittsburgh, Chicago and Baltimore, and in comparison with them the Harlem weeklies are provincial.

There is plenty of truth in the arguments made by the critics of Harlem. Harlem is a piece of New York. And exactly as New York is not the typical American city, similar to one in the Middle West or the Southeast, so Harlem is no black Chicago or Durham, N. C. But as the metropolis of New York attracts America and the rest of the world, so does Harlem, in a lesser sense, make its appeal to the Negroes of America and of the world.

Harlem is the queen of black belts, drawing Aframericans together into a vast humming hive. They have swarmed in from the different states, from the islands of the Caribbean and from Africa. And they still are coming in spite of the grim misery that lurks behind the inviting façades. Overcrowded tenements, the harsh Northern climate and unemployment do not daunt them. Harlem remains the magnet.

Harlem is more than the Negro capital of the nation. It is the Negro capital of the world. And as New York is the most glorious experiment on earth of different races and divers groups of humanity struggling and scrambling to live together, so Harlem is the most interesting sample of black humanity marching along with white humanity. Sometimes it lags behind, but nevertheless it is impelled and carried along by the irresistible strength of the movement of the white world.

Like a flock of luxuriant, large-lipped orchids spreading over the side of a towering rock, the color of African life has boldly splashed itself upon the north end of Manhattan. From the nucleus of a comparatively few years ago it has grown like an expansive tropical garden, springing naturally from the Northern soil.

Four decades ago the artistic and social expression of Aframerican life was centered in West 53rd Street. Musicians, actors and journalists established clubs there. There they socialized among themselves, with other professional persons of their group and with white friends, mainly stage folk.

The black masses then resided in the thirties in the area around the Pennsylvania Railroad station. In San Juan Hill large numbers were wedged in among the Irish population. But Brooklyn was preferred by the respectable and exclusive families. There homes were bought or leased by the old Negro butlers of Knickerbocker families, the reliable bank messengers, caterers and head waiters of downtown clubs and hotels. Brooklyn had this advantage over Manhattan: there Aframericans were not herded together in a single quarter.

And the houses had spacious backyards and gardens in which their children could play.

In Manhattan the Aframericans always led a cramped existence. Even the 53rd Street district was not a congenial quarter. Day and night a thunderous racket came from the elevated trains overhead. And only its proximity to Broadway made residence there tolerable. The blocks around the Pennsylvania Station were overflowing with blacks. And San Juan Hill was notorious for the interracial strife between Aframericans and Irish.

The black people had to expand somewhere in Manhattan. Any realtor who could find a new location would make money. Scouting for an opening, an enterprising Negro realtor, Phillip A. Payton, discovered that there was ample room in Harlem, where many new apartment houses were standing empty.

White Manhattanites in increasing numbers were moving farther northwards and a building boom was under way. But the section of Harlem spotted by the black realtor did not quite suit the better class of whites. It was like the tangible boundary between the East Side and the West Side.

The first apartment house rented to colored tenants was located in 134th Street near Fifth Avenue. It was immediately filled up. Other houses were allotted. And like a pebble making ripples in a pool, the Aframericans began spreading away from that first block into others. But they went westwards among the middle classes of respectable whites.

As the Aframericans pushed forward from Fifth towards Seventh Avenue, the black invasion alarmed the white residents. They feared the permanent quartering of an army of them in the highly desirable section of Upper Manhattan. Patriotic old residents banded together to stem the onrushing black tide. They attempted to buy out houses occupied by colored tenants and have them vacated. They strove to prevent white realtors from selling or renting to black folk. They sought to evoke city ordinances as quarantine measures.

But certain social factors worked in favor of the blacks. Most potent was the power of money. The blacks willingly paid from a hundred to two hundred per cent more than did the whites. And they paid promptly in those days. They were eager to prove themselves good tenants, worthy of living in a better residental district. Penned in the gangster-ruled blocks of lower Manhattan, they were bound to expand or explode. Already there were indications of serious inter-racial trouble growing out of savage incidents in Hell's Kitchen, the Tenderloin and San Juan Hill.

Faced with opposition, the Aframerican realtors resorted to stratagem to develop Negro Harlem. They got "fronts" to make certain contacts and deals. The fair-skinned members of the group were used as decoys. Posing as whites, they achieved better bargains. A Chinaman doing business in the neighborhood was a "front" for many years in acquiring property for Aframericans. Other factors helped. Sometimes a Jewish landlord, affronted by gentiles, retaliated by selling or leasing to Negroes. And when white tenants proved unreliable, a colored family accommodated in the building would frighten them into leaving.

The Aframericans paid a formidable price, however, to obtain and consolidate the new territory. In the lowest bracket of wage earners, they were living in houses beyond their means. They were compelled to do considerable doubling up to pay that rent and otherwise exist. Two and three families rented an apartment together. And all families rented rooms. Every space was utilized—sometimes bathrooms were improvised as bedrooms—to meet the rent. Dignified private houses were made over into rooming houses.

The black masses were attracted from everywhere by the greater living space of Harlem. And soon the churches followed. In the beginning of the movement to Harlem most of the churches were concentrated in the Pennsylvania Station section. Chapels in Harlem were temporarily established in front rooms of private houses. When the migration became an exodus the churches began adjusting themselves to the shift of population. Between 1910 and 1922 all the large churches disposed of their property downtown and moved to Harlem, where white people's churches were bought and a few new churches built.

Even before the arrival of the Aframericans, Harlem was a place of innumerable churches, Presbyterian, Lutheran, Baptist, Methodist, Adventist, Roman Catholic, Jewish and Congregational. The white residents retreated far westward and northward, but their churches remained for a time. And one of the curious spectacles of the earlier settlement of Harlem with Aframericans was the processions of white congregations that returned each Sunday to Harlem to worship God. This unusual Sunday feature came to an end when colored congregations purchased the white churches. Often the transaction was made by a colored congregation's taking over the white church of its own faith. There still remain a few white churches in the midst of the blacks, but the public seem hardly aware of them.

It was the fact that the churches followed the masses that induced conservative colored families to consider Harlem a proper residential section. Hitherto the "quality" Negroes in Harlem were mainly members of the theatrical and cabaret sets. The cabarets were the first establishments to move from downtown to Harlem. And they attracted that theatrical and bohemian set of whites who were *aficionados* of Negro entertainment. The leading cabaretiers of the period, Conners, Barron Wilkins, Leroy Wilkins and Edmonds, operated large and extravagantly decorated places. And soon Harlem became more than locally famous as an amusement center.

The World War brought great waves of southern Negroes to the industrial centers of the North. And many settled in Harlem. At the end of the war the Aframerican population was limited to the district between 130th and 143rd Street, from Fifth to Eighth Avenue. But this quarter had become extremely congested and the residents were cautiously pushing down to 125th Street and over beyond Eighth Avenue.

Suddenly national attention was focussed on Harlem. A grandiose pan-African movement started there by the

West Indian, Marcus Aurelius Garvey, stirred American and West Indian Negroes to wild enthusiasm. Mammoth meetings and enthusiastic parades glittering with gorgeous uniforms were organized in Harlem. Branches quickly spread throughout the states. The movement's slogan was, "Africa for Africans." Its general programme aimed at political, cultural, and commercial relationship between Africans and Negroes abroad, and an Africa freed from European domination.

It was African Zionism. And it received an amazing acclaim from Aframericans. The idea was conceived of a Black Star Line of ships. A stock company was promoted and thousands of shares sold. Aframericans had benefited by plenty of work and higher wages during the war. And they poured their money into the stupendous scheme of African redemption.

As headquarters of the movement, Harlem became nationally and internationally famous.

When the Garvey movement first attracted world attention, 1918-1919, the solid Black Belt extended from 127th to 145th Street between Fifth and Eighth Avenues. From 125th Street to 110th Street, Jews dominated. The breaking of the boundaries coincided with the rise of the pan-African movement. Also the influx of the darker-hued Puerto Ricans and other Latin Americans speeded the change. The Puerto Ricans began penetrating lower Harlem from 110th Street up. And as they pushed up and over from the East Side, the Aframericans surged down to meet them.

The Negro Quarter Grows Up

Vastly different is the Negro Harlem of today from what it was when the First World War ended. Central Park now forms its Southern frontier. It stretches from Morningside Avenue to Lexington and, sweeping up from 110th Street and skirting the Harlem River, it abruptly takes the hill and extends to 164th Street. Then coming down Amsterdam Avenue, it embraces Convent Avenue to 141st Street and turns off, dropping down under the high terrace of the College of the City of New York. It follows the margin of Harlem-under-the-hill up to 129th Street. Then it strikes across further west and zig-zags in and out among white houses and almost seems lost. But hard by the Lincoln school fronting the park at 123rd Street it captures Morningside Avenue and runs down under Columbia University Heights to 110th Street.

Holding the handle of Manhattan, this special African-American area is like no other in New York. It lacks the oppressive drabness of the East Side. It is more comparable with Chinatown, which, although it has slum features, does not exude the atmosphere of the slums. Harlem is like the glorified servant quarters of a vast estate. It has that appearance, perhaps, because the majority of Aframericans are domestics, who live in imitation of their white employers, although upon a lower level. The distinction of Harlem is unlike the huddle of European minorities in New York. The essential quality of the latter is the magic of foreign languages and particular national traits which are emphasized in everyday living. But as Aframericans express themselves in the common American idiom and have shed all the externals of African traits, the distinguishing characteristic of Harlem lies in the varied features and the African color of its residents.

Perhaps it is easier for the eye to appreciate Harlem than for the heart to understand. Harlem is noisy and its noises strike the eye as loudly as they do the ear. Because the district is congested, the street corners and bars provide an outlet as forums and clubs. Children swarm in the streets, although the new playgrounds are full of them.

Groups of children persistently practise the Lindy Hop all over Harlem, as if they were all training to be expert dancers. The allure and longevity of the Lindy Hop are prodigious. Countless other dances of the jazz age have been created and highly publicized, and have tickled the people's feet. But after a hectic time they have been discarded, forgotten. But the Lindy Hop has remained in Harlem, competing for life everlasting with the fox-trot and tango. With its pattern, Harlem's children make fantasy on the pavement. When a new piece is put in the nickel-odeon of a bar and it lilts to the Lindy Hop, the kids come together on the pavement to dance. Since they are not permitted to enter, they sometimes ask adults to put coins in the machine to give them music. Utterly oblivious of oldsters passing or watching, they dance with an eagerness and freshness that is even rustic. They put a magic in the Lindy Hop that it does not possess as an exhibition dance, which primarily it is. They make a folk dance of it.

Visually, Harlem creates the impression of a mass of people all existing on the same plane. Even the natives are generally unaware of the prestige of their own notables. The pace-makers who, fashionably dressed, flash along the avenue in splendid cars have mostly been identified with the racketeering class of numbers "kings" and "queens," bootleggers, hot stuff fences, and the rest. Downtown, a gentleman wearing a top hat or a lady in a mink coat may stir the casual observer to imagine a big banker or industrialist or a dowager or debutante of the exclusive hundreds. But to the average Harlemite, and also to the white police, the top-hatted gentleman and his lady might be a Pullman porter with his lady going to a formal dance at the Renaissance or just a big time procurer.

The first thought of the casual onlooker is not that the gentleman of color may be a professional person or a wealthy realtor. There are many such in Harlem with dinner coats and tails, but there is no opera, no Waldorf Astoria where they may go. There is no other minority group in New York having such an extraordinary diversity of individuals of achievement and wealth who are compelled to live in the midst of the mass. Inexorably the individual is identified with the mass and measured by its standards.

The efforts of the Harlem élite to create an oasis of respectability within the boundaries of Aframerica is strenuous and pathetic. Their number is considerable; doctors and dentists, lawyers and politicians, businessmen, teachers, nurses, successful actors and musicians, government employees and the large corps of social workers. Quite a group of them, but not large enough to establish an exclusive residential district. Wherever they move, the common people follow and threaten to submerge them.

They have succeeded, but just a little, in making a few blocks slightly more desirable than the rest of Harlem. The best result is the block of buildings in 139th Street, between 7th and 8th Avenues, which was designed by the celebrated Stanford White. The houses are private, and when the whites decided to move out, in 1920, a colored group banded together to buy them and keep the section exclusive. The tree-shaded block still retains some of its quiet air of respectability. But it lacks much of the elegance of its lily-white days. The Negroes rent rooms there as they do in every other block in Harlem. And the spacious back alleys with gardens, attesting to Stanford White's fine idea of city planning, are now dilapidated and garbage-strewn. The residents keep a sharp lookout for undesirable intruders. Recently the Colored Fraternal Order of Elks was compelled to vacate its premises in the block, because it was considered a nuisance. But Father Divine immediately set up a kingdom there. The residents attempted to oust him. But Father Divine fought back and declared that God was no respecter of persons. So Striver's Row had to make its peace with the "kingdom" of Heaven. Adjusting itself to the dignity of the block, the "kingdom" is a very decorous place. No heavy stomping or cacophonous shouting is heard there. And daily it dispenses ten-cent meals to many respectable Negroes in need.

Long famed for creating an atmosphere of sylvan retreat in the heart of Manhattan, the Block Beautiful—130th Street between Lenox and Fifth Avenue—has not, like Striver's Row, managed to keep its end up. It still bravely exhibits the little lawn patches before the low porticoed brick houses and the row of luxuriant trees, which gave it the appearance of a nice corner of a German garden town. But its perfect trimness has disappeared. The neat fences are broken, the gates unhinged and leaning awry, the sidewalk unkempt.

The original congregation of the massive grey pile of the Presbyterian Church of the Puritans, at the Northeast corner, held the church for many years after the block was ceded to the blacks. What a tale that block could tell of the strange dark-hued horde sweeping down upon it! But it stood almost virginal white while the Negroes milled around it and headed towards 125th Street. Then in 1922 a Negro bought the first house in the block. Gradually the others went black. And by 1925 the block was entirely colored, excepting the mansion of the Widow MacLean. The Church of the Puritans remained white until 1933. Then it became Aframerican Saint Ambrose Episcopal with a West Indian preacher, a majority of West Indian worshippers and a ritual closely following the Church of England.

The last white landmark of the block, the mansion of the Widow MacLean, disappeared in the spring of 1937. The house was adjacent to the Church of the Puritans and the grounds covered between 130th and 131st Street. The owner had lived in the great establishment 53 years. When finally the Block Beautiful capitulated to the dark invasion and all the white residents had fled, she refused to sell and remained the only white survivor. With a retinue of servants, she maintained the place in grand style, and it suggested a medieval castle with poor retainers squatting in the surrounding land. She became reconciled to the presence of the newcomers and was friendly and charitable to the poor among them.

It was Park Commissioner Moses' idea that the place could be turned into an excellent playground for the poor children of the neighborhood. He persuaded the Widow MacLean at the age of 80 to dispose of the property for that purpose. She agreed and the structure was quickly demolished and the plot transformed into a splendid playground. Now the colored children are joyfully romping on the grounds where the Widow MacLean so recently walked in stately loneliness.

Facing Central Park, the littoral of 110th Street between Fifth and Eighth Avenues is desirable, but not so exclusive as Striver's Row. It was the last residential stronghold of the better class Jews in Harlem. Swarthy Harlemites pushed through to it only five years ago. 110th Street has a particular significance, perhaps mainly symbolic, as a frontier between the white world and the Negro group. It is not by any means a straight clear line, not exactly a color line. Mayor La Guardia, who resides at the corner of 109th Street and Fifth Avenue, may get a pretty good view of Harlem over the border. But his residence is a landmark behind which flows the movement of an entirely different world. The extraordinary social importance of this part of Harlem, its significance to New York and also to America, will be seen as the picture of Harlem unfolds.

From the half lot at 138th Street, between St. Nicholas and Edgecombe Avenue, where the elegant buffstone Dorrance Brooks building, with gloved and smartly uniformed doorman, marks a conspicuous new departure, Harlem climbs up to the hill,—up to the Sugar Hill famous in tune and tale. This is the district which became Aframerican with a resounding theatrical BANG! Like the strangest of orchids upon the broken stem of prosperity, it flowered wildly. It was in

1929 that the Aframericans surged up from the Harlem valley to the heights, commanding a panoramic view of the Bronx. The new expansion was not a people's movement, like that from downtown to Harlem, nor the irrepressible mass elbowing-out of post-war years which accompanied the development of the Back-To-Africa project. It was mainly an operation springing from the urge of Aframerican intelligentsia and élite to create an exclusive residential area.

The build-up of a fashionable and artistic Harlem became the newest fad of Manhattanites in the middle nineteen twenties. And the propaganda in favor of it was astoundingly out of proportion to the economic potentiality of a Harlem smart set and the actual artistic and intellectual achievement. New Yorkers had discovered the existence of a fashionable clique, and an artistic and literary set in Harlem. The big racket which crepitated from this discovery resulted in an enormously abnormal advertisement of bohemian Harlem. And even solid real estate values were affected by the fluid idealistic art values of Harlem.

Sugar Hill has the reputation of being the romping ground of the fashionable set. But the vast majority of its residents are also ordinary Harlemites like those living under the hill. Most of the propertied Harlemites reside under the hill. The houses on the hill are more modern, but rents are exorbitant.

Sugar Hill faces the problem of any other fairly desirable residential quarter of Harlem. The fashionable set cannot keep it exclusive, for it is infinitesimal. Families double up in apartments as elsewhere in Harlem. And racketeers of clandestine professions also set the pace. They are the people who can afford the extortionate rents without caring.

No. 409 Edgecombe Avenue is the best-known building in Sugar Hill. It is supposed to be an exclusive residential house tenanted by some of the prosperous professional persons of the group and high-salaried state and municipal employees. But many of the tenants there also belong to the ordinary working mass of Aframerica. And, too, there are "Rooms to Rent" in these apartments. "409" has something of the atmosphere of a European resort hotel for smart people with small incomes. When a Harlemite says, "I live in '409,'" one imagines that he belongs, or is trying to belong to the Smart Set.

One's imagination is not so easily excited by the Rockefeller colony of houses under the hill, embracing the whole block between Seventh and Eighth Avenue from 149th to 150th Street. These houses, with their lovely, spacious gardens, were built at the same time the smarter set among the Aframericans began the climb to Sugar Hill. And they were designed primarily for the respectable workingman and his family. But the average black worker could not afford the cost of living in them and they were occupied by members of the white-color group—professional persons and city employees and their families. These houses also presaged a new era in the urban existence of Aframericans as typified by New York. Optimistically, a bank was opened in 135th Street and a branch established in the Rockefeller houses. But the project proved a financial loss. The bank was closed and in 1938 the Rockefeller estate sold the houses. This housing project is a brief but enlightening news reel of what actually happens when the Aframerican group moves into better districts.

Sugar Hill is vinegar sour to many of its residents pinching themselves to meet the high rent. Its identification with the hectic pseudo-renaissance period of the Aframerican élite was not an economic asset. If its development had been less spectacular, it might have registered a less dubious social advantage to the group. But the rapacious landlord sharks of Harlem were hungrily waiting on the hill for the disorderly black rush into their jaws. Where white tenants formerly paid reasonable rentals, the blacks were charged up to four times as much. The idea of a miraculous Negro cultural life, although based upon no reasonable group economy, was nationally touted. And the landlords profited by the black credulity and primitive hankering after ostentation.

Excepting the privileged few, the majority of families up there in sweet Sugar Hill are packed together like sardines.

The prohibitive rent makes the unit of private family life the rarest thing. Almost all families take in lodgers. All available space must be occupied. Rooms, rooms and more rooms to let. Adequate clothing and even vital food must be sacrificed to meet the high cost of housing. That exclusive Sugar Hill society of the white writer's imagination is simply a café society. And café society, it is true, is more important in Sugar Hill than in any part of Harlem. The bars up there are more elaborate than those under the hill. During prohibition, following the scramble up the hill, the Italians planted a few well-appointed speakeasies. And spick and span, with blazing lights and comfortable lounges, they came up from underground with Repeal. The Italian bars set the tone for others, both white and colored, which were opened later. As Sugar Hill has precious few of the petty businesses which flourish under the hill, such as grocery stores, candy stores, drug stores, and the rest, its cafés are more attractive in their setting than those under the hill. Cabaret and theater artistes and their friends comprise the major portion of the clientèle with a considerable collegiate leaven. Also, out-of-town visitors favor the hill for its light divertissement. There is not much dancing up there, no cabaret extravaganza. For hot amusement the Sugar Hillies go under the hill on Seventh and Lenox Avenues to the Lido, Renaissance, Smalls', Jimmie Daniels' and Savoy. And they trek to 125th Street where the Apollo specializes in the rich variety of its glorification of the Aframerican brown girl.

Dubbing all of Harlem a vast slum would be offensive to the upper class of Aframericans who must needs make their lives worth living there. It is their tragedy that externally their individuality is almost effaced in the rough scramble of the mass. Slum dwellers do not always see themselves as others see them. Little foxes leap and fleas jump. But both must live in holes and nests. The elastic lump of Harlem below 116th Street has something of the aspect of a flea market. It is the alluring borderline of every type, where all species of humanity mix pell mell. It has something of the quality of the Vieux Port of Marseille, only it is minus the flotsam and jetsam of the immediate waves with the ships arriving and departing.

African, Mongolian, European—all the types of all the races indiscriminately flung together have created a jungle of colors in which pullulate all the imaginable shades of white and black, red, brown, yellow: indigo, chestnut, slate, amber, olive, canary, mauve, orange, ruby and the indefinable. An unaware interracial and international movement dominates the thickly crowded atmosphere. Puerto Ricans and other Latin Americans have tenanted buildings whose façades are still engraved with double triangles and over five thousand years of figures which proclaim their original Jewish occupancy. "Unamerican" signs—*bodega, tienda, carneceria, dulceria, fonda* and *imprenta* are spread across the fronts of stores. Italian Americans have pushed over from the East Side, competing with the Spanish Americans. They have reached up from coal shops and fruit stands to grab and monopolize the lucrative business of bars in Harlem. Greeks have come out from the stinking fried fish joints to install nice restaurants and become the only rivals of Jews in the grocery business. And lastly Negroes are breaking into the candy and cigar stores and express moving business.

World-famed for their promenading ritual, the Spanish have given a special éclat to the tempo of the street. The Aframericans have always delighted in the strut and shuffle. And crossing and mingling steps with the Spanish, together they are making a new movement in lower Harlem.

But it is not wholly a sentimental picture. This patchwork of humanity was planned by no expert mind. It did not evolve from any blue print of interracial and international adjustment. It is a crude, bold offspring of necessity. And it has its sinister side. Around the subway at Lenox and 116th Street, when the sun goes down, there is the feeling in the atmosphere of an apache-dominated quarter of Paris. The bright lights of the cluster of little drinking places and eating joints draw the wasps buzzing together.

The odor of reefers hangs in the air. At any moment the switch blade may flash. The young muggers are on the *qui vive*.

It is mostly in this neighborhood that some of the stupidest crimes in Harlem occur. Like hawks the muggers watch out to rob the men bemused by liquor, going home from the bars. Here too, the pants trick is mercilessly played. Victims are mostly white; imagining they are being introduced to a hot party, they are whisked up to the roof. There they are divested of money—and then their pants to impede their getting emergency help from the police. The exploits of the muggers were so detrimental to the amusement business of Harlem that two years ago it was rumored that the procurers of the borderline had organized to curb the muggers and protect the clients of their ladies.

From the nature of its soil and the arrangement of its fences, wheat and tares will continue to grow together in Harlem. Its Aframerican minority has no counterpart in any other of America's black belts. And it is fundamentally different from the other minorities that have contributed to the making of America's composite. Usually language or religion is the basic bond of other minorities. But in Harlem it is that common yet strange and elusive chemical of nature called color.

Within it are the Ishmaelite remnants of other groups, the nondescripts of miscegenation. From the Caribbean islands of the French, the Dutch, the Danes, the British, they came. From Central America and South America. Each brought something of the characteristic of the dominant European nation, but all bore the common mark of Africa. There are brown North Africans, swarthy East Africans speaking Arabic and ebon-black West Africans wearing their tribal stigmata. All have been forced into the ranks of the original Aframerican group.

Some critics within the group believe that it is doomed to remain an unwieldly, inert and invertebrate mass, precisely because it is a conglomerate color group. Because it lacks a religion or language of its own upon which it may build its self-respect. But the group is a group nevertheless and perhaps it may be to its advantage that it has not the impediment of a separate language and religion with which to contend. The children and grand children of the foreign Negroes are all good Americans. There is no difference between them and those of the original American Negro stock.

The larger problem is the adjustment of the Aframerican as a minority to fit into the frame of the American composite. Probably an examination of the mass movements of Harlem may yield an indication of the trend and direction of the group as a whole.

God in Harlem: Father Divine, 1935 A.D.F.D.

Peace, I thank you, Father. Father Divine is God!" The Deity dwells in Harlem in the flesh, in the small brown body of Father Divine. In this fertile realm of occultists and cultists Father Divine, claiming omnipotence, is supreme. There were many holy Negroes before him and there still is a host. But hailed as God by his disciples, Father Divine stands on a pinnacle above them all. His followers believe and proclaim that the invisible God is made visible in his person. At a mighty meeting in the Rockland Palace, a dancing disciple wildly leaps and shouts, "Father Divine is greater than Jesus Christ!" And with thundering cheers the multitude responds, "Yes, Father Divine is God!"

In many kingdoms of heaven in Harlem the angels unceasingly sing the wonders of their creator. Who is this God of Harlem? He is a near midget of a brown man whose will dictates the ritual of life in scores of New York houses, places named kingdoms, and in hundreds of extensions and connections in city and country throughout several states.

He has no record of his life and declares that there is none: for he has existed always. Beyond the "heavenly rest" of Sayville, L. I., there is no authentic chronicle of him. All is conjecture.

It has been assumed that he was formerly a Joe Baker or George from some place in Georgia, but it has not been proved that he was such a person. He calls himself Major J. Divine or Father Divine.

In 1932 Sayville revealed him to the world as a strange mystic. He had lived twelve years in Sayville, from 1919 to 1931, before fame came to him. Yet all that time he had practiced the rites of his cult.

The Father Divine cult was different from others. Its main feature consisted in its being a collective enterprise. No contributions were solicited. Father Divine presided over the establishment. He found employment for many members. Work, food, clothing, everything was supposed to be provided by him for his followers, whether or not it actually was so.

Now it is obvious that Father Divine could not have originally purchased and enlarged a place in Sayville out of nothing. Where did this money come from? The mystery of his finances has, more than anything else, increased national interest in Father Divine's activities. And the greater publicity vastly increased his spiritual influence and material assets. He has given the public the impression that he has supernatural powers to create money. His followers will not discuss any phase of finance. But as they all work for wages or run enterprises collectively or individually, it is obvious there is no real mystery. The only mystery then is the method which Father Divine employs to attract the huge sums of money to his individual self and dictate the management of his extensive and spreading enterprises.

Everything points to the conclusion that he has a sound basis of operation. There are many people in Harlem who pretend to have known Father Divine before he "materialized" at Sayville. The testimony of the majority may be discounted, like the testimony of psychopathic persons who confess to crimes they have not committed. Some state that Father Divine ran rooming houses in Harlem or Brooklyn before he started out in Sayville.

A middle-aged woman named Mrs. Deanne declares that back in 1914 she lived in a house which Father Divine either leased or owned in Brooklyn. She said that Father Divine had developed a kind of combination rooming house and employment agency. And all his roomers were women. It was a time of great distress and general unemployment. Father Divine devised a plan for a co-operative house. Lodgers received free room and board. The household tasks were performed by those who were not employed at the time, while those who worked supplied the necessaries. Apparently all monies were turned over to Father Divine, as head of the household, to run it.

This account appears plausible. For although Father Divine keeps no record, it is known that when he retreated to Sayville, most of the pilgrims who visited there came from New York. They all said that he had "retired," which must mean that he retired from active work, somewhere in New York. Probably he chose Sayville because many of his followers worked for the wealthy in Long Island.

But the fact of economic interest is that whatever funds Father Divine might have accumulated when he "retired" were not devoted to selfish purposes. The Sayville house was open to his disciples and to all others who wished to accept of its hospitality and abide by the rules laid down by Father Divine.

But in 1931 a crisis occurred at Sayville, after Father Divine and his followers had made their headquarters there for twelve years. At last the good white citizens of Sayville agreed that the house of Father Divine was a nuisance. They were disturbed by the increasingly blatant deification of Father Divine and the amazing tributes to the godhead, accompanied by wild stamping, shouting and dancing. But Father Divine's gospel feasts had always been prodigiously corybantic. It appeared that the major disturbing factor was that considerable numbers of white pilgrims began to join with the blacks in the rampant revels and the worship of Father Divine.

Father Divine was arrested, with others of his followers, and was investigated by the Grand Jury of Suffolk County. The chief count that stood out against him was that white and colored persons were indiscriminately mixed up in the strange fetish worship of the little African-American. This

Photo by M. and M. Smith

Play Ball.

Photo by M. and M. Smith

Harlem inventor.

Courtesy Floyd G. Snelson

Ethel Waters: She got her start in the primitive old-style Negro cabaret, developed into a nationally known music hall artiste, recently amazed Broadway in a signal role

Courtesy Floyd G. Snelson

A'lelia Walker: Heiress of Madam C. J. Walker, who amassed a fortune from the business of Negro Beauty Culture. A'lelia acquired fame as a lavish social entertainer was the feature of the case which was stressed when the Divine cultists were first haled into court.

And it was this item which caused unusual interest in it among Negroes in Harlem and elsewhere. The sensitivity to discrimination, which is often loosely labeled Segregation, is so sharp among the élite of the Negro minority that demonstration of it in any form immediately enlists their sympathy. Ordinarily they would have been opposed to the Father Divine cult as an absurdity exposing them to the ridicule of the white world. But when that cult was attacked on the basis of the national taboo against social relationship between white and colored people, it arrested their sympathy.

A prominent member of the Harlem intelligentsia, Attorney James C. Thomas, offered his services gratis in defense of Father Divine. Mass protest meetings were organized in Harlem. White and colored followers testified to the glory of Father Divine. He appeared in person and Harlem hailed him.

Six months later, in May, 1932, Father Divine's case came up for trial before Judge Smith in the Supreme Court of Nassau County. It was an extraordinary case, inasmuch as Father Divine insisted that he was not an ordinary human being. He had no past, for he kept no record of his life. He had been divinely projected into existence. Devoted Nordic and Negro followers eagerly, fervently declared that Father Divine was God. The judge committed him to jail and ordered that he be examined by a psychiatrist. But in jail, before wardens and doctors, the insignificant-looking little brown man maintained the same vacant exterior and insisted that he had no record of himself.

Ten days later the judge sentenced him to one year's imprisonment and the payment of $500. The sentence was appealed. It was finally reversed by the Appellate Court, which ruled that the presiding judge had injected prejudice in his summing up. Then something occurred which phenomenally augmented the legend of the omnipotence of Father

Divine. Judge Smith suddenly died, three days after he had pronounced sentence on him. He died of heart disease. But to the fanatical followers of Father Divine it was the hand of their God that had struck the judge down. They had always believed that Father Divine could confound his enemies, for he had often triumphed over difficulties. He had worked miracles, curing blind and paralytic persons. And he often declared that those who opposed him would be removed by his power.

The deceased judge had been very severe in handling the case of Father Divine. Said his followers: "He sentenced God to prison and God sentenced him to death." The strange coincidence of the judge's death also influenced that larger credulous public who were not followers, but who believed in signs and portents.

Thus, step by step, from Sayville to New York, because of the civic zeal of a little white community, the way was prepared for the grandiose apotheosis of Father Divine in Harlem. Two weeks after the death of the judge, Father Divine was released and Harlem received him with wide open arms. He came triumphantly. Rockland Palace, formerly the scene of Harlem's biggest balls, was not large enough to accommodate the multitude.

The man who to a limited number of people had been God was transformed overnight into a supreme being to thousands. His conflict with the law had contributed to his higher glory and majestically, despite his size, he entered into his greater kingdom. The heavenly language which had been current among the faithful in the kingdom of Sayville only, became universally popular.

"Peace! It is wonderful! I thank you, Father. Father Divine is God." When he appears, his people become delirious with joy. They shout, they sway, they prance. His words reach their senses like a magic potion. They are strange phrases, an endless jumble of words steeped in metaphysical metaphor and scriptural allusion mixed in with practical advice on daily living. But they are spiritual nourishment for thousands of followers.

Father Divine does not preach and he does not pray. To whom should he pray, being God? In this he is different from all other preachers. He speaks only to reveal his own greatness to his people and to command them.

"Peace! Good Health, Good Appetite, Good Will and a heart full of Merriness, with Life, Liberty, Happiness and Eternal Life. . . . I give you joy and peace. . . . I am your happiness and I am your joy. . . . Whatever you need, let my spirit do it. . . . The spirit of the consciousness of the presence of God is the source of all supply. . . . You have recognized my personal presence in your hearts . . . . I command and demand anything I desire. . . . God in the midst of you is mighty to save. I am here, there and everywhere. Dial in and you shall find me. Aren't you glad?"

And the Divinites respond: "I thank you Father."

Such is the general tenor of all Father Divine's discourses. The phrases are a subtle combination of common biblical phrases applied to himself. Thus when he says, "You shall see God," he uses a phrase from the Bible, but his disciples actually believe that they see God in him. His choice of verbs is not accidental. And when he declares, "You have recognized my personal presence in your hearts," he casts a hypnotic spell over his followers. He does not say, "You *will* recognize," or "You *must* recognize," but "You *have*. . . ."

Within a year of winning his appeal, Father Divine had established in New York a score of kingdoms similar to the one for which he was prosecuted at Sayville. And throughout the States his mission gained large numbers of converts, who set up new kingdoms.

Father Divine flits from one kingdom to the other. Being God, he dwells in all of them at the same time, he says, but he can reveal himself personally only in one place. The kingdoms are acquired either by purchase or by lease. They are renovated, well-furnished and readied for the co-workers or sympathizers of Father Divine. Rooming accommodation may be obtained at $2 a week. Two persons may inhabit a room. But there are kingdoms for men only and kingdoms

for women only. For celibacy is imposed on the disciples.
Married couples are separated when they become co-workers
and dwellers in the kingdoms.

The Father Divine restaurants abound in Harlem. They
serve wholesome food for ten cents and fifteen cents a plate.
A good cut of beef or chicken with two vegetables costs
ten cents and fifteen cents with dessert and coffee. These
meals are served to followers and friends and strangers alike.
They are not in the category of the feasts that are served
every day to the chosen of the true followers in each kingdom. These are the famous banquets where the very best
food is served: a variety of choicest meats—hot and cold—
assortment of vegetables, salads, rich puddings, cakes and
iced drinks.

When Father Divine visits one of the kingdoms in person
he sits at the head of the banquet table and the food comes
first to his hand to be blessed and passed to the guests. This
is real work, for there are always more than a hundred such
guests and Father does considerable strenuous talking besides. Before meals the followers salute him with glorious
singing, dancing, praising of his name. And after the banquet they continue to sing and dance and testify to the
wondrousness of his majesty.

Father's photographs, in many amazing poses, adorn the
walls of all the kingdoms. His significant phrases are printed
as mottoes. Posters and pennants everywhere praise his name.

Through the agency of his Peace Mission, Father Divine
proclaims himself to be against every form of injustice in
the world. The crisis of Sayville, which resulted in his imprisonment, has sharpened his sensitivity to race prejudice.
Huge signs register protests of discrimination against
Negroes, Jews and aliens. Father Divine supports the anti-
lynching bill. He has written a Righteous Government
platform. He sends messages to statesmen, legislators and
other prominent people.

One poster reads: "Father Divine's Peace Mission is in
sympathy with any movement which seeks to abolish racial
discrimination, eradicate prejudice and establish the funda-

mentals which stand for the good of Humanity. We are against War and Fascism. We believe in and practice the principle of the Brotherhood of all Mankind."

In all the New York kingdoms, all of the followers belong to the same type. They are emotionally-inspired congregations of brown and black Americans with a leaven of Negroid Spanish-Americans and West Indians. They are flecked with whites just as ardent. But despite the spirit of abnegation and general fellowship before their God, the Father, the whites appear to the penetrating eye more like slightly uncomfortable visitors. They give one an impression of the missionary type, the God servants who resolutely mingle with and minister to natives of a colony.

There are a few buxom young girls, occasionally a young man or two. But mostly middle-aged folk compose the congregations. They are a happy lot. It may seem to cynical onlookers to be a crazy form of happiness. But their happiness cannot be gainsaid. They are happy singing and shouting and dancing and eating and praising Father Divine. When Father Divine pays a visit to a banquet hall, an enormous crowd attends. His people will wait for a long time singing and dancing, even if he is hours in making his appearance. And when he has arrived, many must continue to wait before they can eat, for the banquet table can accommodate only a certain number at a time. But there is never a sign of impatience. Eagerness there is, but it is to welcome and praise Father Divine. Dancing and singing his praises is as much nourishment as is the food.

The Divinites' dancing, when they are inflamed, is an unforgettable performance. There is anarchy in the movement. In that fervid atmosphere the religious words of the sing-dance fit perfectly the music-hall ditty to which they are adapted. Rampant individual steps punctuate the rhythm. Fragments of every conceivable dance measure whirl about: a rare huddle of Guinea fetishers, an ecstatic Senegalese plunging to the call of the tom-tom, a patter of Moroccan flamenco, an Irish jig, a briefly oblique schottische, the one-step, the rhumba; altogether they make one glorious variation of all the dances of creation.

Faith in the little brown Father makes this dancing wonderful. Some members were formerly strict Methodists and Baptists who never danced, others were derelicts of stage and cabarets and hospitals. But Father Divine made elastic their rheumatic limbs and now they have found their feet to dance again. It is all individual dancing. Here no arms encircle bodies while male and female sway together. But they dance to one another, sometimes unwittingly creating formations like quadrilles.

> "This is my story, this is my song,
>   Praising my Father all the day long."

Thus all the gospel hymns are paraphrased to laud Father Divine.

Sometimes Father Divine himself leads the singing. On such occasions his theme song may be an exhortation to his followers to believe in him always. He may choose these words:

> "Though dark the clouds may be today,
>   My Heart has planned your path and Mine,
>   Have faith in GOD,
>   Have faith always. . . ."

All his followers testify to their faith in him. Sometimes they confess the mistakes of their past lives and praise him for giving the new life.

A black man with a face that is hard-looking but a little softened by his present environment declares: "I killt a man in Alabama. We were drinking corn together with the womens. And my spirit grows big and bigger with hating him. I couldn't stand his looks and his acting among the womens. And I guess he couldn't stand me either. So I fightum. And he fights me and I killum. I runned away up North. But for seventeen years I couldn't get over what I did. He haunted me, that man I killt. I seen him in my sleep and I seen him when I wake. He followed me every place and chased me from job to job.

"I was sick and almost crazy seeing that man I killt, until one day I seen Father Divine. Father he takes charge of me and I surrendered to him. Father turned me inside out and made a new man outa me. I did as Father told me to do. I works as he wished me to work. I sleeps as he put me to sleep. But I don't believe I gived all to Father as I should, for that man I killt came back again. I was scared and went straight to Father and confessed the crime I committed. And Father said, 'Now you have confessed to me, I give you a new heart, I put my power in you and you are not afraid.' And I was no longer afraid. And Father said, 'But I must send you back to Birmingham to tell the Sheriff what you did, and I will make you entirely free.' I was not afraid. Father sent me back to Birmingham. And I went back and told the Sheriff that I did kill that man. And the Sheriff turned me loose. He said, 'After seventeen years you are free, Father Divine made a new man of you. Therefore, go back to Father Divine.' And I come back to Father just as he know I would. I works the way Father wants me to and I sleep like he tells me to. I belong to Father and it is wonderful."

"It is wonderful, Thank you Father," cried the congregation.

A gray-haired white man is moved to testify. He was formerly a chemist. He says he has been ill sometimes and has been quickly cured by the spirit of Father Divine. He becomes ill only when he is not so close in the spirit to Father as he should be. Father knows all and strengthens his spirit in him. He repeats the story of the great accident of his life. It was an automobile accident. Another car forced against a wall the one in which he was riding. The impact crushed him against the wall and his head was flattened out like a pancake. He was taken to a hospital with blood oozing from his nostrils, his ears, his mouth and his eyes. The doctors said he could not live. But in his semi-consciousness he concentrated on Father Divine and immediately the flow of blood stopped. The following day Father Divine came to the hospital and the doctors informed him he could not live. Father Divine replied, "I will make him live." And right away his flattened head assumed its natural shape. "I thank you Father." Undoubtedly the man is a hypochondriac.

Father Divine leads off the singing:

> "An open confession is good for the soul,
> Good for the soul, good for the soul,
> An open confession is good for the soul,
> The half has never yet been told."

The singing over, a yellow-complexioned woman jumps up. She is hefty, big-boned and full-breasted. But there is a vestige of the agony of frustration in her face. She raises her hand and starts: "Father has set me free from the domination of man. Oh, I don't want any man. What is a man and who is a man? There is no telling nowadays in the midst of the masquerade! A man he dresses himself up and struts along the street and imagines he is hot to kill. But what is this thing we have been calling a man? Can you answer me? Can you tell me, eh? In reality he is no better than a piece of bad meat, which the butcher throws away because it is no good for eating."

She shrieks, agitating her shoulders violently: "I don't want any man, for the sinful flesh of man is as cruel as the devil himself playing with the soul of a woman. I'll tell it to the world, a man is a fool believing he is the hottest 'It,' when he is only like a block of ice in the life of a woman. My Father God Father Divine is the only man in my life. He understands the serpent called woman. But he had to quit and circumscribe and forsake the sweet enticement of the flesh and become the spirit of God himself to understand. Yes, Father had to cut it out. SHHHH!"

The woman quivered all over and continued: "Father chased the trouble of man out of my life and plunged his spirit into me. Keep plunging, Father! Oh, my God, I thank you Father."

Although accustomed among themselves to the wildest gestures and eeriest confessions, the congregation seemed to be a little shocked by the savage intensity of the female angel's disavowal of man. There was a kind of awkward lull. The male angels looked slightly sheepish. And indeed, as I scanned the faces of the female angels, it appeared that some were trying to refrain from derisive laughter. Evidently the woman was out of harmony with the universal spirit of Father Divine. And if Peace is the foundation of Father Divine's Kingdoms, Harmony is the pillar.

And now Father Divine speaks: "Peace everyone! Good Health, Good Appetite, Good Will, Good Manners and Good Behavior, and the Reality of Life and Liberty, Truth, Happiness and Harmony which I have established. Upon this foundation and upon this platform you will all stand. In my fellowship, in my joy Divine. For I am sample and example of eternal life. Then take these thoughts into consideration. You must get away from self and selfishness completely if you desire to express Me from any point whereby you wish to convey a thought of what I have done for you. It is all right if you wish to demonstrate what God has done for you, but let My Words be the words of Truth and of Spirit and of Life. . . . Remember, I know those who are out of harmony, who are out of tune. Harmony is the great essential. Only where there is Harmony there is Heaven. Harmonization brings all together in unison in spirit and in mind to be one with your God.

"We often say that Confession is the essential, but Harmony is greater than Confession. It is not at all times especially urgent and necessary to make a public confession. You may tell God anything you want to tell him in your heart. Confession may be considered as the reality of the significance of the particular expressionification of the unfoldment of you. But it must be openward inspirational and not inwardly egoismal and detrimental to the perfect harmonization of all in Me. . . .

"If you are not in Harmony your confession cannot be pervasivisional. But it will remain knotted up and festering in you like a carbuncle. You must harmonize to contact me perfectionally. You must contact me mentally and spiritually as well as personally. That is the mystery. When your contact is made rightfully and righteously you will be attached to me perfectly connected together as the coupling link will couple you rhythmistically to Me. Aren't you glad?"

"By the principle, the impersonality of my Omnipotency, I have actually established in your conscious mentality the impersonal presence of your Savior, not so much as a Person but as a Principle. To those who receive my spirit as it is given by the Personification of the All Principle, I will go home with them and be in evidence with them. You see, that is the Mystery. You will be prosperous and healthy and peaceful and happy if you live forever and always with Me. Isn't it Wonderful? I thank You."

Wildly flapping their hands and leaping, the angels shout, "Thank you Father. It is wonderful." Harmonization is restored. And they burst into singing:

> "Oh, of his kingdom and of his increase
> There shall be, there shall be
> Oh, of his kingdom and of his increase
> There shall be no end."

Father Divine's followers explicitly declare that he is God. Their uplifting of Father Divine to the throne of Deity is shocking to Christians, even to people who are not devout Christians. But the Divine folk also consider themselves Christians. To them Father Divine is a second incarnation of the Christ. Their idea of Jesus is akin to the Mohammedan idea.

Father Divine himself accepts all religions. He says they are different manifestations of his Spirit. He does not say, I AM GOD. But he does not ask his followers not to call him God. Thus, he accepts the title. And he subtly arrogates to himself all the biblical attributes of the Godhead. Pronouns referring to himself are capitalized. And he has declared that he is omnipotent, omiscient and omnipresent, the Personification of the Creator and the Infinite.

But he also speaks of himself and his disciples as One. He in them and they in him. According to his words, therefore, his religion might be interpreted as a primitive pantheism. But he is not a freethinker. He accepts the Bible as a Sacred Book and in his exhortations deftly manipulates the scriptural metaphors to project himself as the personification of God. Only by fully comprehending the popular idea of God, perhaps, can one understand the phenomenon of Father Divine and the thousands (he claims millions) who believe he is God. How many of those who are shocked by this undersized Negro's being called God have ever stopped to analyze the non-intellectual conception of God!

The condition of Harlem itself is a key to the understanding of Father Divine. The hosts of occultists and the industrious preoccupation of all the people with supernatural elements reveal them as eternal God-seekers. They consult the occultists in the hope of obtaining work and food, love and peace and contact with dead relatives. Actually they are seeking intercourse with God. And it is the good God they are chasing, an intimate God who will pity and help them in time of trouble. Before the advent of Father Divine, the legion of mystics and medicine men in Harlem denominated themselves as prophets and priests, shepherds, bishops, confessors and even sons of God. And the masterly types were always successful. But when Father Divine projected himself as God, he eclipsed them all. For he fulfilled a strangely complex but profoundly universal need.

Father Divine has achieved signal success as God by outlawing from his extensive Kingdom of Peace the complex realities which harass men in the everyday world. In Father Divine's mind, in his conception of society and in the Government of his Kingdom there is (1) no sex, (2) no race, (3) no color, (4) no money. Although he inevitably faces these harsh realities in a man-made world, he does not recognize them in his God-made world. Blindly his disciples follow

his lead. Colored and white, they accept his magical interpretation of natural things. The devout disciples do not
even believe in the existence of the body. They are angels
of the Kingdom of Father Divine. Nevertheless, out of this
contradiction, out of the seeming unreality, Father Divine
has founded and built a vast, solid organization.

I tried to obtain from Father Divine a concrete idea of his
unrealistic approach to inescapable realities. Undoubtedly
the fact of his belonging to a special biological type has
vastly contributed to his bewildering triumph as a Deity.
If Father Divine were white and proclaimed himself God,
he probably might have convinced few persons; especially
among Negroes whose conception of God under Christendom
is white. But Father Divine's complexion was an asset,
even among his white followers. I suggested to him that
the national and international interest he had created was
due largely to his being a Negro.

Father Divine replied: "I have no color conception of
myself. I have arisen in Person as an outward expression
to manifest that I am personally living even as I am mentally,
spiritually and eternally living. I came to unify all of
humanity. They all need me: every nation, every tongue
and every people, all the different nationalities and all the
five races collectively. My Power is restoring Unity where
there is Division. If I were representing race or creed or
color or nation, I would be limited in my conception of
the universal. I would not be as I am, that I am, omnipotent."

About domestic life he is subtle. He denies that he is
breaking up married life. He declares that he is helping
men and women to live a higher standard of life. He cites
the Roman Catholic Church. Women live separately in
convents, he says, and men in monasteries. "So likewise I
separate the male angels from the female angels in my
Kingdoms. But I do not interfere with the domestic life
of my followers and well-wishers who do not live in my
kingdoms."

Most of the commentators on the Divine movement have
been puzzled by his methods of finance. Father Divine

scorns the passing of the collection plate. The angels regard it as a mystery. But apparently it is a mystery to which the angels hold the key. It is really the non-followers of Father Divine whom for obvious reasons they desire to mystify. Father Divine delights in deepening the mystery. "Denial of money," he declares, "is angelship degree." Then why should his followers, who love him and who all want to be angels, imperil their chances of graduation by discussing or manipulating money? Why should those who are graduate angels become overconscious of money, when it may cost them the cancellation of their diplomas? Finances are dealt with in the inner sanctum of Father Divine, who provides all. But Father Divine is also a captain of industry. It is strange that those who are curious to have him disclose his financial methods have never realized that if he did so he would be revealing trade secrets, the revelation of which might seriously hurt the entire structure of his Kingdom.

Always alert to every movement of the masses, which they endeavor to manipulate to their own ends, the Communists have approached Father Divine and arranged a working agreement with him. From the Communist platform Father Divine has exhorted the nation to strive for Peace and have faith in him. He has demonstrated with them for Peace and Democracy and against War and Fascism. And although the Communists can muster an impressive array, Father Divine and his followers overshadow them in spectacular display.

The Divine multitudes, headed by Father Divine, parade with the Communists, with white stuffed doves perched on their cars, and flags and pennants advertising Father Divine as God. The Divinites steal the show from the Communists. There is no question about the strength of the cult in Harlem. Father Divine is fully aware of it. And unlike other religious leaders, he is not afraid of the influence of the Communists. Co-operating with the Communists has enormously increased his fame. And the radical difference between his platform and that of the Communists has embarrassed the Communist Party more than it has Father Divine. He has used the Communist platform to denounce trade unionism and extol the principle of the open shop.

After a recent May Day demonstration, in which he participated with the Communists, Father Divine said: "When I am participating with my Comrades, the Communists, whether they know it or not, I know they are fulfilling the Scriptures more than many of the preachers and those that are called religious. . . . The mystery of our demonstration with them the Communists could not understand. But coming out of all of the different organizations, millions are coming up to God. The Communists and all others must accept my message. Every one must recognize it, every knee bow down to it and every tongue confess it. Just what the Communists have been trying to get you to see and do and be, I have accomplished. I have brought you the victory. I have given you liberty with wisdom, health and wealth. I am the great demonstrator and the eternal emancipator! Isn't it wonderful?"

The linking up of Father Divine with the Communists may perplex the casual observer. But in spite of the spiritualistic emphasis of Father Divine's Mission and the materialistic basis of the Communists, both movements, exploiting the principle of the uplift of the down-and-out masses, have a striking similarity.

If one takes the trouble to tear through the gaudy metaphysical and animistic masquerade of Father Divine's Mission and the Communists' highly intellectualized materialistic conception of Society, one discovers the same fundamental principle: the abnegation of all individuality, collective servitude and strict discipline in every domain of life with one man as supreme dictator.

The Father Divine movement is manifestly a glorious Communist cult. . . . And Father Divine is the supreme dictator. The angels who dwell in his kingdoms must obey his commands. He controls their lives within the kingdoms as much as he does their activities in the outside world.

None can challenge his acts and decisions and remain an angel of the kingdoms. All live to glorify his name. No wonder the followers of Stalin have linked themselves with Father Divine! He works with supernatural forces, while they seek to manipulate natural resources. The methods may differ but the purpose is similar. Father Divine in the domain of religion is the "sample and example" of what the Communists desire to achieve in the realm of politics.

.   .   .   .

In 1935 Father Divine was a big show. In 1940 he dominates the most powerful and disquieting social force in Harlem, which indirectly is an influential political factor in the City and State of New York. It was mainly the fetichistic features of the movement, the bizarre quality of the mumbo-jumbo divinity of Father Divine, that excited public interest from 1932 until 1935. Visitors were attracted to a Divine Kingdom as they would be to a grand picnic. The Father Divine vocabulary was in itself a main attraction. His inimitable stringing of the crude slang phrases of the street on a chain of seraphic syllables was a superb mental feast. The improvised shaking and shuffling of angels' feet on the floor of a Harlem heaven was often more highly entertaining than the floor show of a Harlem cabaret. Preachers of all denominations made pilgrimages to Headquarters Kingdom and marveled over the devotion of the angels, their unquestionable faith in the words and works of Father Divine. The banquets, featuring innumerable platters of the best cuts of meat and every variety of vegetable and sweets, were evocative of the festive orgies in Imperial Rome.

But perhaps many who saw the banquets did not observe the other side of the Divine scene, wherein thousands of Harlemites nourished themselves on simple, wholesome meals costing ten and fifteen cents a plate, and three thousand destitute persons were fed free meals every day.

In the meantime, the Divine Peace Mission was encountering its little difficulties. One of its busses had a collision in

1936 and a suit was filed against the mission to recover damages. A former angel of the Sayville Kingdom, Miss Verinda Brown, had deserted to the mundane world, and sued the Mission for four thousand dollars, which she swore she had contributed to it. She declared that Father Divine had not kept his promise to make adequate provision for her. A Mr. Davenport also instituted suit against Father Divine for alienating the affections of his wife. She had renounced his bed and board to enter a kingdom. A children's aid society had brought into court the case of three young girls of the Faithful Mary Kingdom.

Companies of angels from the various kingdoms, marching with Father Divine on his way to the courts of ordinary men, contributed to the greater advertisement of his cause. Only the suit against the bus was clearly won, but collecting the damages was not so easy.

Father Divine startled Harlem in 1935, when he declared that in addition to the urban kingdoms, he was founding in the country a Promised Land for his followers. In announcing his project to a vast assembly of his followers, Father Divine said: "The earth is the Lord's, but He does not claim all Personally. The Communistic ideas must be endorsed. I am not asking you all to buy, neither to help me buy a piece of property. I have purchased the property, several pieces, and they are all free and clear. If perchance you have the means to build a home, the ground, the land, the lots will be given to you free of cost and you will have your deeds for them without a string tied to them. You, my co-workers and followers, have the opportunity of becoming a sample and example for all governments, by co-operative living and a universal pooling of your interests. Having all things in common, claiming nothing for yourself as an individual, and refusing to hoard up riches for yourselves for a selfish purpose, but giving every one a chance to enjoy some of it. This is a concrete expression of the communistic idea. . . ."

Now this new Divine venture was launched at exactly the same time that the W. P. A. was set up. Father Divine acquired his first lots near Kingston on the Hudson in Ulster County, New York. In January, 1936, he held his Righteous Government Convention on the tenth, eleventh and twelfth. The Chairman of the Convention was Attorney Arthur A. Madison, a graduate of Bowdoin College and Columbia University. Mr. Madison had been a follower of Father Divine when his movement came into conflict with the law at Sayville in 1931. He became Father Divine's attorney and advisor and has served in that capacity ever since. Besides legal acumen, Mr. Madison possesses an ingratiating charm which perhaps has helped considerably in carrying Father Divine through his legal battles.

The Divine Righteous Government Platform is significant for the things it declared for and against. It is against (1) New Deal Legislation, which, through discriminatory laws and ordinances . . . deprives the individual of the right to sell his goods for little or nothing if he chooses. (2) Labor unions which intimidate and oppress the workers and compel them to pay dues. (3) Medical science. (4) Employment agencies that charge the employees fees. (5) Tariff schedules. (6) Control of crops and destruction of any foodstuffs.

It demands: (1) The immediate destruction of all firearms and instruments of war. (2) Repeal of all laws and ordinances providing for compulsory insurance, employers' liability or public liability. (3) Abolition of race-creed-and-color discrimination in the Civil Service. (4) Immediate legislation making it a crime to discriminate in any public place against any individual on account of race, creed or color. (5) Abolition of segregated neighborhoods and segregated public conveyances, theaters, schools, and churches. (6) Abolition of regulations requiring Americans to declare themselves destitute and go on relief rolls to obtain W. P. A. jobs. (7) Government control of all idle plants and machinery. (8) That physicians guarantee a complete cure and the life of the individual or be liable for damages in the event of death. (9) Abolition of capital punishment. (10) Legislation imposing the penalty of first-degree murder on all members of lynch mobs, etc.

It was logical that the Divine government should be opposed to medical science and doctors, for his followers believe that they are immune from disease and illness, so long as they have faith in his divinity. Likewise it was against all forms of insurance, for the Divinites are insured in the spirit of Father Divine. All true followers cancel their insurance policies. But its emphatic opposition to several main features of the New Deal was a bombshell in New York's political arena. Father Divine condemned Federal, State and Municipal relief for the needy and objected to the manner in which workers were able to obtain W. P. A. jobs. Said Father Divine: "I have taken my followers off the relief and made them independent, thus saving the Government millions. Not one of my true followers would accept of relief in any form, or even so much as go on the relief rolls in order to get a job. We demand the abandonment of the government regulation requiring the people of America to declare themselves destitute and go on the relief rolls, in order to get jobs."

Such was the position of the Harlem dictator, whom the American Communists had drawn into the Popular Front movement. There was obviously no basis of co-operation between the New Deal and the Divine Deal. And at that time the Communists were the noisiest and most uncritical supporters of the New Deal. They were also shock troops of the newly organized C. I. O., and Father Divine had denounced trade unionism and was seeking to place his disciples in jobs without benefit of unions. Quietly the Communists sneaked out from a united front with Father Divine's Mission. But Father Divine continued to call the Communists "comrades" and to tell the world that he had actually accomplished what the Communists were aspiring towards.

Other lots of land were acquired and soon it was rumored that the Divine Peace Mission was negotiating to take over all of Ulster County. Boundless was the enthusiasm of Father Divine's angels for the Promised Land. Co-workers quickly formed groups to migrate to the country and start

collective farms.   Artisans went along to repair old buildings and erect new ones.   Many had lived in the city all their
lives.   Father Divine put his spirit into them and they were
transformed into farmers.   Other farms were acquired.   Many
had been abandoned because they were unable to pay.   But
Father Divine's workers turned the wastelands into fertile,
productive acres.   They ploughed the land by day and at
evening they sang and danced for joy.   At first the Ulster
County natives objected to the intrusion of the fantastic
zealots.   But they have become reconciled to their presence
and have even complimented their work.   Their industry,
honesty and purchasing power have been lauded by officials
and business men.   The Divinites pay their taxes promptly.
They pay cash for everything and they buy one lot at a time.
Today they own some twenty-odd estates in Ulster County
alone, all thriving and humming with happy activity.   In
spite of the primitive orgies of mysticism which feed the
energy of their collective action, they are practical in making
use of the most modern equipment.   Like the Divine Kingdoms in the cities, the country estates are not solely for the
accommodation of Father Divine's followers.   Strangers are
always welcome and they pay the same minimum cost of $2
weekly for lodging.

If 1936 may be called the year of great joy in Righteous
Government for the Divinites, 1937 was the year of woe.
Misfortune struck the Divine Peace Mission like an air raid.
It struck suddenly, devastatingly in different places and
almost at the same time.   And the trouble came from the
two primary sources which Father Divine in his wisdom had
outlawed among his followers, sex and money.

Non-recognition of sex was the more manageable of the
two.   By setting up separate kingdoms for male and female
followers, Father Divine easily established control over the
eternal Adam and Eve.   To control money was a more
complicated matter.   The majority of the Divinites are
compelled to work for money in the mundane world.   To
control the individual incomes of those angels who are not
voluntary workers in the kingdoms would be a stupendous

project. Therefore Father Divine issued a blanket decree of the non-recognition of money.

This is the aspect of the movement that is a perennial puzzle to observers. But in reality it is quite simple. Father Divine as a Dictator-God refuses to recognize money. The angels accept his dictum, "Denial of money is angelship degree." When they work among mortals and receive wages, they are individuals, but within the kingdoms, they are angels. Supposing they do deposit sums of money with Father Divine! They do so as angels who have no recognition or record of it. They do not give money to Father Divine in the human way. Nor does he receive it in that way. He is their idea of God—God who provides everything, who makes it possible for his angels to work among poor mortals. Mortals may imagine that the angels give their money to Father Divine, because they do not understand the mystery. But the angels from their celestial elevation have an entirely different conception of the transaction. They know that angels from far and near may bring their tributes to the Kingdom of Heaven but none can *give* aught to God, for "the earth is the Lord's and the fullness thereof." And perhaps that may explain why even the peris of the kingdoms of Father Divine have maintained a dignified silence when they have forfeited their "angelship degree." They are rarer than unicorns who dare accuse Father Divine of misuse of funds.

Wars have broken out in all the heavens, and it is inevitable that trouble should also break out in the Kingdom of Father Divine. The wonder is rather that the little God possessed the strength and skill to profess and maintain Peace in his Kingdom. Discord had been secretely disrupting the inner circles of the Peace Mission, when an untoward incident caused the explosion.

About noon on April 20, 1937, at Headquarters Kingdom, 20 West 115th Street, Father Divine was entertaining his angels with one of his inspired messages. Two white men entered the kingdom and one, a process server, approached Father Divine, as he was gyrating and exhorting, to serve

him a summons in a damage suit. Father Divine recoiled
with an unintelligible exclamation. His followers, in-
dignant that their leader should be molested at that sacred
moment when he had chosen to reveal his inspiration to
them, rushed forward and manhandled the men. The process
server was badly beaten and his companion stabbed. Father
Divine, apparently frightened, escaped from the hall in the
mêlée. A police search failed to find him in New York.
An order was released for his arrest, charging felonious
assault. Meanwhile three of his male angels were held on
the same charge.

It was an initial blunder, precisely as silly as that which
precipitated the Harlem riots of March, 1935. A Divine
kingdom has something of the status of a church. The
process server did not even wait until Father Divine had
completed his discourse. He interrupted him in the midst
of it. Nothing like that had ever happened before. No
wonder the devout Divinites were alarmed and acted reck-
lessly. Three days later Father Divine was discovered in
one of his kingdoms at Milford, Connecticut. He was arrested and brought back to New York.

The trouble started a train of tribulation. Out in Los
Angeles that same week a wealthy white disciple, John
Wuest Hunt, whose cult name was St. John the Revelator,
was arrested under the Mann Act for the seduction of a young
follower named Miss Delight Jewel. The Society for the
Prevention of Cruelty to Children instituted an investigation
of the welfare of the children of the Divine kingdoms. The
office of New York's District Attorney announced that some
of the commercial transactions of the Divine Mission were
being investigated.

But the gravest and most startling of all the troubles was
the defection of Faithful Mary, the star angel of the movement. Now the reputation of Father Divine as a miracle
worker and healer of the body and soul of mankind was
largely built upon the healthy personality of Faithful Mary.
She had been a derelict in Newark in 1933 when Father
Divine first discovered her. She was a wreck of skin and

bones from fiendish imbibing of rotgut liquor. She had been put in insane asylums and repeatedly in hospitals, but remained an incurable because of liquor. Often she fished her food out of garbage cans and slept in the gutters of Newark. There was something in her that wanted to be better, finer. But the craving to drink and to be crazy, deadly drunk was stronger. And so she could not of herself develop that better, finer something within. Then she heard of Father Divine. She went to his meeting. She sought him out and gave up her body and her soul to him. He put his spirit in her rotten body and cured her. She developed into a new woman, fine-fleshed, balanced, motherly. And in homage to the miracle-working power of Father Divine, the former Viola Wilson took the new angelic name of Faithful Mary.

As "sample and example" of the effectiveness of the supernatural powers of Father Divine, Faithful Mary was the supreme item. Her testimony was not fraudulent. There are persons in Newark who knew her a few years back when she was a miserable, gaunt and broken creature of the gutter. In Newark, Father Divine blessed her in opening up a kingdom restaurant. The venture was successful beyond Faithful Mary's most romantic dreams. All the Divine angels flocked to her place. Her profits were enormous. And remembering whence she came, she expended some of them in generously feeding, every day, scores of persons who were derelict as she had been.

Faithful Mary is a middle-aged woman, but there is a youthful lissomeness in the rhythm of her big, joyful body. She is a heavyweight, but there is no unpleasant fatness in her brown flesh. She leaps and prances like a splendid horse and tells of the goodness, the sweetness, the wholesomeness that Father Divine has injected into her being. One look at her radiant face and one is convinced that she is sincere and tells the truth.

There is an other-worldly illumination in her features that differentiates her from all the other angels. It is a light that is never seen in the features of Father Divine. He was able to light a torch in Faithful Mary, yet the original fire is not apparent within himself. Father Divine was fully aware of the potentialities of Faithful Mary. After encountering difficulties with Newark authorities, he brought Faithful Mary to Newark in 1934. He had acquired the former Russian-Turkish Bath Premises on 125th Street. He put Faithful Mary in charge, renaming the premises the Faithful Mary Kingdom. It became the most profitable of all the kingdoms.

Often, when Father Divine could not put in his personal appearance at a kingdom, Faithful Mary took his place as the first of his angels. When the extravagant, heavenly high banquets were served, the place of honor beside him was reserved for her. She had more freedom than other angels in her business administration. She wore fine clothes. She had her own car and a chauffeur.

California, not accidentally, is the state which has the largest number of white followers of Father Divine. When they invited him to come and show his person to the Golden Gate in the fall of 1934, he felt unable to heed the request, and he sent Faithful Mary as his representative. She was accorded the reception of a goddess. Gifts of furniture, clothing and jewelry poured in on her. Many of the Divine folk are peacockish in their display of rich raiment in the heavens. They adorn themselves with golden trinkets and precious stones to sparkle in the eyes of God.

Mother Divine faded into the background as Faithful Mary usurped the place of Mother of the movement. She was ostentatiously loved. Devoted angels were happy to weave her beloved name into antimacassars. Posters and pennants publicized her name.

Probably the enormous success of her material enterprises helped to undermine Faithful Mary's spiritual perfection and her psychic allegiance to Father Divine. Early in 1937 discord developed between her and Father Divine. It was a dispute over money. One of the properties of the Promised Land, the hotel and land at Highland Falls, New York, belonged to Faithful Mary. Unlike most of the

Divine properties, which are owned by a group of follow-ers, this piece was purchased solely in Faithful Mary's name. Perhaps Father Divine delighted thus to honor his highest ranking angel.   He could show no greater confidence in his Galatea.   From out of the gutter Faithful Mary had risen to the status of landed proprietor.

But Faithful Mary was not quite the sweet, angelic spirit after this godly gift was bestowed upon her.   It was not the same as when she had been the chief confidential servant, running the big kitchen of God, with a docile staff of angels at her command.   Now she was perplexed by the respon-sibility of ownership.   And perhaps, like most property owners, she became obsessed with increasing her possessions.

At any rate, early in April, 1937, a white follower of Father Divine named William Gottlieb arrived from Ohio. He had in his possession $9,995 which he wanted to invest in the Divine industry.   Gottlieb met and consulted with Father Divine.   But Father Divine showed no eager interest in the Gottlieb money and how it should be harnessed to work in the Divine affairs.   That is the Divine way, accord-ing to those of his angels who know him intimately.   I have gathered these facts from many of his angels:—Father Divine never exerts any pressure upon his followers to extract money from them, often he ignores persons, even wealthy persons, who are eager to turn over funds to the mission.   He prefers such people to devote considerable time in studying his work, visiting the various kingdoms and hearing his messages and the confessions of his angels, before they make any decision. Then, whatever they decide upon, they do entirely volun-tarily.   In the words of Father Divine: "That is the mystery!"

Meanwhile, William Gottlieb naturally came in contact with the Premier Angel, Faithful Mary.   Growing more and more worldly-wise, Faithful Mary eagerly grabbed the Gottlieb money with the intention of investing it in her enterprises.   When Father Divine heard of the transaction he was indeed exceedingly angered.   He ordered Faithful Mary to return the money immediately.   Faithful Mary returned the money under protest.   But Gottlieb did not sustain her for he had no desire to do otherwise than as God wanted it to be done.

Father Divine also ordered Mary to relinquish the property in her name at Highland Falls. This Mary resolutely refused to do. Father Divine fired her as manager of the Faithful Mary Kingdom, and sent her to the kitchen as scrubwoman. Faithful Mary declared: "Even God cannot do that to me."

Father Divine replied: "I made you and I can break you by withdrawing my spirit out of you. You remember when you were a bad, abandoned woman and rotten to the bone. But you were not too low down for me to feel compassion for you. You were sick and emaciated but I put my spirit in you and healed you. I made you lively and well, peaceful, successful and prosperous, fat and healthy in every joint, sinew, limb, bone, vein, fiber, cell and atom of your soul and body. Yet now you dare to say that 'even God cannot do that to me!' Now go down to the kitchen and scrub the floor for your sins." But Faithful Mary chose to hold on to her property and refused to be a scullion. She made ready to vacate the Kingdom. This was on April 19, 1937.

But the following day, before she quit, the hand of fate struck in Headquarters Kingdom and Father Divine himself had to flee New York. Widely publicized, the incident of the process-serving and the resultant beating up of both men and the stabbing of one appeared more serious than it actually was, because of the mysterious disappearance of Father Divine. But as 'God moves in a mysterious way' Father Divine had to make a simple thing complex. Remaining in hiding, he was hunted on a charge of assault. Yet it was practically Father Divine who had been assaulted by the process server in his stupid way. Coincidently, the fanfare attending the arrest of the rich Western Divinite, St. John the Revelator, or John Wuest Hunt, charged with the seduction of Miss Delight Jewel, created the general impression that the kingdom of Father Divine was crumbling. There was confusion among the angels.

This appeared like retribution to the ignorant and unhappy Faithful Mary. It seemed as if a higher power than Father Divine was administering punishment to the man who had declared himself to be God. And so she seized the opportunity to denounce him and promote herself to leadership of the cult. By her action Faithful Mary obtained the maximum of publicity. Her denunciation was bitterly feminine. She accused Father Divine of all the crimes of Satan; the seduction of herself, the rape of juveniles, blackmailing rich followers into giving him money, taking the profits of all the kingdoms, kidnaping children, putting his evil spell upon women and men alike and bewitching them to imagine that he was God.

The poor, frightened angels were stupefied by the un-Divine utterances of Faithful Mary. Only about half a dozen in her immediate entourage sided with her. She had ambitious schemes of salvaging the Divine Mission and setting it up on a new foundation without a God. But within three days of his disappearance Father Divine was discovered in one of his Kingdoms in Milford, Connecticut, and brought back to New York. His lawyers quickly effected his release under bond. All the angels hailed him. And his kingdoms continued to function as heretofore.

Unfaithful Mary was the name now applied to the fallen first angel. She tried to start a rival cult, but her efforts remained unblessed. Her hotel in Highland Falls was deserted by all the followers of Father Divine and remained empty. She furnished a house on Fifth Avenue and 123rd Street, but there were few guests. There was no rush of people to consume her good food. She journeyed to California, but this time she was a failure. The newspapers, white and colored, gave her valiant support. The Hearst organs were notoriously sympathetic. But everything she attempted ended in a sputter. Finally she was nearly killed in an automobile accident. And all the angels believed that it was the power of Father Divine pursuing her. She believed it herself.

For one year Faithful Mary lived "in the world of the

flesh" to which she had returned. She again took up drinking. Later she confessed that the reporters started her off
by inducing her to take egg-nog, so that she would testify
against Father Divine. But she became lonelier and sadder.
She said the spirit of Father Divine pursued her with a
warrant for her arrest. After one year she was compelled
to give herself up, and she wrote to Father Divine, asking
him to forgive her and take her back into his kingdom.

Father Divine has accomplished miraculous feats. But
nothing he has done has so fortified his position and elevated
his authority than compelling the humble return of penitent
Faithful Mary to his Kingdom. It has been gossiped about
that Father Divine pursued and pleaded with her to return
and made a secret deal with her, because his kingdoms were
falling to pieces without her. Faithful Mary publicly denied
this report. But the gossip was silly. During the year in
which Faithful Mary was out of the movement, every venture
she attempted to promote was a failure. And she dissipated
her funds. Naively she said that "Hearst reporters" promised
to make her a "pile of money," which they never did. But
during that same year Father Divine increased his following,
established new city kingdoms and added new lots to the
Promised Land. Even if he did persuade Faithful Mary to
return, it was eminently his godly duty. Father Divine has
stated that he is always ready to welcome again the angels
who have backslid. Faithful Mary was no exception. His
kingdoms are wide open to the world—all who care to enter
them.

On New Year's night, 1939, ten thousand followers and
sympathizers crowded Rockland Palace to celebrate the
return of the prodigal angel. The multitude of angels
capered and shouted "Peace, God is Wonderful!" Lustily
they sang the song of welcome:

> "I have never seen such happy days,
>   Since Father drew me safe back home,
>   From mansions to mansions, I've never seen
>   I have never seen such happy days,
>   Since Father drew me safe back home."

Faithful Mary made a complete recantation of the charges she had brought against Father Divine. She accused "Hearst reporters" of making her crazy with liquor, when she "began to get conflicted." And she went crazy in the head and said bad things about Father Divine. The reporters told her: "Hearst is going to give you a big lump sum of money. We are going to fix you up to make a good job and you can go into the movies and also broadcast. . . ."

Mary said that she and the reporters drank egg-nog and "I went plumb crazy, mad, fighting, every time it hit the bottom of the stomach. . . . They says, 'We wants a story. Maybe we can get something on Father, we can drive him out of the United States or give him time.' Prompted and under the influence of eggnog, Mary said, she lied about Father and the Peace Kingdoms. They made her sign a paper, but she lied, lied about Father and herself and young girls. Even before she went into court she had to drink first.

Mary told the long story of her futile flight away from Father Divine. From the time she left him, she said there was always a loud noise "like June-bugs singing in my head." And the spirit of Father Divine pursued her everywhere, in her bed, in her car. But she kept on trying to run away. She was afraid of Father Divine's catching up with her, for she could not face round to look at him, because of the low lying things she had said. Finally Father Divine caught up with her: "I was running through a barbed wire fence and my dress caught and before I could snatch it from the wire, Father came through the fence wtih his head looking right at me. And when I went to bring my arms down, Father had come suddenly under my arm. . . . Now truly the hour was come. . . . Oh, I am a prisoner of the Lord and today at the Judgment Bar I confess. I want to thank Father for allowing me to come back to the fold."

Faithful Mary has a pleasing voice, and as she recited her story in the charming Negro vernacular of the South, it was full of the poetic power, intensity and sincerity of Francis Thompson's divine poem, "The Hound of Heaven."

Now back in the fold, she is no longer the premier angel of the Peace Mission. She has returned to Newark, where under the direction of Father Divine she very humbly operates a house of peace. More than any other she is typical of the potentialities of the Divine people. Their collective initiative is enormous and they accomplish practical wonders under the leadership of Father Divine. But when they are not herd-driven by his power, they are lost souls. Many observers recognized that Faithful Mary was a key person in the Divine organization. But she was a key fashioned by Father Divine. And when that key fell out of his hand, it was worthless, it could open no other door.

．　　　．　　　．　　　．　　　．　　　．　　　．

1937 may be reckoned as the year of greatest tribulation for Father Divine. But 1938 was his banner year when he rallied to a thumping triumph in winning back Faithful Mary, acquiring the Krum Elbow estate and becoming the neighbor of President Roosevelt. The dictator of the Divine Deal carried his mystic-social experiment to the very boundary of the estate of the New Deal's founder. Father Divine's gesture appeared like a challenge to the New Deal and received national notoriety from that angle.

There could be no minimizing its symbolic significance. For the first time since its emancipation the Negro minority had broken away from the Republican Party on a nation-wide scale when it voted Democratic in 1932. Father Divine's is the only national Negro organization of any importance which has opposed the New Deal. Under the New Deal the Negro has received especially benevolent attention from the Washington Administration. They have official representation in the W. P. A. and N. Y. A. set-up. It is said that the percentage of Negroes benefiting from Federal relief is higher than that of any other group. In Harlem it is estimated that 60 per cent of Negroes are on relief and 20 per cent hold W. P. A. jobs. The rest, excepting the fortunate few in private employment, must be with Father Divine. In the South the status of Negroes under Federal relief has developed serious differences between the southern conservatives and the northern liberals of the Democratic Party. Under two administrations the Negro minority has remained Democratic; the only sign of change in its political horizon is the drift of Pennsylvania Negroes back to the Republican Party.

Now Father Divine believes that his movement is the natural collective successor to rugged individualism. He is fully aware of the break-down of the social system and the resultant misery of millions. But he believes that the Divine plan is the way of salvation. He is a vociferous advocate of laissez-faire and a rigid upholder of the status quo. It is only in his method of operating that he conflicts with authority and conservative opinion. Father Divine is not only an arch-conservative, he is a primitive mystic and is opposed to medical science and its advantages to the human race as much as he is to governmental regulation of industry for the benefit of workers and public.

He declares that he has saved the State of New York twenty-five million dollars since 1932 by taking his followers off the relief rolls. He would put the Divine plan in place of State and Federal aid. Militantly he also challenges trade unionism. He places his followers through his private employment agency. Frank Crosswaith, Chairman of the Negro Labor Committee, has charged Father Divine with undercutting the average wage standards. Crosswaith has discovered in Harlem some clothing industry operating shops in which the followers of Father Divine were working for much less than the union scale of wages. Father Divine declares that he has forbidden his flock to accept less than ten dollars in weekly wages! He says that by operating cheap lodging houses and cheap restaurants he has made it possible for his people to room and board for $5 per week!

The Divine Deal may be undermining the American standard of living, as Crosswaith says, but Father Divine's fanatics prefer it to the New Deal. I heard a brown woman testify to that at one of the banquets. She was a stout, fervent soul, about ten years short of middle age. "Peace!"

Photo by M. and M. Smith

Where the exclusive of Negro Respectability reside: the famous architect Stanford White's row of houses in 139th Street between Seventh and Eighth Avenue. Nicknamed Strivers' Row because of its smartness and desirability when Negroes first took over in the early nineteen-twenties.

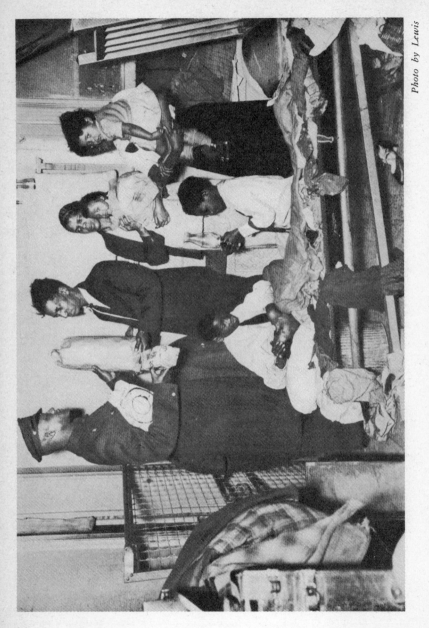

Police officer victualling a needy family.

Photo by Lewis

she cried. "Thank you Father, for being my true Relief. Oh Father, when I say Peace, I mean Peace, the Peace that you and you only can bring to the world. For I was a miserable and unhappy woman, Father, all the time I was on that Relief.

"The investigators they were all like detectives, Father, acting like I had committed a crime. They acted as if I didn't even birth myself my two children, as if I had killed my husband perhaps or had him in hiding some place, when he had runned off with a cat of a gal. I had to tell them more about my life, more than if I was on trial before the judge, and I never did keep no daily record of my life.

"Dear Father, the investigator searched my ice box and examined the toilet. Father I felt as if I was stripped of all my clothes and standing naked before them investigators. I wondered what else they might have been wanting to look at. And, oh, Father, I was ashamed of my life. Father, it is an awful feeling that to be sick and tired of your life. To feel that when you are down and out you are nothing better than a criminal.

"I got so, Father, that I hated the sight of that investigator. And one day Father, the devil him got the better of me and made me mean and mad and I hit the investigator wham in the mouth. Oh, and then I was sorry, Father, and I prayed to God to forgive me. I went down on my knees and wailed like a baby. And you revealed yourself to me; while I was kneeling and crying, Father, and said I should lay my burden down and get up and follow you. And I followed your spirit like a little lamb, Father, and it brought me into your bodily presence. And you have taken the trouble out of my life and put your Peace in my heart. Right away you removed me from the Relief and gave me a decent job. It is truly wonderful! I am a new woman. I am not ashamed anymore. I am happy on my job and I am happy with you, Father, and with all in you. I thank you, Father."

And the angels sang:

> "Father is the victory,
> Father is the victory,

Father is the victory that
Overcomes the world."

Thus Father Divine has assured his angels security and happiness. The Divine domestics are apparently well liked by many householders in New York. Father Divine receives letters praising their punctuality and honesty. Father Divine does not tolerate laziness. He declares forthrightly: "Even if you think I am slothful, if you think I am impractical, if you think I am unprofitable, good for nothing, my mind is that everyone of you should be practical, profitable and good for something . . . and produce more and earn more than what you could in the mortal world. If you cannot and will not and do not desire to do it, you are not attached to me!

"If you say you love him,
Get a job and go to work.

"What said I through the apostle by inspiration? 'He that does not work should not eat.' Then go to work in a practical way and see that you are at least as profitable as anyone else could be out in the world.

"The little honey bee can give you a mystery of what I am telling you. He goes into all of the flowers and seeks something. He may get something from the bitter as well as the sweet, and some sweet and some sweeter, but he gets it all together into what you call honey. Then I say, Go to the little honey bee, thou who are slothful and impractical as the bumble bee who knows everything and never makes honey. Oh how glorious it is to be a real honey bee instead of being a bumbling bee! Learn the lesson of the little honey bee."

Father Divine has been criticized for breaking up families, for separating husband and wife and children and parents. I have met several unhappy men in Harlem whose wives had left them to live in the Kingdom of Father Divine. One poor fellow had retained an undergarment as a souvenir, which he fondled disconsolately while I was visiting his dreary room. But the plain truth is that most of the angels in the Kingdom went to live in them because their homes were already broken up. There are plenty of broken homes in Harlem and even Father Divine's numerous kingdoms could not accommodate all the lonely hearts. Some live in the "Y" buildings, many in the innumerable lodging houses that cater to the restless population of Harlem.

Not all Father Divine's followers live in his kingdoms. Those who do are the co-workers or angels, who must renounce the responsibilities of family life. The children of these devoted disciples are not deserted by them. They are sent to the children's farm, where they live collectively. The plan appears to be similar in many ways to that under which large groups of children in Soviet Russia are brought up. Of course, there are older children who, untouched by the new faith of their parents, do not want to follow them into the Divine Kingdom; they do make something of a problem. I have lately observed a considerable number of adolescents at kingdom meetings, although this was not noticeable five years ago. Perhaps these are the grown-up children of followers. I could not determine what the psychic effect of the cult on their lives would be. But ordinarily they seem better cared for than a good many of the children of Harlem who are sent to dime-a-day nurseries or who roam the streets by day while their parents are at work. Father Divine has some capable teachers among his following, who undertake the education of the children. I know one who was a teacher in the New York City school system. Her husband is an engineer in Soviet Russia. She had planned to join him there, but in 1936 she changed her mind and resigned her position to join Father Divine. When her Communist friends disapproved of her action, she said that they had chosen Stalin as their God and she preferred Father Divine.

Father Divine has ordered all his illiterate angels to attend night school. They are numerous in the Harlem W. P. A. schools. He is interested in their political education and insists upon their exercising the right to vote. Five years ago the Metropolitan press asserted that Father

Divine had enormous political power in Harlem, which was a determining factor in the Negro vote. That was an incorrect appraisal. Harlem's vote went overwhelmingly New Deal. Father Divine's influence was most powerful in the religious arena, where he was drawing hundreds away from the regular churches into his kingdom.

Since then he has founded his Righteous Government forum, and today in 1940 he *is* a political power to reckon with. In the industrial field his Divine plan is working in its special way. It is possible that the Communists who sneaked out of their compact with him when he denounced the New Deal and trade unionism may be secretly supporting him, now that they are opposed to President Roosevelt. Divine's prestige has risen high since he launched the project of the Promised Land and finally acquired Krum Elbow. Negro journalists who formerly ridiculed him turned their pen to praise. The Negro intelligentsia may be skeptical of the cult, but they admire the Divine courage and cleverness in circumventing the great American taboo and bringing white and colored people together in intimate collaboration.

In five years Father Divine has won over a mountain of ridicule to command considerable respect. Convincing evidence of this is the *New Day,* the weekly organ of the movement. The diversified advertisements therein tell their own story of the enormous social influence of Father Divine. The magazine consists of a hundred odd pages and carries over four hundred local and national advertisements. Among the national advertisers are Pillsbury Flour, Weston's Biscuit Company, A & P Food Stores, Rand Stores, Loft's Candy and Woolworth's.

The Woolworth stores rarely advertise and so it is of some significance when they have a national advertisement in Father Divine's magazine. I was informed by an employee of the 125th Street Woolworth's that the Divinites are their best Harlem customers. Sometimes a kingdom will send in an order for fifty dollars worth of goods at one time. That does not appear such a large amount if one does not bear in mind that Woolworth is a 5 and 10 store.   Another national advertiser is Spear's Furniture at 3rd Avenue and 121st Street, with five branches in New York, Brooklyn and Long Island and two in Pittsburgh.   Spear's has the entire inside front cover of the magazine.   It is a huge installment plan establishment.   As Father Divine is resolutely opposed to the installment plan and prohibits his followers from making installment purchases, I asked the business manager of the *New Day* why the advertisement was featured.   She replied that she had sought Father Divine's advice and he had consented to the publication of the advertisement.   He said his followers could make cash purchases from the store and that the magazine is also read by non-followers who may want to take advantage of the installment plan.

Father Divine is enormously adaptable and receptive to the ideas of the outside world in spite of the apparently stringent regulations by which he rules his Kingdom.   He is prehensile in grasping whatever comes within his reach to make it serve the interests of his movement.   Divinely elated though he may be in the creation of the Promised Land, at present his greatest pride appears to be in the *New Day* magazine.   He often mentions it in his messages, commending it to the faithful.   Says Father Divine: "Because it carries my message verbatim, you can see most distinctly it is sweeping the universe.   It is not merely a national publication, it is international in nature."

He has always shown a keen interest in literature.   "Years ago," he says, "when I started through the different libraries to find some books of truth that would convey a high light of my divine teaching, I found the Robert Collier writings. This Robert Collier was a great metaphysician.   I sent these copies of his books to my followers: "The Christ in You," "The Impersonal Life," and I also sent Bruce Barton's books—the one who is Congressman now from New York City—"The Man Nobody Knows," "The Book Nobody Knows," and "The Life and Teachings of the Master of the Far East."

Here is Father Divine's idea of language: "There shall

be no division after awhile in language.   There shall be one language.   Now isn't that wonderful!   Now I did not say specially it must be broken English as I am speaking, but whatsoever language Divine Love and God's Omniscience finds sufficient and efficient for the purpose will be adopted. . . .

"Our English language is but a dialect according to the intellect and understanding of the Infinite.   And I say, how dare mortality in its limited finite mind to try to correct the Infinite One, the Almighty God?   How dare they try to criticize the grammatical expressions or grammatical errors as they may term it to be!   For the languages of men universally in this civilization, they are only dialects of me. I shall stop every dog from barking, those of you who think you are superintelligent, you who are the deans of the different colleges and institutions.   A good many of you attempt to criticize the omniscience of the Infinite One because his condescension to come in his likeness as he came was insignificant according to the versions of men. . . .   You cannot interpret the different dialects in the heathen land and yet you think you are intelligent. . . .   I will let man see the folly of his intelligence.   Who has known the mind of God that he or she might correct him?   I have not done a thing yet to what I will do.   I shall cause you to observe things that could not be considered.   I will even bring them out in that which is termed your own language."

And that is Father Divine in the grandeur of his glory in the year 1940 A.D. F.D.   He has magnificently created his kingdom on earth.   He has ushered in his own millennium, with angels of all complexions and races cavorting in his heavens in the Metropolitan heart of New York.   His arcadian extension of the Promised Land is abundant with all the milk and honey and perhaps locusts that enchant the dreams of the lotus lovers of Paradise.

His size, his color, his race, the subtle combination of ignorance, mystery and arrogance all have contributed to his elevation to the throne of Deity.   His followers are hypnotized by the strangeness of it all:—God must be like that!

Not so long ago he was only a piece of stick or stone. What appears most ridiculous to the outside world is the secret of his success and the source of his strength. By outlawing sex from his kingdom he neutralized the unsavory popular reaction which is the inevitable concomitant of intimate association between colored and white persons. And by setting himself up as a Deity his authority remains unchallenged.

The one thing missing now in this glorious creation is the Goddess. Mother Divine does not fill the place next to the Deity as fittingly as did Faithful Mary. The return and confession of the penitent Faithful brought forth a thousand new angels with jewels to stud the solid golden throne of Father Divine. But none has taken the precious place that Faithful Mary never will have again.

Who will get that place? Every king needs his viceroy and my prediction is that the place of Faithful Mary will fall to an archangel. Perhaps a white instead of a dark angel. No one has been so unswervingly devoted and loyal to Father Divine all through the years of his trials and triumphs than his confidential white secretary, John Lamb. Recently Mr. Lamb has pushed noticeably forward in platform speaking, besides continuing indefatigably in his secretarial duties. In former years he was always self-effacing, silent and smiling, even a little demure through all the volcanic emotions and heavenly antics around him.

Father Divine is a primitive God who has declared that he has stricken and will strike down all those who oppose and seek to injure him. He has forgiven Faithful Mary, but he does not forget that he was betrayed by a member of that species of humanity through which he chose to reveal himself to the world in bodily form.

After Faithful Mary had confessed, he said significantly: "Jesus came in the likeness of those who were called Jews . . . and they received him not. I came to the Americans and a good many who are commonly called Afro-Americans and they received me not. . . . If they will not come unto me, I may turn wholeheartedly and completely to those commonly known as Jews, for they are the ones now suffering. . . ."

Since that memorable night the faithful John Lamb has made many speeches and Father Divine has often sung the praises of the Lamb. Said he in one of his inspired messages: "Prejudice is the serpent! Prejudice beguiled the woman and the woman beguiled the man. But 'I looked, and lo, a Lamb stood on the Mount Zion and with Him was an hundred and forty and four thousand having their Father's name written in their foreheads.' Can you see the mystery? My spirit can lead and guide you and you will follow the Lamb—the Lamblikeness of God. The Lamblikeness of God is the Lamb of God. You will follow that degree of my expression. Can you see the mystery? The Lamblikeness is your leader. Then follow the Lamblikeness. For the Lamblikeness is your leader whilst God is in many different expressions of his majesty and allness."

If Father Divine should some day withdraw his bodily form from this world, his Peace Mission may continue to flourish, even as has Mrs. Eddy's Christian Science. His spirit is in all his angels, and in the event of his "withdrawal" they might simply agree to elect the worthiest among them to the throne of God.

The Occultists

Negroes, being human, love religion and also being animals, they wallow in animism. The religious heart of the Negro is his golden gift to America. The religion of the Negro is nationally regarded as an exotic phenomenon. The attribute of black folks' religion is not the same as that of white folks' religion. Some chroniclers believe that Negro religion is the nearest thing extant to the primitive religion of Jesus.

When black baptists of the South are celebrating a grand baptism down in the river, the whites make a special picnic day of the event to enjoy the spectacle. It is the same spirit which prompts the whites in the North to visit a church or a cult when the Negroes are prancing in Harlem.

Educated Negroes are roiled by such an attitude towards Negro religion. They fondly delude themselves that there is no difference between black folks' religion and white folks' religion—just as they can hypnotize themselves into thinking that there is no difference between white and black.

They have ready-made explanations. They can show with satisfaction that white people manifest some religious variations similar to the Negroes'. For the Kingdom of Father Divine in Harlem there is the Temple of Aimee Semple MacPherson in Los Angeles. For the occult mysteries of Harlem there are the Rosicrucians. And they can lean upon the support of social scientists who take the measure of all human expression with an identical economic yardstick and reduce all of psychic phenomena to a basic materialistic formula.

The organized Negro church is a great American institution. Founded in 1816, the African Methodist Episcopal Church is the greatest of all the denominations. Its spiritual and social achievements in the domestic and foreign fields are substantial and inspiring. But the religion of the Negro people stirs and swells and rises riotously over the confines of the Negro church and pours over into glorious streams of cults and fetich tributaries. It is immersed in African magic.

The innumerable cults, mystic chapels and occult shops which abound in Harlem are explainable only by tracing back to the original African roots. For Africa remains the continent of magic. From the northernmost tip of Tangier all the way down to the Cape, the African atmosphere is saturated in magic.

Millions of natives may come under the sway of either of the great rival religions of Islam and Christianity; but it is on pagan terms. Their profession of faith is pervaded by occult imagery. The fetich gods rule their hearts and the secret ritual of jungle magic is evoked to appease the obscure yearnings of the mind, which civilized religion cannot satisfy.

The cruder the magic, the greater its influence in Africa. I was amazed at the unlimited extent of the psychic influence of the Guinea fetichers over the more civilized people of northern Africa. The Guinea fetichers are the most powerful of magic makers. Their ritual is an elaborate extravaganza of music and wild dancing and shouting. Among their members and supporters are some of the great families of notables and nobles. Educated persons, high officials, sheriffs and even sultans are members of the cult. The Guinea fetichers are supposed to be in close contact with the diabolical powers. And they exorcise the evil spirits that have made their habitation in the bodies of human beings. They excel in strange maladies and are credited with curing persons who have been stricken by the principals of evil. They purvey charms. A leathern bag of Guinea magic stuff may be discovered hung around the neck or the shoulder of children of the best families.

Whether they are West Indian or southern practitioners of the occult science in Harlem, their ritual is basically similar in form and style to the performance of the Guinea fetichers. They may impressively promote themselves as numerologists, magicians, oraculists, metaphysicists, or plain spiritualists. But under the high-sounding titles they are the same old delvers in West Indian obeahism and voodooism.

In Harlem they have refined their work and enlarged their scope. The former basement dives of the obeahman and the conjure woman, once weird with the accumulated relics of animals' skins and bones and feathers and the black pot brewing evil-smelling stuff, are now transformed into mystic chapels in which burn candles and oils and incense.

Distraught persons resort to them for solace, to get information on finding jobs, love, friendship and conjugal felicity, lucky playing numbers charms to ward off evil. It is not so strange that these occult establishments should exist in Harlem. Like gypsies, they may be found in every place. But it is significant that such an increasingly large number should flourish there. Many of them advertise in Harlem's newspapers. But the exclusive and successful ones do not advertise. And these constitute the majority.

An indication of their luxuriant growth is the unusual springing up of sacred shops in Harlem. These are the depots which supply the ritualistic paraphernalia of the occult chapels. At first glance they appear no different from similar establishments downtown which furnish special religious articles for priest and altar.

But a little investigation discloses astounding differences. Behind the pictures and the statuary of biblical figures, there are the more important appurtenances of mumbo-jumbo. The shelves look like a pharmacist's, loaded with vari-colored jugs of oils with euphemistic labels such as: Jupiter, King Solomon, Felicity, Love-charm, Commander, Concentration, High John, Rosemary, Chapel Bouquet.

There are candles of every hue which are used in the mystic rites of candle-lore. Divination is done by the flicker of the flame or the shape of the tallow after the wick has burned out. The color of the candle is of special importance, as also the day on which it should be burned.

Yellow candles are burned for true devotion; green for material gain; purple for self-mastery, power and domination over others; red to win and increase love; pink to invoke celestial happiness; white for communion with the departed; orange for lucky dreams; blue for peace and harmony; black to ward off evil. Incenses, magic herbs and roots and an array of dream books of numbers complete the stock.

There is no connection between the occult chapels and the open cults, such as Mother Horne's and Father Divine's. The chapels are designed for intimate séances. Most of them are hidden away in apartments and known only to special devotees. There is as much difference between the occultists and the cultists as there is between the human ghost and the human soul.

Cultists, such as Father Divine, somehow follow the tradition of the prophets. But the Harlem occultists are the true descendants of the fetich priests. They attract their following by exploiting the method of a deft combination of cosmic mysteries and jungle apprehensions. Upon their altars in Harlem, pagan and Christian symbols are ranged together. But the priest or priestess is partial to oriental vestments, either Hindu or Persian, Arabian or Egyptian.

Over their pagan apparel the cross hangs upon their breasts. But they appease the wishful thinking of their devotees, telling their thoughts with roses and stars and birds' feathers and the symbol of the serpent, even as with the symbol of the cross. The lavish use of incense, oil and candles is a powerful opiate to the senses. And in that close atmosphere a rosary of meaningless words may seem beautifully true to those who recoil from facing forever the drab reality of their existence. Messages from the dear dead, interpretation of dreams and lucky numbers are eagerly accepted. And adequate remuneration is given in return. Like drug addicts accustomed to their special stimulant, the devotees must have their occult medicine.

I am drawn to Harlem's occult chapels by the same curiosity which impelled me to visit the candle-lit shrines of marabouts in Africa. One I visited recently is situated in the middle sector of Harlem, on the third floor of a tenement. Half the flat has been transformed into a chapel. It was suffocatingly crowded. I found standing room at the back. The atmosphere was narcotic with the heavy aromas of burning oils and incense. In the audience women predominated. They whispered excitedly, eyes strangely glittering, like pentecostal pilgrims awaiting a miracle. The walls in light blue were covered with mottos and rubrics— "Trust and Hope," "Love and Live," "Life is Mystery,"— and embellished with stars, crosses, crescents and hearts cut out of colored paper.

Up front there was a white altar, loaded with colored candles burning in little glass jars, and behind it, on the wall, a crude painting of an elaborate Tree of Life and Hope. The priestess was a brown woman of commanding height and bulk. She was robed in black and white, with voluminous sleeves and a long white train. Her headdress was fitted like that of a woman of ancient Egypt and all her movements were sidelong. She was assiduously assisted by a tall black man, costumed in red and gold. He straightened the train whenever the priestess seemed in danger of becoming entangled. He handed her the magic-making items she needed. On the altar were set the symbols of divination: a cross, a star, a crescent and roses.

When I entered, the priestess was engaged in a pantomime before the altar, clasping and unclasping her hands, bowing her head and stretching her large-sleeved arms to look like wings. At intervals she glided around the altar. Then she started an unintelligible incantation. When she stopped, she picked up a star and gazed intently at it. And in dark deep tones she declared: "I can see the limitless dimensions of omniscience. It is a long straight stroke. Is it the divine whip of the archangel of retribution? Or is it a staff? I feel interference. Let mine eyes be as the sight of the serpent."

Slowly she began gliding again around the altar, one hand

thrust out before and the other behind her as she said: "I see through the rose of revelation and I discern a pattern of lightning. It is a bright triangle. There is the letter Y. I hear sweet voices singing. I see little children dancing. The grass is green and tender, oh, I glimpse a silver M. Oh, I see another M clear as the sunny water of the stream of heaven! It is the month of May."

The women sighed together. "But there is a shadow," the priestess intoned. "There is a hand and a long finger pointing at May. Oh, clear like the jewel of the Madonna, I can see R. Yes, it is a name, Mary—a message for Mary. Five women, each named Mary, showed their hands. "But it is one message for one person only," said the priestess. "And it isn't you, and it isn't you and it isn't you," she sing-songed pointing at each Mary. She swayed back and forth and glided around the altar. She clasped the star to her forehead. Then she flung back her head and threw her hands straight upwards.

"I see a garden in the sky, a beautiful garden. Now there is a lady walking in the garden. Oh, but it is painful, painful. She walks with crutches. Oh, she is very painful, but she must walk in that garden. Now she is stooping—it is painful, very painful, but she picks a rose." As she chanted, moaning, the priestess acted out the part of the lady in pain in the garden. She was a good actress. And now she cried: "Oh light of my vision! My eyes are dazzled by a wonderful flash in the sky. And it brings me the name, Rosemary! Rosemary!"

A good-looking brown girl fell out of her chair in the front row and writhed on the floor: "Oh mother, my mother, my mother in pain!" she wailed. The woman started keening and moaning, but in subdued voices, like persons sobbing in a sick-room. The priestess lifted up the girl, embraced and comforted her: "Don't cry. Your mother is no longer in pain. But the good spirits revealed her to me by her former life here on the earth. Those are the ways of the spirit to convey hidden secrets. I saw your mother in pain, but I have also seen her uplifted from pain. She is happy

Photo by James L. Allen

Photo by M. and M. Smith

Night Club Scenes.

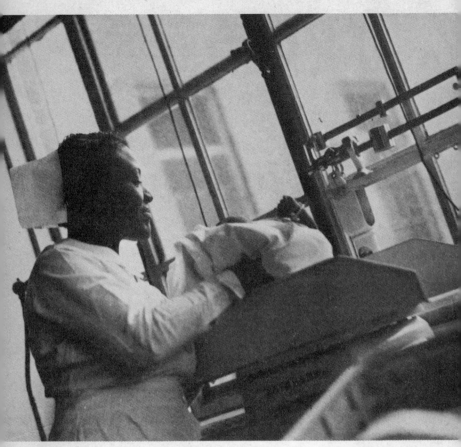

Harlem Nurse.

and laughing with honey on her tongue. Her message to you is, walk straight and beware of the joy-riding lovers in Harlem."

"Thank you, mother, for your message," said the girl. Composing herself, she extracted a five-dollar note from her purse and handed it to the priestess. "This is mother's gift," said the priestess, holding the note before the altar. "And any of you all who feel compensated by the action of my spirit in contacting and revealing the unknown tonight, may contribute something for the good spirits. I feel that my inspiration is boundless tonight and those who desire more personal and secret revelation may wait and see me after the meeting. The fee is only one dollar for a private revelation. And I am giving you two consecrated numbers, 618 and 901."

The women crowded round the altar with contributions.

A few of the prominent occultists are known in the wider field of the community's life. Madame Josephine Becton is the wife of the famous evangelist and cult leader, George Wilson Becton, who was mysteriously murdered in 1933. She established the Becton spiritualist chapel as a memorial to her late husband. Professor Bennet has visited Europe and has there had remunerative séances. He says that he made his greatest success in Scotland. In Harlem he has been identified with straight business ventures. He was one of the chief promoters of an Actors' and Travellers' Club.

The most interesting of all perhaps is Madame Fu Futtam, the last wife of Sufi Abdul Hamid, the former labor agitator and cult leader. Madame Fu Futtam is the top-ranking occultist. Very industrious in the art of clairvoyance, she has published a series of dream books with interpretive numbers, which have made a fortune for her.

Probably she owes some of her success to her striking oriental features. She was born in Panama and has oriental blood of some sort. She is neatly small and birdlike and when robed for a séance she resembles a dark Chinese girl.

Since the Sufi's death she has had aspirations for a higher expression of the mystic urge within her. She had given her

hand and her fortune to the Sufi when she persuaded him
to give up the hard and always conflict-stirring job of Negro
labor leader to return to the more tranquil business of
preacher of oriental mysticism. They established an ornate
Temple of Tranquillity. But, within a year of their union,
before they could profit materially from the new spiritual
adventure, the Sufi was killed suddenly, tragically.

Now alone, but an ardent votary of the Sufi idea, Madame
Fu Futtam is striving to establish a small mystic Temple
of Tranquillity for the needs of Harlem. She says that
the core of the idea is the worship of the female principle
as the all highest of the universe. By persevering in these
ideas, human beings may finally reach the acme of perfect
tranquillity. Madame Fu Futtam does not approve of the
clash and clamor of the traditional Negro cults. Negroes
are a naturally noisy people, she says, and the religious
exploitation of noise has made Harlem a bedlam. But
she aspires to cultivate tranquillity in Negro character in
the hope that Negroes might grow within and develop their
spiritual forces like the oriental peoples.

Madame Fu Futtam has abandoned her former name in
favor of calling herself Madame Abdul Hamid. But I
imagine that, with her charming Chinese face, she was more
appealing as Fu Futtam, perched like an illuminated tropical
bird in her oriental inner sanctum. Such a setting seemed
perfect for her tiny, svelte form and her demure attitudes.
I cannot imagine her successful transfiguration into a cultist,
even in a Temple of Tranquillity.

I must confess to a greater interest in the introvert occultists than in the heaven-raiding cultists. Some of my
friends are very "psychic" and I enjoy attending séances with
them. Occultists react differently to different persons. Immediately one enters, they apprehend one's presence whether
one is a positive or a negative subject. Their mystical
clairvoyant faculties are enhanced by contact with "psychic"
persons. The women, especially when they are as pleasing
as Madame Fu Futtam, have the seductive fascination of
serpents. And probably they exercise the rare art of the

snake charmer to subdue and soothe distraught souls. To those who find spiritual comfort in dim-lit rainbow colors and the opiate odors of incense, the intimate atmosphere of the occult chapel may offer as much solace as the shrine of a great cathedral does to others.

The Cultists

While the performances of the occultists rarely reach the glare of publicity, the cultists often steal the Metropolitan headlines. Strange cults have always been numerous in Harlem. The Negro church has gone a long way towards letting its people go to the extreme of spiritual license. To hold their people the preachers are partial to their excessive demonstration of primitive emotionalism in the pews. Indeed, many preachers prompt and lead the shouting and the stomping of the old-time religion.

But the church is no adequate outlet for the burning religious energy of the black masses. Therefore the cults multiply in Harlem. In bygone days the cultists were taken with tolerance and humor by the ordained ministers. Many of them chalked their messages on the pavements and did their stunts with banjo and tambourine. They were the spiritual spice of the Harlem scene. Their performances on the sidewalks at eventide did not much disturb the respectable congregations in their fine buildings. They were more the rivals of the political street speakers than of the preachers.

One picturesque figure was the tall and stately Barefoot Prophet, who was beloved by all of Harlem. In summer and in winter he walked the streets barefooted and white-headed. And whoever had a spare coin dropped it in his box. His method was the undemonstrative one of accosting an individual on the street and asking if he were all right with God. In the same quiet manner he went into all the poolrooms and saloons, talked to a few individuals and accepted contributions.

The myriad cultists blazed the glory trail to heaven, frenziedly tramping and shouting to the stars from basements and abandoned stores. There were such sects as the Cross-bearers. They were a group mostly of women who had crosses sown down the full length of their backs. They shouted deliriously of the burdens they were forever doomed to carry on their backs. And they vigorously danced with that emphatic downward stroke of the head, common among the native women of West Africa. There were the Ordeal-By-Fire Disciples, who licked flames with their tongues, somewhat similarly to the Dervishes of Mauretania, who consume fire on their great feast days. Daddy Grace and the radio artist Mother Horne compete with Pentecostal Pilgrims, Orthodox Ethiopians, Moorish Science Templars, Black Jews and many others, Christian and non-Christian; the black masses thrive upon heterodoxy. To the Harlem intelligentsia and the respectable church-goers the cults were local circuses. But in recent years two cults have arisen in Harlem so different from all the rest, that they have compelled serious attention. They are the World's Gospel Feast, which was promoted by George Wilson Becton, and the Peace Mission of Father Divine.

George Wilson Becton was the first of the great cult leaders to excite the imagination and stir the enthusiasm of the entire Harlem community. He was the supreme Godsman. He started his career in Harlem just when the high tide of its carnival was receding. That was in the beginning of the nineteen thirties. Harlem was the wild playground of New York. A territory abandoned to big law-breakers, it was the "widest-open" spot when Prohibition was in force and was the headquarters of the great gangsters trafficking in bootleg booze and narcotics. At night its speakeasies drew together around the same bar the sophisticates and aristocrats of New York, the hoodlums and criminals. Like gypsies summoned for the divertissement of distinguished guests, Negro performers provided rare entertainment. The spirit of the times was reflected in the state of hectic ferment among Negroes.

Becton invaded the notorious realm of freebooters with his twelve young disciples and a splendid orchestra. Becton was tall, handsome and college-educated. Harlem cultists before his time were all illiterates. But Becton spoke the language of the educated Negroes, although he knew how to reach the hearts of the common people. He styled his mission "The World's Gospel Feast." His meetings were not the loose, corybantic revels of Father Divine's "kingdoms." They were patterns of order and grace. The congregation waited in a hushed silence which was broken by soft strains of music. Pages in fine robes led the singing. The orchestra plunged the congregation into joyful swaying, as they sang gospel hymns to the titillating music of the dance hall. And Becton's commanding presence dominated the scene. Women, responsive to his agile movements and his well-modulated, persuasive voice, swayed like reeds.

Becton was an inspiring preacher, and ordained ministers welcomed his irresistible evangelism in their pulpits. Only a Becton could provide the spiritual excitement to compete with the ungodly distractions of the times. Thus he was called to the Salem Methodist Episcopal Church, whose pastor was the Rev. F. E. Cullen, the father of Harlem's poet Countee Cullen.

Becton invented the phrase, "the consecrated dime," by which he diverted tens of thousands of dimes from the numbers racketeers to the church collections. He was adequately remunerated. He purchased two houses and his own apartment provided Harlemites with delectable gossip. Among its special items were his golden slippers and his broad golden bed. A golden gate led from an immense music and reception room into his private rooms, which he called the Holy Chambers. His white-and-gold bathroom resembled an oriental bazaar with fine cushions. The tub was concealed in casements. Becton sometimes dined there. with disciples and special guests.

The order of his household was extraordinary. The cook was called "dietitian," the valet was "intelligent officer," the chauffeur "city guide." Becton set the fashion for

Harlem's boulevardiers with his expensive, finely tailored clothes.

As a prestidigitator of primitive piety, Becton was magnetic and magnificent. He was aloof, exclusive and worshiped by his followers. He advocated celibacy, even as Father Divine did later. After preaching, he never mingled with the congregation to shake hands. One of the chosen of his twelve disciples would throw a cape around him and he would retreat by a rear door.

Becton increased his prestige by making impressive hegiras to other Negro cities, and his return to Harlem was always triumphal. But Becton paid the price of his unprecedented success and bizarre life. He was always a subject of suggestive gossip and there were strange rumors about his emotional grip upon women and men. He had enemies. Other preachers were jealous of his holy business. Also he had remained for some years estranged from his wife.

One night in Philadelphia—it was May 21, 1933—he was kidnaped by two white men and "taken for a ride" in his own car. Later the car was discovered in a sinister side-street with Becton's body punctured with bullets. Within four days he died in extreme agony.

With the death of Becton, the Harlem field was wide open for Father Divine to conquer and expand the glorious domain of his wonderful Kingdoms of Peace.

Harlem Businessman

It is significant that the original founders of this Harlem had no intention of building a great Negro quarter. Phillip A. Payton and his associates had another vision, when they formed the Afro-American Realty Company in 1904. They *did* consider the acquisition of property in Harlem as a pioneer effort. But their aim was to make it serve as an instrument in abolishing residential restrictions against Negroes, so that individuals of wealth and consequence, according to their material assets and cultural accomplishments, could enjoy the luxury of acquiring homes in any desirable section. The plan must have been approved by powerful influential white New Yorkers, for it was conspicuously published and praised in the Metropolitan Press. Apparently there was increasing concern among the liberal groups of whites of that period that the best Negro citizens were being condemned to live among the worst elements of whites, who were militantly contemptuous of Negro respectability.

To illustrate the progress of Negroes as propertied persons in New York, these twenty were listed who owned property valued at $20,000 and upwards:

William Russell Johnson	$20,000
Charles W. Anderson	20,000
Samuel R. Scrotton	40,000
Norman E. Epps	40,000
James E. Garner	40,000
William R. Heyliger	40,000
J. Hoffman Woods	45,000

John D. Nail	$50,000
Charles A. Dorsey	60,000
Charles H. Lansing	60,000
Mrs. Phillip A. White	70,000
Mr. Leonard Frazier	70,000
Daniel Brooks	75,000
F. H. Gilbert	75,000
Phillip A. Payton, Jr.	80,000
Lemuel S. Williams	100,000
Dr. P. W. Ray	100,000
James C. Thomas	125,000
William H. Smith	200,000
Mrs. James Barfield	200,000

The hegira of the respectability of white Harlem when the cultivated stratum of Negroes aspired to be their neighbors compelled the latter to create a Negro colony. Well-off Negroes were attracted to invest in Harlem property. During the boom years of the First World War and the golden nineteen twenties the properties held by Negroes were enormously increased. Today, despite the 10-year economic crisis, there still are about 200 Negroes owning property which runs in value from $20,000 to $500,000. Many of the incautious were left high-and-dry when the expansion boom contracted and suddenly subsided like a river returning to its bed after wildly overleaping its bounds. The catastrophe swept away some of the oldest Negro firms. Others were cruelly crippled. The St. Phillips Episcopal Church (colored) owned an entire side of a block on 135th Street between Lenox and Seventh Avenues. This property was caught in a net of financial difficulties and the trustees, while still holding the title, were compelled to place it in the power of a white brokerage firm for a number of years. The property is worth about $900,000.

New firms have superseded the old. The largest is the Augustine Austin Antillean Company which controls an estimated million and a half dollars worth of property. Among other realtors names that are popular among Harlemites are Dr. Godfrey Nurse, Mrs. Branch, Walter Miller, Clarence D. King, Captain Joshua Cockburn, Kenneth Bright, John W. Walker.

The last named is the only Negro member of the Real Estate Board of New York. His property rates about $200,-000 in value. He is one of the few realtors who withstood the shock of the collapse of real estate values in Harlem. Of the many Harlemites who tried the cooperative housing plan he is one of the rare ones who made a success of it. In 1925 he decided upon turning one of his tenements into a cooperative house. He gathered together a group of dependable tenants receiving regular wages and sold each an apartment to be paid by instalment. Walker himself supervised the project and thus eliminated the cost of a manager. When the house was first turned over to the group it rented at $14 per room. It has been gradually reduced and today is $6 per room. Mr. Walker advocates the cooperative plan as one practical way of tackling the housing problem for Negroes, or for any low-salaried group.

The Rockefeller Dunbar apartments failed of their original purpose because the high managerial salaries of a large staff were too great a burden. Negro property is put in a special category in New York's Real Estate. It is taboo to the large responsible firms. As it comes under a ban, it must be exploited by a special group. Mortgages are expensive and banks are not co-operative, because black houses have a lower value than white houses. It is an inexorable law of real estate that as soon as Negroes move into a building or a block, which was formerly white, the value depreciates. The property may not immediately deteriorate, but the landlords insure themselves against that eventuality by enormously increasing rentals as soon as Negroes take over. It must truthfully be admitted that deterioration sooner or later is a natural correlative of Negro occupancy. For unlike small conservative white families, the majority of Negro families must let rooms to eke out the rent. And roomers cheapen a Negro house as much as they do a white house.

Many among the professional groups of Harlemites imagine that the Negro has done exceedingly well in the matter of displacing the whites and acquiring churches and homes in Harlem. The late James Weldon Johnson optimistically sums up this attitude in "Black Manhattan": "The question inevitably arises: Will the Negroes of Harlem be able to hold it? . . . the Negro's situation in Harlem is without precedent in all his history in New York; never before has he been so securely anchored, never before has he owned the land, never before has he had so well established a community life."

Undoubtedly the bulk of Harlem's intelligentsia, the hundreds of medical doctors and dentists and lawyers and city and state employees would support this viewpoint. What then is the cause of the chronic sickness of Harlem, which is pre-depression and has become only more acute since the depression?

It is apparently the lack of community commerce among the residents. This feature, more than anything, strikes the eye and invites sarcastic or cynical comments from every intelligent visitor. There is no other American community in which the huge bulk of local business, from the smallest to the largest, is operated by outsiders.

Once a white observer commented to me: "The whites gave up their churches and homes to the Negroes but held on to their businesses." But the statement was not quite correct. Harlem was exclusively a residential quarter when the Negro moved in. There was not a single store on Seventh Avenue. Fifth Avenue had an occasional store, and the few grocery stores and drinking and eating places were all on Lenox Avenue. The little tradesmen, Greeks, Italians, Jews and others, followed in the wake of the Negro invasion to Harlem because they discovered there a fallow field.

In the Puerto Rican section of the negro quarter, from 116th to 110th Street between Lexington and Lenox Avenues, the aspect is altogether different. Like Arabs, the Puerto Ricans wedged themselves into every available space, in basements and front rooms of first floor apartments, and carried on business until they were able to acquire larger stores. Today 99 per cent of the community commerce is done by Puerto Ricans and other members of the Spanish-speaking colony. Yet they started moving into Harlem in considerable numbers only about 1925, twenty years after the Negroes had established themselves there.

An analysis of the popular movements of Harlem show that they all spring from the simple instinctive urge of the Negro masses to support some form of community enterprise. This urge was put into motion by the churning propeller of the romantic Back-To-Africa movement of Marcus Garvey. When the Garvey organization purchased two trucks the people were exuberantly enthusiastic; when it acquired an old boat and manned it with a Negro crew, they went delirious. It was the same spirit that inspired the Sufi campaign and other campaigns for jobs. Under the shibboleth of peace and prancing it also infuses the Father Divine Mission. It injected that tempo and éclat in the numbers game in Harlem which went out of it as soon as white gangsters took it over.

These manifestations of the Negro masses have been condemned by white and colored critics as chauvinism and race hatred. But such social phenomena are purely human and American, showing the desire of Negroes to develop similarly to other American groups. The clandestine numbers game compelled Negro operators to set up candy and cigar store fronts to run it. The experience has taught many of them that it is even more advantageous to run such stores legitimately without the numbers business. The candy and cigar stores have been the best barometer of Negro business within the last ten years. They are the most numerous. Next in line are the restaurants and grocery stores and taverns. But excepting the taverns only a few of these little businesses measure up to the standards of those of their white competitors.

There is not a straight first-class restaurant in Harlem. And this fact is surprising, because Negroes make excellent cooks, waiters and caterers to white people. Some of the taverns serve good food, such as Eddie's, Chicks, the Hollywood, the Old Colony and the old Monterey. But many people, even the most modern, do not always like a crowded barroom atmosphere, which is not conducive to a quiet conversational meal. All other restaurants are small, stuffy lunch-counter places. The only congenial place in Negro Harlem, where a person may go with a guest to sit and converse at leisure and enjoy the atmosphere of a dining room with good food and courteous service is the Spanish restaurant El Mundial on 116th Street.

Cafeterias have been popular in New York for about twenty years. There is not a Negro-owned cafeteria in Harlem. The two run by whites in 116th and 125th Street respectively are always crowded with Negroes. They are spacious and airy, clean and comfortable. Negroes come from all parts of Harlem to eat and keep rendezvous in them. Then, too, there is no tipping in a cafeteria. Negroes must tip in their own places, for tips are a part of waiters' wages. But the tipping custom, annoying to whites, must also be to Negroes, since the majority are in the lowest income group.

In the more ambitious business field, the Belstrat Laundry Company was for many years the outstanding enterprise. It was launched in 1921 by David Doles, Colin Doles, Ellis Wright and L. A. Baron. The capital stock was $5,000. At present the capital stock is $150,000. It employs about 75 persons, all Negroes. Besides its Negro clientèle, it serves a considerable number of white people. But it is like a candle flickering in a small corner of the vast dim depot of Harlem.

Here again a little self-criticism might be good for the Negro soul. Negro women are celebrated as laundry workers, and 75 per cent of women laundry workers are colored. A large percentage of them work in hand laundries, which do not require any considerable outlay of capital like the Belstrat, which is a steam laundry. The wages and working conditions of laundry workers are notoriously poor. Yet no Negroes thought of operating their own laundries, like the Chinese and small white proprietors, until Father Divine started to reign as God in Harlem. Excepting the cheap restaurants, the "Peace" laundries are the most numerous of the businesses of the Divine Mission. Scores of them have sprung up since Father Divine launched his Righteous Government Plan in 1936. He taught bewildered middle-aged Negro women to work cooperatively by establishing small laundries in which they work in groups. And although the Father Divine businesses are largely cut-rate, his Peace laundries are not. They compete fairly with the Chinaman and the small white laundry owner, charging the same 10 cents each for shirts and 6 or 7 cents for sheets. They are making good business, for their laundering is tiptop.

The plain truth is that it is only in the last seven years that the Negro Community has been awakened to the possibilities of the small business in the basement or a pushcart in the street. Working in the well-stocked kitchens and dining rooms of the whites downtown, without thought of social catastrophe, the average Negroes were extremely snobbish as servants of the wealthy. They were contemptuous of Tony who served them in Harlem with ice and vegetables and the Jew who bought their junk.

It was Arthur Reid, founder of the African Patriotic League, whose propaganda changed that attitude. Reid was one of the promoters of a Negro doll factory during the halcyon reign of Marcus Garvey. People had mocked at his idea of Negro dolls, but his adventure was a success until Negro pride went low with the Depression. Then Reid turned to the pavement to preach development of Negro business. He started about the same time Sufi Abdul Hamid began his job crusade.

Negroes stirred from their lethargy and shed the snobbery of comfortable domestics. They found other uses for the basements than the concoction of obfuscating rot-gut liquor. They stored there, instead, blocks of ice and toted them thence to serve customers in the neighborhood just as Tony did. The competition became so sharp that some of the white dealers hired colored delivery boys as fronts. Other Negroes acquired push carts and started selling fruits and vegetables and fish on Eighth and Lenox Avenues. Some were so successful they expanded and opened fruit and vegetable shops. It is no longer unusual to see colored and white vendors with pushcarts offering their wares in fair competition. And there is no friction.

West Indians are foremost in these little businesses of push carts, fruits and vegetable stands, candy stores and grocery stores. American Negroes are more numerous in the restaurant trade, bars and grills and barber shops. Because of their energy and tenacity in this line, their American cousins call the West Indians the black Jews of Harlem. They even credit them with superior business acumen. But the truth is that the English-speaking West Indians, like the Spanish-speaking, show aptitude in this sphere because of their background. In the English speaking islands the Negroes are over 90 per cent of the population. The small white aristocracy are all high officials, heads and subheads of departments and large landed proprietors. The upper layer of the wealthy mulatto group are politicians, big merchants and civil servants. Enterprising Negroes therefore enter the field of petty commerce which is wide open to them and in which their competitors are immigrant Chinese and East Indians whose standard of existence is on a lower level than the Negroes'. When these Negroes migrate to America they see in the black belts a special field in which their native background is helpful.

The most ambitious development in recent Negro business in Harlem is the Powell-Savory Corporation. The company takes its name from the two physicians who head it. It operates the Victory Mutual Life Insurance Company, the Brown Bomber Baking Company and the *Amsterdam News,* local weekly newspaper, and smaller enterprises, among which is the Personal Finance Corporation.

An interesting aspect of the three major enterprises is the fact that Drs. Powell and Savory stepped in when the companies were insolvent, and started them spinning again along the road of success. The two physicians were outstanding in their professional work in the community and had never had any training or experience in business. Yet they have shown extraordinary acumen and capability in the world of affairs.

The Victory Life Insurance Company was first organized as a Chicago stock company in 1923. The director was a Negro manufacturer and banker, Anthony Overton. Its capital stock was $100,000 and its surplus $100,000. It became bankrupt in 1932 and went into Federal receivership. Dr. P. M. H. Savory of New York was the largest single stockholder, having an investment of $40,000. He, Dr. C. B. Powell and Undertaker John W. Duncan were untiring in their activity to refloat the comany. They succeeded in their effort in 1934, when it was reorganized as a mutual company. It was the first company of its kind to be redeemed from receivership. The Victory Mutual is the third largest Negro life insurance company. The central offices are housed in a $250,000 building in Chicago, but the largest volume of business is done in New York, where the two chief heads of the organization reside. Other branch offices are in Brooklyn, N. Y., Buffalo, New Rochelle, Washington, D. C., Cleveland, Toledo, Cincinnati. In the last annual report of December 31, 1939, the company's assets were $921,-825.55, its total liabilities $792,694.44. The New York region does about $5,000,000 business in a year. The company has about 400 Negro employees.

The Harlem weekly, the *Amsterdam News,* was acquired by the Powell-Savory Corporation late in 1935. The former owner, Mrs. Sadie Warren Davis, was a sympathetic, middle-aged mulatto woman, instinctive and emphatic in her likes and dislikes, primitively personal in her social attitude, and was not a figure in smart Harlem society. She was not highly educated but she was very race-conscious and had a real respect for education and intelligence in her group. And so she assembled together on her paper the best journalistic talent in Harlem. When her staff joined the Newspaper Guild and demanded recognition as a unit, she could not understand their desire to organize. She saw nothing in the labor movement but a white folks' racket. She considered it a personal affront to herself, especially because she had to treat with white officials of the Guild, some of whom were ineptly or perhaps deliberately lacking in tact. Mrs. Davis felt that she had worked hard enough to publish a community newspaper in the face of white contempt and ridicule, and resented white persons dictating the wages and hours under which her staff should work. Her employees went on strike. Great, spreading Heywood Broun, President of the Newspaper Guild, led the pickets on the line, and the downtown Communists came uptown in relays, the local staff projected effective community propaganda, and in a few weeks the *Amsterdam News,* losing circulation and harassed by creditors, went into receivership.

As soon as the *Amsterdam News* went down in the fight, out-of-town publishers moved to get hold of it. The Communists were interested, but their own Harlem *Liberator* had just died from lack of nourishment and they were very busy launching the Popular Front. At this point Drs. Powell and Savory stepped in and, taking advantage of the situation, they acquired the paper and kept it in the community. It was a clever move, for a weekly organ was an invaluable asset to their various business ventures.

With no previous newspaper experience the publishers have done a good job. Under the able realistic editorship of Harvard Graduate Earl Brown the paper is sharper and snappier than previously. From 11,000 the circulation has increased to 50,000, jumping from a provincial Harlem weekly to take third place among the six or seven national Negro newspapers. The *Pittsburgh Courier* published at Pittsburgh, Pa., leads with over 130,000 circulation, and next but much farther behind is Baltimore's *Afro-American*, put out by the interesting Murphy clan of that city.

Negro newspapers are largely chronicles of local events which are of special interest only to the members of the group. Social items often take precedence over news—parties and receptions, the splashing of prominent members of the smart set. Next in importance are the grim stories of the discrimination and prejudice which Negroes must endure throughout the States. Sports and the stage are widely featured. And petty local crimes within the group are headline features. There is much criticism of the *Amsterdam News* for its sensational dressing up of these crimes with documentary photographs. But obviously they make a popular appeal. It is a first-class achievement to publish a successful Negro newspaper, for it is the strangest of hybrids in the newspaper field. A Negro weekly is something like a small-town newssheet but the latter has the advantage of a small town location. The Negro weeklies are published in the large cities and must compete somehow with the white dailies which Negroes read more than they do their own newspapers. Many of the highly intellectual Negroes do not read Negro newspapers. Indeed I have heard individuals say they are ashamed to carry a Negro newspaper in public! The Negro weekly approximates to the magazine type of publication. But the majority of its readers are not the magazine reading type, not even of the popular brand such as Liberty. And so the Negro publisher faces the problem of making his special newspaper unusually attractive and exciting for its readers. More than any Metropolitan newspaper the *Daily News* is read in Harlem. The *Amsterdam News* might be described as a special weekly Negro edition of the *Daily News*.

The Brown Bomber Baking Company is the latest venture of the Powell-Savory Corporation and the most challenging of all. It takes its name from the popular sobriquet of Joe Louis, who is a director of the Victory Mutual Life Insurance Company. The clever idea popped into the head of Mr. Macy Maconeal that he might do good business selling a loaf of bread in a Joe Louis wrapper to Negroes. But he had no capital. Therefore he imparted the idea to a white baker who saw a possibility in it and agreed to furnish the bread wholesale at a moderate price.

When the Brown Bomber bread was first put on the market in January 1939, it was greeted with a good deal of intellectual criticism. Its critics thought it would have difficulty competing with the popular brands of established companies selling in Harlem. They said that bread could not be sold on racial sentiment. But the common Negroes were curious about the Brown Bomber bread and asked their grocers for it. In its initial stage, however, the venture was not profitable. It was about to be liquidated when the Powell-Savory corporation took over. A stock company was organized with a capital of $100,000. It established its own plant, improved on the quality of the bread and injected a community loyalty, colored with racial sentiment, in its advertisements. The Brown Bomber is hitting a strong new stride in Harlem. It looks as if it might become the brightest thing in Negro business.

The two men who direct the Powell-Savory companies see in the Negro community a long neglected field of business endeavor. They are neither sentimentalists nor chauvinists about race. And they are not defeatists. They are aware that in the white world there are different elements that make business enterprises possible and successful. They know that good will means much and sentiment too, and that a name may have distinction and selling quality among white as well as among colored people. They see the possibilities of the Negro community in terms of business. And that is a new point of view for professional Negroes.

Besides the Powell-Savory Corporation's Victory Life there is another important insurance company. The United Mutual Benefit Association was organized at the height of the Depression in 1933. It is the only Negro insurance association chartered in the state of New York. It specializes in the industrial type of insurance and has a special weekly plan designed to meet the needs of the average Negro worker. Also it carries on extensive activity in the field of Negro real estate. It has 125 persons on its permanent pay roll, and part-time employees brings the total to two hundred. Its officers are President Charles N. Ford, Vice-President Gilbert A. Miller. Democratic District Leader and Assemblyman Daniel Burrows is one of the trustees.

No report on business in Harlem would be adequate without mention of the Madame C. J. Walker Company, manufacturers of hair preparations. For years it was the greatest Negro business, having branches throughout the States and

the West Indies.   The founder of the business, Madame
C. J. Walker, was reputed to have made a fortune of over a
million dollars.   She employed hundreds of Negroes in her
factories in Indianapolis and New York, in her schools of
Beauty Culture established in all the large cities, and as
agents here and in the West Indies.   And she built a mansion
valued at $250,000 in Irvington-on-the-Hudson.

Indirectly her fame crossed over to Europe.   It was the
Walker System from which originated the attractive coiffure
of Josephine Baker that was so fascinating to Parisians—so
much so that a French company adopted the name for a
pomade, Baker-fix.   This pomade was widely sold in France,
Spain, Italy and North Africa.   The attention of a traveller
in these countries was often arrested by huge colored posters
of Josephine Baker advertising Baker-fix.

Madame Walker was first in the field.   She was considered
a benefactor to the women of her race.   Before her rise to
fame, articles for bleaching black skin and refining Negro
hair were purveyed by Southern white firms.   About 1904
Madame Walker produced a salve which was peerless in the
process of straightening and softening kinky hair.   She said
that the secret of it was revealed to her in a dream.   She
started to manufacture it in a little frame house in Indianapolis.   The demand for the product rapidly increased.

She built a large factory in Indianapolis.   In 1914 she
moved to New York.   She bought a house in Harlem in
which she established a school of Beauty Culture.   Before her
time, nappy-haired Negroes were apologetic about their
fibrous scalps.   Any measures taken to improve the primitive
condition of the hair were carried out in secret.   Madame
Walker revolutionized Negro Beauty Culture, and respectable women of her race were no longer ashamed of
treatment to improve the hair.

Advertised by attractive agents and in Negro publications,
the Walker products became essential to Negro society.   Her
schools of beauty attracted students from the most cultivated
Negro families.   Around her gathered some of the most arresting types of Negro beauty, even those who did not require

special treatment for their hair. That was before the great national growth of beauty shops. When the Marcel wave was the fad among white women, the Indian mane was the rage among colored.

At the peak of the Garvey Back-To-Africa movement, the agitators conducted a vigorous campaign against the revolution in Negro hair. Today it is Father Divine who carries on the crusade. His followers are forbidden to recondition their hair. But Harlem wags say that Father Divine might not be so opposed to hair culture if he were not entirely bald. In the pioneer days it was mainly the women underwent the treatment. Men who did so were generally connected with the stage. Laymen who took to ironing the hair were regarded askance. But when so many innovations were precipitated after the First World War, colored men of all classes openly adopted the hair-straightening process.

At that time Madame C. J. Walker had reached the top of her career. She was not an arbiter of fashionable Harlem society as her daughter was destined to be. But in her mansion on the Hudson she presided with Queen Victoria-like dignity over the conservative element of the Negro group. Her advertisements in Negro publications were the largest and costliest of any Negro business.

Besides the salons of beauty for colored ladies, today all the barber shops feature the novel process of hair refining. The spreading of the hair-straightening custom among Negro males has spawned that singular phenomenon of the stocking on Harlem's head. Harlem's head is full of vaseline. For in the process of unkinking and ironing and plastering Negro hair, the barbers consume a vast quantity of vaseline. After one's hair is straightened and rolled and glossed, a half length of stocking is tightly affixed to keep it in place. Boys and men go about Harlem with a stocking on their head, sometimes they wear their hats over it. They go to bed with the stocking on, so that they may awake in the morning with unruffed hair.

Perhaps there is no place in which so much vaseline is absorbed as in Harlem. The manufacturers are aware of it.

Their extensive advertisements in the Negro newspapers are illustrated with good-looking, sleek-haired Negro boys with jars of vaseline at 10 cents.

The texture of Negro hair is not merely a matter of physical appearance; it is also of social importance. And does not concern only Negro Americans. Cubans and Haitians are equally obsessed with it. Among the latter, Negroes are categorised according to the quality of their hair. Dark persons with Indian-straight or curly hair are graded higher than similar types with burr-like mats. And a light-complexioned Negro with coarse, kinky hair is often an object of pity and ridicule. It is amazing but nevertheless true that the subject of "good" or "bad" hair consumes much thought and energy in the Negro group. I know many white persons, Americans and Europeans, who were puzzled about it. Many of them prefer Negro hair when it is thick and rough, like a hard brush. But cultivated Negroes consider such white persons offensive and patronizing or even degenerate!

Madame Walker died and her daughter A'lelia inherited her fortune. A'lelia lavishly entertained white and colored bohemians with broad, unconventional gestures. Her prestige was highest at the peak of the Negro literary and artistic renaissance of the nineteen twenties and she was famed as the hostess of Harlem. When the industrial crisis struck, her fortune was hard hit. The mansion on the Hudson was sold.

The beauty business in Harlem has seen many changes. The Walker system was challenged by many others, some superseding it. Other beauty establishments have graduated hundreds of girls. Beauty shops are as numerous as barber shops in Harlem. And at present the whites have a big hand in it. They furnish the elaborate primping places at their price just as they do the barber shops.

The Business of Numbers

Playing numbers is the most flourishing clandestine industry in Harlem. It is the first and foremost of the rackets and the oldest. Exciting the masses' imagination to easy "hits" by the placement of tiny stakes with glittering quick returns, it squeezes Harlem in its powerful grip. To the Negro operators it is not so enormously profitable today as in its halcyon period, when its foundations were laid and it spread with impunity, not fearing white competitors and the action of the law. At that time the operators ("kings" and "queens" as they were called) each had a turnover of a quarter of a million dollars yearly. But after a span of unbelievably fabulous, gold-years, the law of the land at last became aware of them and Federal and Municipal investigations compelled well-known operators to retire to private, comfortable and even luxurious lives. Through fear or careless management the business of some slipped from their hands and they were reduced to penury. And others were driven from the field by white overlords.

Through all the changes Harlemites have played the game increasingly and apparently will as long as Harlem exists. Numbers is a people's game, a community pastime in which old and young, literate and illiterate, the neediest folk and the well-to-do all participate. Harlemites seem altogether lacking in comprehension of the moral attitude of the white world towards its beloved racket.

In its early years these whites in and around Harlem who were aware of the game were tolerantly amused, and contemptuously called it "the nigger pool," or "nigger pennies"! "Numbers" was the only game on which a penny could be put up as a wager. But a lucky penny makes 6 dollars for the player, minus the small percentage for the collector who places the bet. The white world never imagined that the pennies of Harlem's humble folk were creating fortunes of thousands of dollars and "kings" and "queens" in Harlem.

But suddenly in 1928 the nation became aware of the state of affairs when a wealthy Harlem Negro, Caspar Holstein, was kidnaped and held for $50,000 ransom. Holstein was considered to be worth half a million dollars. He was outstanding and upstanding in the community. He operated the Turf Club, which was the rendezvous of Harlem's fastest set. He owned the premises. Prominent in Negro Elkdom, he was exalted ruler of one of the best lodges. He was known as Harlem's philanthropist—the only one! He donated money to Negro colleges and charitable institutions. He provided scholarships for brilliant Negro students, who were too poor to enter high school and college. Through his club he tided needy individuals and families over difficult times. And although he used his personal income, he did not attach his name to such gifts.

There was also an artistic side to Holstein's extraordinary activity. He was *persona grata* among Harlem's élite. And he gave pecuniary assistance to struggling and aspiring writers and artists. In collaboration with the Negro magazine, OPPORTUNITY, he set up a fund for literary prizes. He did not exclude white organizations from his generosity and thus he contributed donations to the League for Mutual Aid. Holstein was born in the Virgin Islands and when the island of St. Thomas was devastated by an earthquake, he gave a large sum of money, organized relief, shipped food and clothing to the victims, and lumber and skilled workmen to rebuild the houses.

Locally Holstein dealt in real estate, but everybody was aware of his real business as a race-track broker and a numbers banker. He was one of the big six among the numbers bankers. He was liked, he was respected, he was trusted.

Sometimes faced with the payment of unusually large sums to winners, some numbers bankers defaulted and fled Harlem. But Holstein was renowned for his reliability. He paid fully the heaviest winnings. His fame spread and his business increased.

The kidnaping occurred on the night of September 21, when Holstein was leaving a friend's house in 146th Street. A white man approached, flashed a detective badge and said that Holstein was wanted at police headquarters in Harlem. Holstein replied that he would go willingly, although he knew of no reason why the police should want him. Another white man came up and between them they walked Holstein to a waiting car. In the car a third accomplice was sitting beside the chauffeur. All were white. Holstein was roughly shoved in. The car started, but instead of turning south toward the police station, it headed north to the Bronx. Aware then that he was tricked, Holstein struggled with his captors. They covered him with their guns, overpowered and blindfolded him and drove to a hideout in the Bronx.

The gangsters had reasoned that Holstein, carrying on an illegal business, was just another gangster who would gladly toss them a large sum and hush up the affair. But Holstein enjoyed being munificent voluntarily; otherwise he was a very stubborn man. He insisted that his property was in collateral and that he did not possess any considerable amount of negotiable funds. Ascertaining that Holstein dealt regularly with the Chelsea bank in Harlem, the kidnapers telephoned there to ask if Holstein's cheque would be honored for a large sum. But already the bank was notified that Holstein had disappeared in a suspicious manner, and it gave a non-committal reply. Holstein's close associates had telephoned the bank. They were worried by his absence even for a short while, without any of them being informed of where he was. For his affairs demanded his constant personal attention.

Soon Harlem was agitated by the rumor of Holstein's kidnaping. Some thought that rival numbers bankers had had him "taken for a ride." But a message was received at the Turf Club demanding a payment of $50,000 for his release. The police started hot on the trail. The Negro sergeant (now Lieutenant Battles) was then the glamor boy of the police in the eyes of Harlemites, at a time when Negroes on the police force were a rarity and none was an officer. Battles was a friend of the kidnaped man and knew the places in which the right information could be picked up. A bootleg basement spot in 125th Street yielded the clue.

It put the police on the trail of one Michael Bernstein, a beer runner of the Bronx. Scenting the police on their heels, the kidnapers released Holstein on the fourth day of his detention. But upon his return to Harlem, Holstein pretended that he did not know who were his kidnapers or where he had been held. He said that he was blindfolded when he was taken and could not identify his captors or his environment. The police intensified their activity and within a few hours Michael Bernstein and his accomplices, Peter Donohoe, Anthony Dagustino and Moe Schubert were apprehended. But in court Holstein still refused to identify the men. His attitude was evasive. He admitted that he had been beaten and tortured to reveal the extent of his bank account, but said he had not been permitted to see his captors. Holstein's reticence fed the gossip that his kidnaping was perhaps a hoax engineered by himself.

But he was not the type of man who would foolishly give his clandestine business a sensational publicity which finally helped to ruin it. Always he was extremely reserved about his affairs. Had he desired, he might have allowed his vanity to feed and inflate itself upon his charitable acts, but many of his large gifts were covered under anonymity. Often when he gave donations under his name to respectable institutions he suggested that it should not be published, because he was averse to placing such institutions in a compromising position. Many "innocents" among the respectability of Harlem were quite unaware of his real business affiliations. Although he was one of the fabulous six of Harlem's numbers operators, he never paraded his prosperity in the flashy big-shot-of Harlem way of the "kings" and "queens." He was very conservative in his appearance and his habits. He dressed quietly, like a dignified broker, and abstained from drinking liquor and smoking. To obtain his release, he made a deal (which was eventually confirmed) not to squeal on his kidnapers.

The Holstein case hit the front page and won national notoriety. It was the first time a wealthy Negro was kidnaped and held for ransom. It made the world aware of another phase of Harlem. For ten years Harlem was nationally advertised as the headquarters of the Garvey Black-Star-Back-To-Africa movement. And carried forward by the impetus of the ascendant literary and artistic bohemianism of New York, the Negro renaissance spurt of the latter nineteen twenties had stimulated national interest in the creative possibilities of Harlem. But Holstein's kidnaping flashed the searchlight on a Harlem underworld, different from the drab ugly tenements nauseating with odors of fried pork chops and rot-gut gin. This was an underworld comparable within its dimensions to the dazzling dynamic underworld of the whites, a world in which the shrewd enterprising members of the Negro minority chiseled out a way to social superiority by the exploitation of the potentialities of their own people. That "nigger-pool" was not such a contemptible thing after all. And it was destined amazingly to stimulate the speculative propensities of the Negroes and establish itself as the new game of the white and black masses of all the United States.

And now others besides the big racket monopolists of the white underworld discovered an interest in the Harlem game. Federal agents ferreted out information about the "kings" and "queens" of the black masses, who paid no income taxes. And as they probed, they uncovered startling facts. The secret "nigger-pool" was no child's play. But, disarming as black laughter in Harlem, albeit loosely organized, it was a formidable parasitic growth within the social body of the blacks.

And the great black bottomless pool had spawned independent auxiliaries. The avid playing of numbers enormously multiplied the appetites of the credulous in the science of numerology. Harlem was set upon a perpetual hunt for lucky numbers. House numbers, car numbers, letters, telegrams, laundry, suits, shoes, hats, every conceivable object could carry a lucky number. Any casual thing might become unusual with the possibility of being endowed with a lucky number: a horse in the street, the first person you meet, an automobile accident, a fire, a fight, a butterfly fluttering on the air, a funeral, even a dog posing against a wall! And dreams! Harlem is haunted by numbers.

Dreaming of numbers is an inevitable condition of the blissful state of sleeping. And so the obsession of signs and portents in dreams as interpreted by numbers created a business for local numerologists. They compiled books of dreams interpreted by playing numbers. Dream books of numbers were published by Prince Ali, Madame Fu Futtam, Professor Konje, Red Witch, Moses Magical and many others. Such are the best sellers of Harlem.

"Hot" lucky numbers are peddled on the streets. Some are offered with a phial of oil or a box of incense to elude the curiosity of the police. But many are brazenly sold in a little piece of folded paper. And the occult chapels have multiplied and increased their following by interpreting dreams by numbers and evoking messages from the dead with numbers attached to the messages and by figuring out signs and portents by numbers.

The religious playing of numbers naturally increases the development of mysticism in Harlem. The numbers must be guessed and played at hazard. When such numbers do not win, the addicts of the game will readily resort to those psychic types of persons who profess to be mediums of numbers. It may be crudely manifested in Harlem, but this mystical abnegation is not a Negroid monopoly. It exists among the international gamblers of Monte Carlo as well as the *aficionados* of the Spanish lottery. In fact I have been amused in foreign parts by some gamblers taking me as a kind of fetich and touching my skin before placing a bet.

The early history of the founding and growth of the numbers industry in Harlem is unknown to the millions who ardently participate in the game today.   It has a Mediterranean background and might parallel the story of a small smuggler in Spain or Sicily building himself up to great power by the active cooperation and admiration of the common people.

In the first decade of the Negroes' big trek to Harlem, 1910–1920, a few Puerto Ricans and Cubans joined them and established barber shops in the black belt.   They had a large patronage, chiefly among the British West Indians, many of whom had worked in Cuba and Central and South America, before coming to the United States, and thus were familiar with Latin-American customs.   Then the Spanish-American colony did not border on the Negro district as it does today, but was concentrated in the east nineties.

The numbers game had its first start in these Spanish barber shops.   Originally it was known as *bolita* or *paquerita*. The British West Indians called it "numbers" and popularized it.   It was introduced to Harlem by a Spaniard from Cataluña, who was nicknamed Catalan by the Spanish-speaking Harlemites.   Catalan devised his system of playing the numbers from the financial figures of the Stock Exchange. Familiar as he must have been with the method of the Spanish lottery, this could not have been a difficult job. The playing number was deduced from the totals of domestic and foreign sales.   Its computation was not mathematical. Figures were arbitrarily chosen and put together to make a unit of three.   To the uninitiated it was an extremely puzzling thing; to the players who were given the key, it was simple.   As the financial figures printed in the newspapers are exact, there could be no trickery.

The numbers game has gripped all of Harlem precisely because there is no obvious trickery in it.   It is an open, simple and inexpensive game of chance.   Any winner gets an enormously sweet profit.   Who would not thrill to a Cinderella penny placed on a number, say 391 and bringing the player 6 dollars?   Make it 10 cents and it is 60 dollars, if you win. And the average Harlemite reasons that he may as well invest a dime on a lucky number as he might in a glass of beer or a piece of candy.

Of course the operator of the numbers game is more fully insured against loss than the moguls who run the gambling Bank of Monte Carlo. For a thousand different numbers are played every day and only one can win. And there is only one chance in a thousand of a person winning. Yet not a day passes but somebody does win. The stakes may be small or big, more often small, but still that is a great incentive for everybody to play.

Catalan was the sole numbers operator in Harlem for many years. The barbers gathered up the numbers slips and the money for him and he hired a few collectors to pick up numbers here and there. Nobody knew the extent of his wealth. He was unassuming and lived modestly. Once he went to Spain and it was rumored that he purchased there a fine piece of property. But shortly after the ending of the World War he returned to Spain again to settle down.

Before leaving he made over his business in Harlem to a Cuban Negro named Messalino, who was his chief aide and confidant. Messalino was quite a different type of man. He was flashy, amiable, man-about-town. As lieutenant to Catalan, his flair for extravagance was checked by the latter's thriftiness and simplicity of living. But when Catalan made his exit, deeding to Messalino the Harlem field, the latter splashed forth gorgeously. He bought a big car and hired a chauffeur in uniform. He entertained lavishly. Catalan had checked accounts and paid winners from his small apartment. Messalino rented an office and installed clerks with adding machines and typewriters. He expanded the game, exciting community interest and making all Harlem numbers-minded. He was the first of the dazzling line of numbers kings.

With the speculative propensities of the simple people aroused, other Negroes became aware of the huge operating profits and Messalino was challenged by rival numbers bankers. The post-war expansion of Harlem brought the considerable Puerto Rican colony to the border of the black belt. And new rival bankers sprang from their group. The common people became enchanted by lucky numbers and Harlem a huge factory humming with the alluring activity of the game.

The operation of the game became more complex with its hectic spread. An army of collectors was organized to solicit players. Over the collectors were controllers, who received the money with the slips, which they turned over to the bankers. Each collector was remunerated with 10% of monies collected. And from any client who played the lucky number he was entitled to 10% of his win. The controller's reward was 5% of the total sum turned over to the banker. A competent controller is a powerful asset in the setup and may have as many as 50 collectors in charge.

The chances of winning were increased by the combination plan of six ways of playing a number. No. 915 could be played thus:

$$915$$
$$519$$
$$159$$
$$195$$
$$591$$
$$951$$

A player might put six cents on this number, alloting one cent to each component.

The magnetism of the game was heightened by its illegitimate link to the Stock Exchange. Harlem folk thought that they too had a little part in the ramifications of the stock market. The widespread playing and the increase and rivalry of bankers had brought into existence a type known as the tipster. The tipster made it his business to discover the lucky number prior to the publication of the financial reports in the newspapers. This was done by establishing contact with minor employees of the Stock Exchange, who perhaps were not aware of the purpose for which the figures were used.

The tipster played the number himself and also informed a few confidential persons, who agreed to share their winnings with him. The tipster did not always receive full advance information, sometimes he could give only the first and second figures of the lucky number. At other times his lead was wrong, as the earlier Stock Exchange reports were subject to correction before final publication.

However, the tipster idea was a profitable one, and in the dizzying era of Prohibition the tipster was a mighty man in the numbers business. One ingenious Harlemite actually rigged up an office in the Wall Street district and was highly regarded as "the Negro with a office in Wall Street." He organized a syndicate to play his tips. The bankers were afraid of him, as his tips were generally good winners. Sometimes he played both ends against the middle by tipping off bankers and players. The informed bankers held in their collectors on such occasions and remunerated the tipster. Sometimes the method was employed to break the smaller competing bankers and run them out of the racket. In the hectic Harlem of the late nineteen twenties, "the Negro in Wall Street" became an affluent Harlemite. He purchased a yacht, upon which he played host to members of Harlem's smart set. His prosperous reign continued until the Seabury investigations of 1931, when the Stock Exchange discontinued the publication of the Clearing House reports from which the lucky numbers were computed.

．　　　．　　　．　　　．　　　．　　　．　　　．

The advent of Prohibition gave impetus to the growth of the numbers racket. As the widest-open bootleg area in New York, Harlem was a rich field for other rackets. From barber shops the numbers business spread to scores of cigar and candy stores, which were actually bootleg joints. Like the bootleg liquor business, the firmly established numbers game received the proper police protection as soon as the law caught up with it. Many of the Harlem police played the numbers regularly. And bankers and controllers paid handsomely for protection. They paid district captains and leaders who had powerful influence with the police and the courts.

In those days the collectors of slips had no fear of being arrested. If they were arrested, there were special lawyers to handle their cases and there were special numbers bondsmen who were well paid by the bankers to obtain bail for offenders. If the cases were too flagrant to be dismissed, the sentences invariably would be light. Arrested collectors used substitute names. When they were important officials of the game, the bankers provided real substitutes to be sentenced in their place. It was the bounden duty of the bankers to provide legal aid for their employees. If a banker shirked this responsibility, he would be boycotted by all collectors and his business ruined.

The Seabury investigation of 1931 turned the light and the heat on the operators of the game and their protectors. The "kings" and "queens" of Harlem were paraded before public opinion. But a few of the biggest ones eschewed the spotlight. Some of them, Cubans, Puerto Ricans and British West Indians, preferred a sea change instead and skipped to their respective islands. But many inside facts were extracted from those who faced inquiry.

One of the leading "queens" who testified was a Madam Stephanie Saint Clair, who later became the spouse of the Harlem labor and cult leader, Sufi Abdul Hamid. She revealed that the operators of the numbers game were often double-crossed by their "protectors." In spite of sums of money paid for their protection, collectors were regularly arrested to provide business for bondsmen and lawyers.

From then on Harlem's banker "kings" and "queens" were doomed to an agitated reign. For the white lords of racketeering decided to put in a controlling fist. They organized a syndicate to dominate the Negro operators. The big boss of the syndicate was Dutch Schultz. He summoned the Negro bankers to get into his syndicate on his terms or get out of the racket.

The small fry of the Negro bankers paid the tribute but the bigger ones resisted. Their motives for resisting were as much moral as financial. Curiously the Negro racketeers put the white gangsters in the class of unregenerate criminals. They felt that they who had a respectable enough status in the colored community could not join an association of white criminals! Some of these Negroes had amassed a fortune, enough to retire from the business. One man went into the garage and taxicab business. A Cuban returned home to buy an estate and enter politics. And a British West Indian went back to buy up an entire township of his island. One big "king" attempted to carry on an independent game. His collectors were beaten up by gangs. His best controller was scared out of Harlem. And one night the top of his car was shot away by machine guns when he was motoring in the Bronx. He gave up the fight.

The numbers game in Harlem now came under the undisputed control of the big white booze raiders. The game was efficiently organized. And it was more smoothly operated. The lucky number was taken from the Mutuel reports instead of the organs of the Stock Exchange. Thus the tipster was eliminated. There was no syndicate to break bankers, who disappeared when they could not pay off. But the winners were exceeding few compared to the golden harvest years of the reign of the Negro kings. And the éclat in the atmosphere, which formerly made Harlem hum like a beehive, went out of the game forever.

When Prohibition was delivered the *coup de grace* in 1933, Harlem, the vast depot of bootleg, was eclipsed. The bottom fell out of the gigantic underworld business which Dutch Schultz and his cohorts had built up. And now instead of secondary importance the numbers game assumed the proportions of a major racket. The large corps of gangster employees had to be paid wages and politicians and officials their graft.

To meet expenses Dutch Schultz attempted to reduce the cost of operating the numbers game. He had established the extensive chain of Dutch Masters cigar stores in Harlem as fronts for the running of the numbers business. And under him the game had its widest expansion in other cities

United Press International Photo

Marcus Aurelius Garvey.

Photo by Lewis

Sufi Abdul Hamid.

Photos by M. and M. Smith

Schomburg Collection of the 135th Street Branch Library.

Photo by Woodard Studio

In 1937 Harlem welcomes Lij Araya Abebe (left) and Dr. Malaku Bayen (right) representatives of Emperor Haile Selassie.

with thousands of whites participating. But in Harlem he depended exclusively upon colored controllers and collectors.

In an economy drive Dutch Schultz tried to get them to take a reduction on their percentages. The Negroes refused. Schultz tried to coerce them. They went on strike and paralyzed the playing of numbers in Harlem. They maintained that if colored bankers had paid the high rate for many years, they would not work for less under white bankers.

Dutch Schultz was powerless to take action against them. For in Harlem the numbers game is an intricately intimate transaction. Most people play with friends or relatives only. Sometimes a collector is a person out of work, who picks up numbers from his friends. The friends get others to play and so the person is helped collectively. When the controllers and collectors went on strike, Dutch Schultz attempted to replace them with white ones. But the whites couldn't make the machinery work. The numbers business was not so easy to handle as the booze business. Most collections are made in the privacy of the players' homes. And excepting bohemian and courtesan circles, colored folk are not comfortable with whites penetrating into their homes. The strikers were supported by the players.

Dutch Schultz found himself up against a formidable passive resistance. And his murderous gorillas were powerless to help him there. Finally he withdrew his demands and consented to the controllers and collectors operating on the old basis. But some of them did not return to work for the white syndicate. They had learned that Dutch Schultz was in reality not so mighty and were no longer afraid. It was the beginning of the end of Dutch Schultz's supremacy in Harlem. New Negro bankers started secret operations in their homes. Others withdrew from the syndicate. It disintegrated and when Dutch Schultz was assassinated in 1934, the numbers business in Harlem had already passed out of his control.

But the come-back of Negro bankers could not revive the glory of the "kings" and "queens" of Harlem. The phrase fell into disuse and "numbers bankers" or "racketeers" became current. The new crop of native operators did not do enough business to dazzle the world. The game had spread amazingly underground and developed into a clandestine national pastime. The invisible white syndicate now held the power and the secret of the gaudy "kings" and "queens."

But one unusual aspect of the illicit game is its siring of a legitimate respectable bantling. When Dutch Schultz horned into the numbers arena and the Negro operators went on strike, the business of the little store fronts run by the latter faced ruin. But many held on and increased their stocks of candy and cigars with hot dogs and soda drinks. The men left their wives or children to carry on while they hunted work elsewhere. The transformed places won the patronage of new clients. The owners were surprised to discover that they could successfully compete with whites who formerly monopolized such small businesses in Harlem. Today there are hundreds of such places, which do not need the numbers game to exist.

Caspar Holstein was one of those who quietly dropped out of the numbers racket when the national searchlight was trained on it. Aside from the kidnaping case, he had managed to keep out of the spotlight during the notorious period of the investigations. He stayed on in Harlem, using his assets to do other things. His real estate holdings had increased and he had acquired the Liberty Hall property of the Back-To-Africa movement, when it went bankrupt.

He gave much of his time to the social welfare of the Virgin Islands. From 1917 until 1931 the government of the islands was administered by the United States Navy. The people agitated for the return of civil government, which they had had under the Danish administration of the islands. Holstein had actively assisted the islanders in their efforts. An American Negro Commission was appointed to investigate and report on the islands in 1927. A civil governor, Paul M. Pearson, was appointed in 1931.

But the change from military to civil administration did not come up to native expectations. The new governor proved unpopular and a mass movement developed against his administration. An active participant in the movement, Holstein organized the Virgin Islanders here. He carried his crusade to the islands personally in 1935 and was wildly acclaimed by the population at the time of his visit. That year Governor Pearson was removed from his post.

For his aggressive part in Virgin Isles politics, Holstein drew the enmity of powerful politicians. Nemesis pursued him upon his return to New York. In his legitimate enterprises he had employed dummies, who now double-crossed him, involving litigation and heavy loss of property. His fine club became the scene of strange brawls and shootings and it was forced to close. He was under constant police surveillance and was arrested a few times, but could not be convicted. Finally in 1937 he was indicted as a numbers operator, although he had long since quit the racket. He received an indeterminate sentence and remained in prison for nearly a year.

Always a reserved person, even when his affairs projected him in the limelight, he is more withdrawn than ever since his release. Sometimes he may be seen entering his Turf Club, which is now deserted and unlit. Or he may be discovered sitting aloof in a café on Seventh Avenue, severely dignified and appearing as if he were in the wrong place, as he does not drink or smoke.

Perhaps he, more than anyone, is familiar with the small beginnings and the gigantic octopus growth of the numbers game in Harlem. But tight-lipped in retirement even as when he was big boss, he would be the last person to tell all he knows. Even if he likes one enough to loosen up a little, he is ever wary and delivers himself in generalities.

Said he: "When I was kidnaped and the police were hot on the trail of the gang, I overheard them debating one night whether they should turn me loose or bump me off without leaving a trace. They said it was no use making me promise to hold my tongue, for 'a nigger will always talk.' But one of them argued that if I didn't talk when I was tortured, then maybe I wouldn't to the police. He said maybe I was different and it would be plain stupid to bump me off and get nothing for it but a mess of trouble. So I was turned loose and I didn't talk."

The Business of Amusements

The amusements of Harlem have a big hand in the business of the community. For three decades Harlem cabarets have held their special fascination. That was one paddock exclusively for Negroes' gamboling. There they maintained a monopoly. It was the side entrance which they opened to obtain a share of New York's enormous liquor business.

In that pre-Prohibition era there were two Negro-owned taverns among the scores in Harlem. The Irish ran the rest. The Negro patronage was large and buttressed by their overwhelmingly happy spirits. The Negro cabaretier made a special instrument of the cabaret to attract and hold the restive customers of his race. He created an intimate theatre of relaxation for colored boy and girl, in which the respectable family man could spend an evening away from home and where bachelors were beguiled by darkly singing damsels, to the chinking of glasses, the erotic suggestiveness of Negro music and wailing "blues" of the entertainer. The Negro cabaretier remained unchallenged in his cockpit, because it was so special. White visitors were privileged guests introduced by Negro friends.

Barron, Conner, Leroy, Edmunds and others built up an attractive business and made Harlem famous with their special type of entertainment.

Prohibition crippled this lucrative affair. The Irish made their exit from Harlem; the Italians came in. Harlem went on consuming its liquor under Prohibition and the Italians were unmatched at subterranean purveying of it. When the big brains of rum-running made a vast depot of Harlem, the lesser brains found it convenient to operate speakeasy places. The Italians broke through the special circle of the Negro cabaret. They established well-appointed, attractive speakeasies with moderate-priced drinks and employed Negro entertainers. They were more engaging, freer and more intimate in their relationship with the Negroes than were the Irish. Under Repeal they have captured the cream of Harlem's drinking trade and remain far ahead of all competitors. They run the best paying bars and they have created the specialty called the "shorty," which is a purely native Harlem product. It is a kind of double-double drink and the customer gets twice as much in a "shorty" as he does by ordering one drink at a time. Besides this the Italians are promptly generous with "the drink on the house," when the customer has imbibed his third.

Repeal has brought Negroes back into the cabaret field. But against the Negro-owned Smalls Paradise and Brittwood, there are the white-owned Elks Rendezvous, Victoria Café, 721 Silver Grill, Speedway Gardens, New Capitol and Massapequa. And it is the latter places that attract the gay colored crowd.

Happy or unhappy, Harlem dances abundantly. Negroes excel and joy in dancing, and it is a gift of theirs in which all the world delights. But there is not a Negro-owned dancing hall in Harlem. Working downtown by day, kitchen maids, porters and errand boys keep fit by dancing at evening. But who profits from the business of their careless dancing feet? Internationally famous for a decade and a half, rendezvous of famous and infamous cosmopolites, of privileged and titled and nondescript bohemians, celebrated in smart unconventional publications, the Savoy is the vast depot of dancing for the commonalty of Negroes. Many whites imagine that it is Negro-owned! It appears so natural and matter-of-course to them that a people so congenitally avid of dancing as Negroes should at least own a community dancing hall! The Kremlin-dominated comrades-in-arms have often chosen the Savoy as the scene of some of their elaborate interracial fiestas. Always proclaiming themselves to be the only true defenders of labor, they appear curiously ignorant of the fact that the Savoy is an open-shop institution.

Behind the exciting baroque fantasy of Negro entertainment lies the grim reality of ruthless jobbery. When Negro entertainers are launched in the national field of entertainment, their business managers are whites, who are no benevolent god-fathers. It is said that even the famous jazz bands such as Duke Ellington's, Claude Hopkins', Fats Waller's, Count Basie's, Lucky Millinder's, Cab Calloway's, Jimmy Lunceford's and Louis Armstrong's, receive a remuneration on a lower scale than white jazz bands, even *though they may perform in the same houses*. The colored performers are paid at an estimated *Negro* rate. I have not been able to ascertain if this is also true of the highest colored stars such as Ethel Waters, Paul Robeson, Marian Anderson, Roland Hays and Bill Robinson. Quite recently the *Pittsburgh Courier's* sardonic columnist, George S. Schuyler, contributed an illuminating and authoritative article on this subject. Mr. Schuyler exposed the manner in which Negro musicians were exploited under the economic distinction made between white and colored performers. The white musicians have no scruples in taking advantage of the Negroes' vulnerable position. Schuyler reproduced excerpts of letters from Negro musicians as evidence. And he concluded by advising Negro entertainers to organize among themselves to protect their interests. This was very significant because Mr. Schuyler has consistently opposed separate Negro organization as potential segregation.

Up on the higher level of the drama, Harlem is also retrograde. During the years when Negro cabarets expressed the community folk art on the lower level there existed a little higher the Smart Set Company of Homer and Whitney Tutt, which produced broad comedies of Negro life. They were an indefinable burlesque-variety combination. But for years they played to enthusiastic Negro audiences in New York, Boston, Philadelphia, Baltimore and other large cities east of Chicago.

More ambitious was the performance of the brilliant group

of actors called the Lafayette Players. They were the first hopeful augury of an indigenous Negro theater in Harlem, although their vehicle of expression was popular Broadway melodrama. Even so, perhaps unawares, they injected into the Broadway pieces a distinctive Negro quality of color, humor, idiom, gesture and movement. And they packed the Lafayette Theatre with applauding Negro audiences. Often the enthusiastic Harlem folk stole the show from the stage in venting their appreciation of Negro actors parading their version of white roles. Some persons are under the impression that the Lafayette Players Company was exclusively an all-Negro set-up from top to bottom. On the contrary, it was under the direction of a white manager, Mr. Frank Schiffmann.

After successfully imitating Broadway in Harlem, some of the Lafayette Players had the opportunity to demonstrate the quality of their talent downtown. Charles Gilpin popped out as a new star to dazzle Broadway in Eugene O'Neill's "Emperor Jones." Edna Thomas did a brilliant piece with Lenore Ulric in "Lulu Belle," and more recently she did striking work with Jack Carter in the labor melodrama "Stevedore." Others among the Lafayette Players who performed on Broadway and in Europe are Laura Bowman, Abbie Mitchell, Percy Verwayne, Frank Wilson.

The exciting promise of a Negro group theater emerging from the Lafayette Theatre petered out. Today in its place is 125th Street's Apollo with its ostentatious revues and midnight shows. It is the only theater in Harlem which attracts the masses as formerly did the old Lafayette.

Harlem Politician

In the political and municipal garden of New York, some juicy plums fall into the lap of the Negro group. A considerable number of persons hold positions with salaries ranging from $2,500 to $12,000 a year. Among them are Police Lieutenant Samuel K. Battles; Jane Bolin, Judge, Domestic Relations Court; Harry G. Bragg, Assistant State Attorney General; Elmer Carter, Member, Appeal Board of State Unemployment Insurance; Eunice Hunton Carter, Assistant District Attorney; Hubert T. Delaney, Tax Commissioner; Joseph DeCourcy, Municipal Chemical Analyst; Lieutenant Jay Clifford, Customs Inspector; Monroe D. Dowling, Assistant Superintendent, State Unemployment Insurance Division, Eugene Faulkner, City Marshall; James Ferbee, Deputy Clerk of Court, Rev. John H. Johnson, Police Chaplain; James W. Johnson, Chief Office Deputy Internal Revenue; Eugene Kinckle Jones, Jr., Assistant Queens County District Attorney; Mrs. Vivian Mason, Supervisor, District Office of Welfare Department; Ferdinand Q. Morton, Civil Service Commissioner; Myles Paige, Judge of Special Sessions; A. Maurice Moore, Municipal Purchasing Agent of Drugs and Chemicals; Aiken A. Pope, State Unemployment Insurance; L. D. Reddick, Curator, Schomburg Collection, 135th Street Branch Library; Vernon C. Reddick, Deputy State Assistant Attorney General; Francis Rivers, Assistant District Attorney; John W. Ross, Member, State Tax Commission; Harold Simmeljkaer; Clerk to a judge of Supreme Court; W. D. Simmons, State Department of Labor; J. Dalmus Steele, City Marshall; Darwin W. Telesford, Secretary to Supreme Court judge; Lester F. Walton, United States

Minister to Liberia; Battalion Chief Wesley Williams of the
Fire Department; John Wilson, City Architect; Max Yergan,
Negro lecturer to the College of the City of New York. The
military is represented by the Commander of the 369th Regi-
ment, Colonel Benjamin O. Davis, assisted by Major Chaun-
cey M. Hooper.

There are many more who fall under the $2,000 a year
class of employees.

There are ten librarians of whom one, Mrs. Regina Andrews, wife of Assemblyman William T. Andrews, is head of
the 115th Street Branch Library.

The Public School system has about six hundred colored
teachers, seventy-five Junior High School teachers and thirty-
five Senior High School teachers. There is one Harlem Pub-
lic School Principal, Mrs. Gertrude Ayer; one Assistant
Principal of Harlem Evening High School (also teacher of
History in the Bushwick High School) Dr. Willis N. Huggins;
one Head of Physical Education, Tilden High School, Frank
Turner; one Head of Department of Languages in Harlem
Evening High School, Dr. Wilfred A. Rankin; and two
Assistant Principals of Public Schools, John B. King and
Dorothy Hendrickson.

The United States Postal Service employs upwards of 3,500
persons in all categories, some are supervisors, others in
similar responsible positions. One, Major Rufus A. Atkins,
is Superintendent of Harlem's College Station; another, Alexander King is Assistant Superintendent of the Church Street
Annex. There is a union, the All-Negro National Alliance
of Postal Employees, which won official recognition in 1936.
Officers of New York City's Branch are President Wayman A.
Evans, First Vice-President J. Carl Canty, Second Vice-President Albertus B. Foster, Third Vice-President Elmer E. Arm-
stead, Financial Secretary James S. Jackson, Recording Secretary Douglas H. DesVerney, Treasurer John M. Christian,
Reporter Reginald E. Young.

The Negro group has the largest number of nurses in
New York's municipal hospitals. There are well over a thousand colored nurses. Harlem Hospital has the biggest con-

tingent with an estimated three hundred and fifty graduates and students; Sea View Hospital in Staten Island is second with three hundred and twenty; Lincoln Hospital in the Bronx has about two hundred and fifty. There are seven supervisors among them. There are three hundred colored nurses in the City's Department of Health. The majority of the nurses are members of the National Association of Colored Graduate Nurses. Not until 1922 did the city employ its first Negro nurses, when a number of them entered Harlem Hospital. This was achieved largely through the political activity of former Alderman George W. Harris.

Also through Mr. Harris's effort the first Negro doctors entered a New York City hospital in 1920, when six were appointed to Harlem Hospital. Today, among the two hundred doctors attending this hospital, fifty are Negroes. Harlem has its own police surgeon in Dr. Louis T. Wright, diplomate of the American Board of Surgeons. Dr. John B. West, District Health Officer, is administrative head of the Central Harlem Health Center. A few of the distinguished Harlem medical men are Drs. Harold Ellis, diplomate Psychiatry and Neurology, Chester Chinn, diplomate Board of Otolaryngology and Ophthalmology, John Finlay, diplomate Obstetrics and Gynecology and Peter Marshall Murray, diplomate Obstetrics and Gynecology. Others active in community health and social work are Drs. Charles Harris, E. P. Roberts, Peyton Anderson, Henry O. Harding, Paul A. Collins, Ernest Alexander and Gerald Spencer.

Harlem's one hundred and fifty doctors exchange social and professional courtesies in their organization, the Manhattan Central Medical Society. The President is Dr. Charles C. Middleton. One-third of Harlem's doctors have clinical experience in the Harlem Hospital. Sensational charges of careless treatment and fatal neglect of Negro patients in this hospital have appeared periodically in the Negro Press. But as the hospital is City-controlled and its administration perforce affected by political influences, most of the scandal stories may be discounted as motivated or colored by politics. Nevertheless Harlem Hospital is apparently the most congested in New York. According to official statistics it has six hundred and forty-two beds. In 1939 there were 19,579 in-patients and 461,768 out-patients. No other New York hospital, excepting Bellevue, had such an enormous influx of clinic patients. But Bellevue is in a special category and serves the world, so to speak. It has 1964 beds and accommodated 476,583 clinic patients in 1939.

Perhaps nothing could be more efficacious in relieving the overcrowding of Harlem Hospital and benefiting the entire Negro minority locally and nationally than the establishment of a large first-class all-Negro hospital in Harlem. The Negro group has more than enough first-rate doctors to staff such a hospital. There was a project to found a Negro hospital a few years ago, but before it was launched the idea was killed by the obstreperous and extremely vocal and effective group of Negro intellectuals who style themselves the "anti-Segregationists." They maintained that a Negro hospital would be an incentive to the greater segregation of Negro doctors.

Preposterous is the situation in which the entire Negro minority is placed by its irrational intellectuals and their canny "radical" white supporters. I predict that nothing could be more effective in breaking down the barriers of Segregation and compelling white doctors to recognize the merits of colored colleagues than the establishment of a great Negro hospital in Harlem. Throughout the country there are expert Negro specialists in all kinds of diseases. If the best of them were brought to work together in a great institution, the nation would soon be aware of them. Moreover such an institution could become an asset to the American medical profession. White doctors would be more attracted by the outstanding work of their colored colleagues, just as white educators and intellectuals were drawn to Tuskegee to study the great work of Booker T. Washington. In the arena of New York's politics, the Negro's part, often of major importance in deciding an election, was until recently only auxiliary. Like others elsewhere, New York's Negroes remained loyally Republican for decades following their emancipation. And so Negroes were naturally excluded from political privileges in the Democratic fortress of New York City.

It is interesting that the Negroes began shifting to the Democratic Party about the time of the great race riots of 1900, which coincided with the hegira of the group to Harlem. Perhaps they instinctively felt the need of more local political protection. The first Negro Democratic group was the United Colored Democracy. It was organized by Chief Edward E. Lee, who got his title from being a head bellman. In welcoming the Negro group into the Democratic phalanx, Tammany Hall Leader Richard Croker said: "Your people are a poor people. Tammany Hall is a poor man's organization. The colored man rightly belongs in Tammany Hall. I'll start you off by appointing a leader. Thereafter elect your own leaders and Tammany Hall will recognize him. And although your vote is only 10 per cent, I will place a colored man in every department of the city government."

Thus the Negro minority began its career in New York's democratic politics. The chieftains of Tammany Hall adhered to the principle laid down by Richard Croker and rewarded Negroes with patronage. As far back as 1905, a Negro was named assistant district attorney. But the manner in which the appointments were made by the Democrats in the local arena was little different from that of the Republicans in the national arena.

The Negro positions were appointive. Negro votes were delivered a little differently from the way white votes are. White leaders and sub-leaders directly represented their people in the Tammany organization and therefore felt responsible to them. But the Negro people were represented by Negro "leaders" who in turn were represented by white leaders in the Tammany organization. And so the Negro leaders did not feel directly responsible to the Negro people who made their appointments possible. In Tammany politics as in Republican it was the same old chronic sickness of indirect representation, the eternal tapeworm in the belly of Negro life.

The white leaders of the predominantly Negro districts often opposed the appointment of Negroes to responsible political posts through a Negro organization that did not directly represent the voting power of Negro people. Their opposition was not moral or idealistic, but purely expedient. For frequently when they desired an appointment for a deserving Negro democrat, who had labored loyally for their election, it was given instead to someone recommended by the United Colored Democracy.

President Wilson's re-election campaign of 1916 focused the attention of powerful politicians on the potentialities of the Negro vote. War-industries migration had enormously increased the population of Harlem and in two Assembly Districts, the 19th and the 21st, the Negro vote was becoming preponderant and decisive.

The Marcus Garvey movement had stirred a more independent spirit among his people. Political-minded Negroes, agitating for direct representation, stuck sharp pins in the tough hide of Tammany Hall. In 1917 the first Negro Assemblyman, Republican Edward A. Johnson, was elected to the State Legislature. John C. Hawkins, another Republican, was elected from the 21st Assembly district in 1919 and re-elected in 1920.

Tammany waked up a little and rubbed its eyes to see that its system of indirect recognition and patronage of the Negro minority was inadequate. The Republicans, despoiled of their Negro vote in the South, had no desire to relinquish it to strengthen the Democrats in the North. Tammany countered. In 1923 it supported the candidacy of Henri W. Shields, who was elected to the State Assembly.

But tasting a little of the rarer food of politics, the Negroes were developing a gourmet's appetite. They started agitating for district leaders in the predominantly Negro areas. Republicans were the first to appreciate the significance of the agitation and Colonel Charles W. Filmore was elected the first Negro leader of the 19th district in 1930. But this was not of significance to Negroes, for New York is a Democratic city. And so began the campaign to elect a Negro Democratic District leader.

The leaders of Tammany were not ready for such an eventuality. A Negro District leader might prove extremely embarrassing, even disrupting to the Tammany organization, they thought. Tammany conceded something which appeared more highly distinguished than district leadership. It created the 10th judicial district and requested the United Colored Democracy to name two Negro candidates for municipal judgeship. Head of the organization, Civil Service Commissioner Ferdinand Q. Morton, recommended two attorneys, Charles E. Tony and James S. Watson, who were elected over their Republican opponents.

They were the first Negroes to serve as judges in New York. The term was 10 years and the salary $12,000. Harlem is proud of its two municipal judges, who have excellent records. Mr. Justice Watson possesses the judicial mind in its finest form, balanced, temperate and charming. He is a native of Jamaica, as fine a colonial product as any, with great reserve and self-effacement, the result of an elementary English education. He was a student of the same law firm as Elmer Rice, who later chose the theater instead of the court-room to express himself. While they were studying together Elmer Rice remarked to Judge Watson: "You are the whitest man among us."

Since the first Negro was elected to the New York State Assembly, in 1917, nine more have been elected, besides ten aldermen. Harvard graduate George W. Harris was the first Negro alderman. He was founder and editor of the New York News, which, established in 1913, soon became the leading Harlem weekly. He entered the aldermanic race as an independent Republican in 1920 and was elected. Harris's pioneer effort resulted in the nomination and election of Negro candidates for aldermen on straight Democratic and Republican tickets. But the Negro group lost ground in the political shuffle of 1937, when the Aldermanic set-up was revamped and the old style of voting was replaced by pro-

portional representation. The Negro minority has no representative now in the present City Council.

In the State Assembly it has two representatives: Attorney
William T. Andrews of the 21st District, first elected in 1935,
is serving his third term; Leader of the 19th Assembly District, Daniel L. Burrows is serving a second time. Burrows
is 33, one of the youngest men in the State Legislature. And
the second Negro to achieve the distinction of becoming a
Democratic district leader. He has been in and around politics for 17 years, holding a number of political appointments
such as Clerk of the Board of Election, Clerk in the N. Y.
County Registrar's office and Deputy Clerk of the State
Senate.

Burrows is to the common run of Harlemites what Governor Smith was to East Siders. Born in Virginia, he was
brought to New York as a child and grew up in the rough
and tumble manner of the ordinary Harlem child. The
19th Assembly District has always seethed with black-and-
white strife and intrigue. For over ten years Negroes have
vociferously expressed their dissatisfaction with Tammany's
disposition of the district. But they couldn't work in unity
to win what they wanted. Perhaps the Negroes were more
concerned in getting rid of District Boss Martin J. Healy
than in electing a Negro leader.

They organized several independent clubs. Burrows, with
W. R. Bain, organized the Yucatan Democratic Club in 1935
with the express purpose of defeating Martin J. Healy. They
succeeded, but in his place got Harry C. Perry, another white
man and formerly leader of the 2nd A. D. But Perry was
not destined to last, for the issue of Negro leadership had
become acute. In the 1937 campaign there were four Negro
candidates and Perry won the leadership. Supported by the
District leader, Burrows ran for the Assembly and won.
Perry paid scant attention to Negro grievances. He knew
that because they were so divided among themselves, the
white candidate would win every time.

Negro unity was spouted in the air of Harlem all during
the two-year interval. But again in 1939 there were as many

Photo by Lewis

The Angels acclaim God Divine in Harlem.

A. Philip Randolph.

candidates as ever. Deposed Leader Healy and the then
Leader Perry had supporters among influential Negroes
whom they had favored. But the general demand for Negro
leadership of the 19th district was so positive that no Negro
dared oppose it.

Young Assemblyman Burrows was in the running. But
no one took his candidacy seriously. The rumor was started
and passed around that he was Perry's stooge and in the race
only to throw his strength to Perry in the final lap. This
seemed plausible enough, as Burrows was supported by district leader Perry as a candidate for the Assembly. But
Burrows is a fox, and as different from Herbert L. Bruce,
Negro leader of the 21st district, as a mongoose from a mule.

There were four colored candidates in the running and
one white. The inevitable deadlock ensued. Burrows represented a minority, but he held the key to the puzzle. If he
gave his votes to Mr. Perry the white candidate would win
again. The inside story is that Burrows was told by Tammany to quit the race. Mr. Perry is a half-brother of
the Leader of Tammany Hall. But even if Burrows was
willing to forego the distinction of being the second Negro
in the history of New York to become a Democratic District
leader, he would have wrecked his political career among
Negroes by throwing his strength to the white candidate.
Gone are the days when a Negro can *openly* betray his people and still remain their leader. Instead Burrows demanded
that Perry relinquish his votes to him. Perry was aware that
he could not win and, convinced that the game was played
out, he withdrew from the race.

Burrows is the most popular politician in Harlem today.
The common people love him, because on the surface, he is
simple, unaffected and friendly. But in reality he is an
extraordinary sharp and shrewd politician. Following soon
after his election in 1939, there was held a Communist-
Front labor meeting under the auspices of the C. I. O.
(Burrows was probably unaware that it was) at the St. James
Presbyterian Church. And there he announced that his
union was the Harlem Labor Union. This is the inde-

pendent Negro union which is a copperhead alike to Socialists and Communists. The crowd broke loose and wildly applauded him. He's got what they like. It is with a chuckle that they say in Harlem that he double-crossed ex-District Leader Perry.

The campaigns for district leadership in Harlem have been ginger stuff. In spite of its shortcomings, the Marcus Garvey movement germinated the idea of really responsible Negro leadership in the people. And it has sent forth its shoots everywhere. The first Negro to become a democratic district leader, Herbert L. Bruce, is a fanatic about Negro leadership. Unlike Burrows, he had no political experience and no inclination for the game. He was a red cap for many years. With a partner he opened the old Monterey Restaurant in 1929, which was one of the best in Harlem. When Prohibition was repealed they added a bar to it. Bruce was dragged into politics in 1933, when The Beavers' Democratic Club was organized in the 21st district by former assemblyman and alderman Henri W. Shields. The club was founded expressly for the purpose of electing a Negro leader. The majority of the professional men in the district supported it. Bruce helped finance the club and Shields asked him to become his campaign manager. Mr. Shields ran for the district leadership. Because of the racial angle, it was a sharp fight. Officially he lost, but it was generally believed that he was counted out. However, Shields refused to ask for a recount, although the members of the club demanded it. He lost favor with them and Bruce assumed the leadership of the club.

In the 1935 campaign, Shields threw his support to the regular Tammany Chicopee Club. The insurgent Beavers put up Bruce as their candidate for the district leadership. He won overwhelmingly. When his strength became obvious during the campaign, he was secretly offered inducement to quit. But the tactics which formerly succeeded with certain Negro leaders did not with Bruce. He checkmated all attempts to bribe, count him out or disqualify him after he was elected.

After he had beaten his white opponent, the rival club petitioned the boss of Tammany not to recognize the election. A delegation of Negroes and whites from the district tried to convince the Tammany leader, Mr. Dooling, that a Negro leader would increase antagonism between the colored and white residents and ruin the district. Mr. Dooling offered to divide the district. Bruce rejected the plan. He declared that he was elected by popular vote as a leader of the white and colored residents of the district and he intended to remain a full-time leader.

The Irishman respected the Negro's courage. Dooling turned to the delegation and said: This man put up a hard fight for the election and won fairly. Tammany Hall will recognize him as the leader of the entire 21st District.

Bruce possesses enormous tenacity of purpose. He is loyal to loyal friends, but a formidable hater of his enemies. He is compactly built and bull-doggish in appearance. He is a successful leader. Although he won his leadership on a racial issue and is therefore a Negro leader of the blacks he is keenly aware that he is also the district leader of whites, who make up about one-fourth of his constituency. The whites were apprehensive that they would be subjected to unfair treatment from a Negro leader even as the Negroes were neglected and deprived of their percentage of patronage under a white leader. But Bruce has won a little of the whites' respect by recognizing their title to a share in the spoils, while endeavoring to placate the Negroes who have for such a long time been shelved.

His job is no relaxing in a feather bed. It is complicated by the fact that although he tries to be a loyal Tammany man, he is also a New Dealer. He had a walkover re-election in 1937. But his fight to retain the leadership in 1939 is memorable for the bitterness it engendered among Negroes.

Racial Groups

Herbert R. Bruce is a West Indian and an orphan. Born in the Barbadoes, he was brought to New York when he was 5 years old. He was educated in the Public schools and grew up in Harlem. There is a sharp struggle for place and elbow room between the educated West Indians and native-born Negroes. It is not keen among the ordinary types of both groups. The natives call the West Indians "monkey-chasers" and the West Indians call them "coons" and they fight or laugh over it. But they work together, play together, marry one another and share equally the joys and sorrows of the group.

The educated American Negro is brought up in the old tradition of special protection and patronage for the talented members of his group. He regards the West Indian as an outsider, who should not share in the special patronage. But the native-born Negro is perhaps not so keenly aware of the subtle changes and shifts in the social system as is the West Indian.

I think the same state obtains among European immigrants, who are often quicker than some white native-born to appreciate the new currents and opportunities in the social set-up. The educated native Negroes resent the aggressiveness of the foreign-born Negroes, especially in politics. The first Negro Democratic Presidential elector, Dr. Godfrey Nurse, is a West Indian. And that the first Democratic District Leader should be also a West Indian! It was natural that the exclusive tenth among the native-born would be a little resentful.

Mr. Mal Frazier, boss of the Mimo Club, was put up as candidate to oppose Bruce. Bruce was pictured as a West Indian provincial, using his leadership to protect West Indians only! A forged letter was sent out over his signature requesting West Indians to vote for him because he was one of them! Despite this propaganda the voters went to the polls and gave Bruce an overwhelming vote of confidence.

It was amazing because, as his opponents said, 90 per cent of the Harlem vote is American Negro.

The rivalry between West Indians and native born is more amusing than tragic. They both are subject to the same discriminatory practices as a minority group. The American-born Negro derives great fun out of the West Indian accent. This accent is a colonial variant of Scotch and Irish, in Jamaica a curious hybrid Cockney. Strangely enough, the native born Negro does not appear to find funny the accent of South-Eastern Europeans and Levantines who may be his employers, and of the Irish policemen and political bosses who lord it over him. Yet some of these accents are hard as a fist in one's face in comparison to the liquid dialect of the West Indians.

An influential white person told me of a young Negro who was seeking his help to secure an important appointment. The Negro was well educated and fitted for the position. But before approval of his application, the white person sought to learn something of the applicant's character from a distinguished Harlemite. The Harlemite replied that the young man was of good character, but he was a West Indian. The white man was puzzled, for he was not aware that there were any sharp differences between West Indian and native-born Negroes and desired to know why. His informant said that it was because the West Indians were taking good jobs away from the native-born Negroes. This feeling of resentment against the West Indian immigrant does not seem to extend to the European immigrant.

The West Indians might find consolation in the fact that immigrants in all countries are more or less resented and patronized by the native-born. But they are more inclined to think of Aframericans as Negroes like themselves than as native-born Americans! In France, for example, the considerable colonies of Spanish, Corsican and Italian that concentrate in the Midi are tolerated but never quite accepted by the French. Yet they are all Latins. The first generation of immigrants are precisely in the same dilemma as the West Indians in Harlem.

Prejudice against first-generation immigrants may be stupid, but it is a universal human trait. And it must be said that the West Indians are largely responsible for their unpopularity among the educated Afro-Americans. Many of them lack the bonhomie of the natives and are considered too serious-minded by the latter. There also is too much pretense among West Indians. They boast irritatingly of better social conditions for Negroes in the islands, which cannot hold under analysis. The English do not have laws against intermarriage; they do not have Jim-Crow laws separating Negroes from whites in public places and conveyances; they do not disfranchise Negroes; they do not establish a rule of refusal to serve them in hotels, bars, etc. But in reality all such restrictions more or less obtain in the islands. This is easy. The large masses of Negroes live in such a poverty-stricken condition that they cannot aspire to the better life of the British aristocracy of the military and high government officials. Only the members of the entailed mulatto aristocracy can afford to intrude in the privileged area. This mulatto group of wealthy landed proprietors and business men is the controlling factor in the political and industrial life of the islands. It has in the United States no counterpart that could be cited in comparison.

West Indian masses do not eat the same food nor enjoy the same amusements as do the white aristocracy. There are no poor whites except the regiments of English soldiers, who live in camp apart from the natives. Here in the United States there are poor whites, rich whites and poor Negroes and wealthy Negroes. Rich and poor, white and black, all alike eat ham and eggs and potatoes and cornflakes and white bread. The bootblack rubs shoulders with the bank clerk at a hot-dog counter. That doesn't happen in the West Indies.

Unlike the West Indian, the American Negro is a minority in the midst of the white man's activities. His wages may be much lower than white wages, but it is incomparably higher than West Indian wages. It affords him the privilege of participating in the ordinary creature comforts of American life, just as the white bootblack. But he is often barred from such because of his complexion. It creates a resentment of which the average West Indian is oblivious until he lands in this country and participates in the life of the Negro minority.

Again, the West Indians are incredibly addicted to the waving of the Union Jack in the face of their American cousins. Of all the various peoples who migrate to America, the West Indians may be classed as the most patriotic to their homeland. All immigrants come to America to seek an opportunity for better life. They may come seeking employment or education; whichever it is, they seek something that is denied to them in their native land.

The Irish came with a hatred of the English who oppressed and exploited them. Poles and Russians fled from the mailed fist of Russian imperialism. Jews fled persecution. They all came incensed against the social orders which degraded them. But the West Indians seem strangely lacking in this spirit of resentment. They remain romantic about the régime that oppressed them. Yet they are black and suffer even so much more than white immigrants of the same category.

.   .   .   .

In Harlem there is a miniature Chinatown at the bottom of Lenox Avenue. And there are Japanese who run the neat Sandwich Shops, which feature American and Chinese, but no Japanese food. There is a small colony of Haitians and a pocket of Martinique Negroids.

But the Spanish element, predominantly Puerto Rican, is the most important and provocative bloc of people in relation to the Negro group. It is of special and complicated interest because of the considerable numbers of Negroids within its fold. This Spanish-speaking mass embraces the area from 110th Street to 116th Street, between Lexington and Seventh Avenues. Some of them live beyond Seventh Avenue and above 116th Street and extend on the East Side as far down as 96th Street. But the popular movement of their life pulses in the first-named section.

Puerto Rico is one of the rare Caribbean islands where color has never been a major problem. Extensive miscegenation has occurred there. And here in Harlem the white and the yellow and the brown Puerto Ricans (there are not so many black ones) insouciantly mingle on equal terms. Nevertheless the pressure of American mores is having its effect upon them. The American Negro cannot comprehend the brown Puerto Rican rejecting the appellation, "Negro," and preferring to remain Puerto Rican. He is resentful of what he considers to be the superior attitude of the Negroid Puerto Rican. He is not aware that basically it is also a matter of language, that in Spanish Negro is the word for black and therefore brown cannot be black. The Aframerican also holds to the popular notion that all West Indians are colored and imagines that the white Puerto Rican or other white West Indian is merely the Caribbean counterpart of the near-white colored American.

Besides his natural adherence to his own language group, the colored Puerto Rican is motivated by economic necessity. By insisting that he is Puerto Rican and Spanish, he may, like the swarthy Sicilian, escape a little from that stigma which fixes the American Negro in a specific position in the social set-up. For the Puerto Ricans also have their social problems. Their avenues of employment are limited, as are the Negroes in the same field. Housing conditions are bad, often worse than among Aframericans, and are a menace to health. And politically the Puerto Ricans are not so flexible as Aframericans in party-politics and in winning favors from influential politicians. Of recent years, however, there has developed a strong movement for political cooperation between the two groups.

The community life of the Puerto Ricans, with the rest of the Spanish-speaking group, is more compact and purposeful than the Aframerican. The Aframerican efforts towards social adjustment in Harlem have been handicapped by invidious notoriety. The Puerto Ricans also have had a grim experience in establishing themselves in Harlem, but it was unaccompanied by spectacular publicity. The Puerto

Ricans concentrated their energy in building up a bulwark of small business. The Negroes have centered theirs upon moving into big and costlier apartment houses. In replacing the former residents and businesses the Spanish group encountered strenuous opposition. There were disputes and bloody fights, and much difficulty in renting shops.

Today the Spanish quarter in Harlem is as definitely Spanish as the Italian quarter is Italian. Unlike the Negro quarter it does not consist of a large professional stratum at the top and masses of laborers at the bottom with a void between. The Spanish group contains a bulging belly of middlemen—traders. There are 300 grocery stores, 200 restaurants, 50 dry goods stores, and cigar stores, laundries, tailor-shops, shoe-repair shops, pharmacies, bakeries, bars, dancing halls, two theaters and many bookstores. The casual observer may imagine that there are far too many. But competition is keen within the Spanish group itself. The word *"barato"* has infinite nuances to the Puerto Ricans, for it means so much to their group economy. Its equivalent, "cheap" or "good bargain," is of far less significance to the Negro group.

The Puerto Ricans will not pay the exorbitant rents that are exacted from the Aframericans. Therefore, apartments are much cheaper in their quarter. Some Harlem landlords have a rule of not renting to them. They consider the Negroes better tenants. In many instances the Spanish-speaking tenants of a house have been evicted and Negroes installed at higher rentals.

The Puerto Ricans unwittingly aided the Negroes in their expansion below 116th Street. When white Puerto Ricans moved into a house, the brown ones followed and that inevitably opened the doors to the Aframericans. However, until quite recently there were houses in 110th Street facing Central Park that had dark Puerto Ricans as tenants but refused Aframericans. When the landlords gave the signal and they became "houses for colored tenants" the rents went up. Harlem has many such interesting contradictions. Quite a number of native whites still live in the Negro quarter in isolated houses carrying signs: "Apartments for Whites Only." When some open up to Negro tenants the signs are changed: "Apartments for Respectable Colored." There are even colored landlords who rent only to whites and hang out signs: "For Whites Only."

A singular aspect of the Spanish scene, which appears imitative of the Aframerican, is the diversity of "store-front" churches. For a Roman Catholic people this is an arresting development, for all such churches are Protestant. There are Pentecostal, Evangelical, Church of God, Adventist, Jehovah's Witness and other churches. I have not yet come across the Spanish Church of Christ, Scientist. The worshipers in these places are as noisy as Aframericans in theirs. There are, in addition various occult or spiritualist chapels, redolent with incense and aromatic oils and burning colored candles.

But there are other aspects which give obvious distinction to the quarter. The cafés have introduced a new spirit of social amenity in the life of Harlem. They are the nearest approach to popular men's clubs in the community. There men come together after dinner and engage in long conversations over cups of coffee or glasses of wine. These cafés have no equivalent in the Aframerican bars, where customers are expected to spend the time imbibing one drink after another and not in conversation.

As elsewhere there is in the Spanish quarter, the inevitable petty criminal element. It was one of its juvenile members who ignited the fuse that exploded the Harlem riots of March, 1935. But it is interesting to note that the notorious gangsters and public enemies among Latin Americans do not belong to the Spanish-speaking group. In Harlem its crimes are mainly misdemeanors. Often the offenders are unjustly treated and nourish resentment for being held in jail for days because there are no Spanish interpreters.

In the congested blocks prostitution is rampant and brazen with apache overtones, and must naturally be repugnant to native Americans. But it is also objectionable to respectable Spanish-speaking residents and especially to the business people. *Chulos* and *cabrons* on the street corners spit aloud the filthiest epithets, especially when women are passing by. Perhaps this exhibition is a corruption of the ancient Spanish custom of the right of males to flirt with females on the promenade. In Spanish Harlem it has degenerated into an extremely obnoxious practice. It could easily be checked if there were Spanish-speaking policemen on the beat. Unfortunately there are none. And the English-speaking policemen have no comprehension of what is being said and done around them.

Signs of literary culture are more evident in the Puerto Rican than in the Aframerican quarter. A number of book stores are stocked with Spanish classics and contemporary literature, and also English books. Negro Harlem has one only and that recently established: the Blyden Bookstore owned by Dr. Willis Huggins.

As far back as 1921, the 135th Street branch librarian, Ernestine Rose, remarking the infiltration of Spanish-speaking persons into Aframerican Harlem, recommended and obtained the appointment of a Spanish-speaking assistant. But the Spanish-speaking population, enormously increasing in Harlem about 1925, settled in the 116th Street section. The assistant, Miss Pura Belpré was transferred to the 115th Street branch library. Under the direction of Head Librarian Leah Lewinson the branch accumulated a collection of Spanish literature. It contains 2,600 volumes and is extensively used by Harlem's Spanish readers.

Perhaps the most distinctive contribution of Puerto Rico to the literary culture of Harlem is the Arthur A. Schomburg collection of books and manuscripts which, although housed in the Negro Division of the 135th Street Library, is pertinent to any discussion of the Spanish-speaking group of Negro Harlem. The Schomburg collection is the most important library of books by and about Negroes in the world. It consists of 10,000 volumes and 3,000 manuscripts of letters, poems, addresses, sermons, historical documents, etc., written by or about well-known and little-known persons of the Negro group. Many of the volumes are extremely rare.

There are books in all the major occidental languages: Spanish, Portugese, French, Italian, German, Russian and Latin.

Through the active interest of Branch Librarian Ernestine Rose, cooperating with the officials of the National Urban League, the Schomburg Collection was purchased by the Carnegie Corporation in 1926 and turned over to the New York Public Library. The directors of the Library established a Negro Division in the 135th Street branch and the collection was there installed. In 1932 Mr. Schomburg was appointed curator. The collection is accessible to readers and research workers and is extensively used. Ironically, this priceless affirmation of the culture of the Negro group has been disparaged by some of its intellectuals as a segregated institution.

The story behind this incomparable collection is as remarkable as the collection itself. Arthur Schomburg came from Puerto Rico to this country at the age of 23, seven years before the United States acquired the island of Puerto Rico. In appearance he was like an Andalusian gypsy, olive-complexioned and curly-haired, and he might easily have become merged in that considerable class of foreigners who exist on the fringe of the white world. But because of his African blood, he chose to identify himself with the Aframerican group, and soon he was married to an Aframerican woman. He worked at various "Negro" jobs, such as bell-hop and elevator boy. After he had gained experience in New York he obtained a position as messenger for the Bankers' Trust Company. His excellent command of Spanish earned him promotion to the Latin-American Mail Department. Finally he became head of the bank's mailing department.

In the Negro colony he was attracted to a circle of eager-minded intellectuals, Aframerican and West Indian. The leading members were John Edward Bruce, a prominent Freemason, David Fulton, Dr. York Russell, eminent physician, the Rev. Dr. Charles D. Martin of Harlem's Moravian Church and William Ernest Braxton, a remarkable painter.

They founded in 1911 the Negro Society of Historical Research. Schomburg was elected secretary and librarian. Lewanika, King of Basutoland, South Africa, was the Honorary President. The membership included Negroes from the Barbadoes, Brazil, Capetown, Costa Rica, Cuba, Gold Coast, Lagos, Liberia, London, Panama, Puerto Rico, Sierra Leone. The aim of the Society was to create in New York a cultural center for the promoting of research work and the collecting of literary and historical items of the Negro race. Within a year of its formation the Society acquired 300 books and pamphlets.

These founding members also began collecting individually: John Edward Bruce, Arthur Schomburg, The Rev. Dr. Charles D. Martin and Henry P. Slaughter of Washington, who at present possesses the finest private collection. Schomburg's Spanish background was a priceless asset to the Society in its research work. It helped him to unravel the threads of that African Negro contribution to modern civilization, which came by way of Spain, through its conquest and 700 years' domination by the Moroccans. One of his invaluable finds was the rare volumes of the Negro Juan Latino, famous Latin scholar and professor of poetry at the University of Granada in the 16th Century.

Yet Schomburg was not typically literary. His private taste in books was inclined to the esoterically erotic. But he possessed a bloodhound's nose in tracing any literary item about Negroes. He could not discourse like a scholar, but he could delve deep and bring up nuggets for a scholar which had baffled discovery.

When he received $10,000 for his collection from the Carnegie Foundation he must have been highly gratified. But the honor of being rewarded for a noble work must have meant even more to him, for when he became obsessed with the urge to buy Negro books, often denying himself creature comforts, so that out of his moderate salary he might acquire a rare item, he was not actuated by the possibility of pecuniary profit. Nor were any of his colleagues. There was no national interest in Negro books, and Negro writers were a liability.   But they were hoodooed by the strange magic of one special branch of literature, which was greater than they had imagined.

Schomburg's first thought after disposing of the collection was to travel to Spain and visit the libraries of Seville and the Escorial and search through antique books and manuscripts for more material about the Negro.   Perhaps a psychologist might have been interested in plumbing him to discover whether the Spanish-European or the African-West Indian was uppermost in his character.   Intellectually he was proud of his Spanish heritage and fond of Puerto Rico, yet he cultivated no social contact with Harlem's Puerto Ricans.   He strangely combined a simple, disarming exterior and obscure inner complexes.   And his emphatic character and lusty appetite for life were amazing.   He had large, expressive eyes and the body and energy of a powerful Spanish bull.   He was thrice married, each time to an American Negro woman, and he reared 7 children.   He was full of wonderful love and admiration and hate, positively liking his friends and positively disliking his foes.   He died in 1938.

Marcus Aurelius Garvey

The movement of Marcus Garvey in Harlem was glorious with romance and riotous, clashing emotions. Like the wise men of the ancient world, this peacock-parading Negro of the New World, hoodooed by the "Negromancy" of Africa, followed a star—a Black Star. A weaver of dreams, he translated into a fantastic pattern of reality the gaudy strands of the vicarious desires of the submerged members of the Negro race.

There has never been a Negro leader like Garvey. None ever enjoyed a fraction of his universal popularity. He winged his way into the firmament of the white world holding aloft a black star and exhorting the Negro people to gaze upon and follow it. His aspiration to reach dizzy heights and dazzle the vision of the Negro world does not remain monumental, like the rugged path of the pioneer or of the hard, calculating, practical builder. But it survives in the memory like the spectacular swath of an unforgettable comet.

Leaving the Caribbean island of Jamaica, Marcus Garvey arrived in New York in March, 1916. He did not come as "a Numidian lion" (as he was once described by Mr. William Pickens of the National Association for the Advancement of Colored People) to lead the Negro people. He came as a humble disciple of the late Booker T. Washington, Founder of Tuskegee Institute. Garvey had hoped to establish in Jamaica an institution similar to Tuskegee. He corresponded with Booker T. Washington about his plan and was invited to visit Tuskegee. But the Founder of Tuskegee died suddenly before Garvey's arrival in the United States. Garvey then planned to raise funds and return to Jamaica to establish his institution.   There, in 1914, he had organized the Universal Negro Improvement Association, which failed.

Marcus Garvey was born in 1887 in the village-town of the most beautiful region of Jamaica, called locally The Garden of Jamaica.   His father was not a peasant, but an artisan, a carpenter who, during Garvey's early years, lived comfortably by his work.   Garvey was given an excellent common school education.   Modeled on the English plan, the elementary school system of Jamaica is sound.   And Garvey received extra education, presumably the pupil-teachers' course of training, which, depending on the ability of the student, may be very thorough.   Garvey has stated that he studied at the University of London, but the truth of this statement is doubted by persons who knew something of his earlier life and his enormous capacity for exaggeration.   However, by substantial, catholic reading and traveling, Garvey provided himself with a higher education, perhaps greater than he might have derived from an institution.

Like all ambitious provincials, Garvey was attracted to Kingston, the capital of Jamaica.   There he went as a lad to learn the trade of printing.   He was so proficient that at twenty he became a master printer and foreman of one of the largest local firms.   This was no easy achievement.   Indeed it was extraordinary.   Printing is a first-class trade in Jamaica and some of the foremen of the big plants were imported from Britain and Canada.

A mere youth, the youngest foreman printer in Kingston, Garvey held down this position of responsibility and authority until in 1909 a printers' strike took place in Kingston. All the rank and file printers were native blacks and mulattoes. Being foreman of his plant, Garvey had not been informed of the strike and the walkout of his men took him unawares.

Nevertheless, he was a native son himself; he understood the grievances of the strikers and voluntarily supported their demands for better wages and shorter hours.   The strikers welcomed Garvey and he quit his job to join them.   He was the only foreman who did.   Grateful, the strikers elected him to lead the strike. He did the job efficiently, organized public meetings and for the first time demonstrated those extraordinary oratorical talents which were to magnetize the Negro people and stir the world.

The employers finally won the strike. They broke it by introducing the linotype machine and importing key printers from abroad. Most of the men compromised and returned to their jobs. But as the one foreman who joined the strikers, Marcus Garvey was boycotted by all the employers, who were white, and nevermore could he obtain another job as a printer in Jamaica. It was probably this bitter experience which later made him contemptuous of workers' organizations and the labor movement in general. And when he was able, as a universal leader, to sway thousands of Negroes, he ignored all efforts that were made by various quarters to bring about an understanding or working agreement between the forces of labor and his racial mass movement.

The following year, after the strike, Garvey established a periodical called *Garvey's Watchman*. Also he organized an annual Elocution Contest. The Elocution Contest was a success and still is conducted in Jamaica. But the newspaper failed. Garvey emigrated to Central America. He tried to establish another paper in Costa Rica, where there is a considerable population of English-speaking West Indians. This venture failed, precipitating difficulties, and it is said that he was arrested and deported from Costa Rica.

Next Garvey is discovered in London in 1912 or 1913. There he became associated with an Egyptian author, Duse Mohammed Ali, who published the monthly *African Times and Orient Review*. He visited the British Museum and contemplated the relics of the culture of ancient Egypt. He studied the tribal cultures of West Africa and South Africa. He read many books about native West African empires, such as the Empire of Benin, which became extinct. He studied the colonization system of Africa. Duse Mohammed introduced him to other Africans in London: cocoa and copra and palm oil merchants and their student sons.

In July, 1914, just before the outbreak of the World War,

Garvey returned to Jamaica. His head was big with the idea of an African Redemption and Colonization scheme. Garvey had been quite irritated by the complacency of the Africans in London. They appeared to him to be apologetic black Englishmen rather than Africans proud of their race and country. Garvey believed that the Africans should be awakened with new ideas and a world outlook. And he had proposed to Duse Mohammed the plan of an international organization of Africans and Negroes of the New World.

Back again in Jamaica, he founded the Universal Negro Improvement Association. The native intelligentsia did not respond to Garvey's efforts. The majority of educated British West Indians are more conservative in their patriotism than many Britons and feel little kinship with the natives of Africa. The Jamaica intelligentsia ridiculed Garvey's pan-African dream.

But the common people were receptive. So Garvey preached to them. But he felt that if the common people were to grasp fully the significance of his movement, they needed a wider education. There were no facilities in the West Indies for the education of such people. So Garvey planned to establish an institution similar to Tuskegee and accordingly corresponded with Booker T. Washington. The Universal Association had already failed from lack of public support when Garvey left Jamaica for the United States.

Garvey had been converted to the Roman Catholic faith in his youth and he carried letters from members of the Catholic hierarchy in Jamaica commending his work. His first public meeting in New York was held in the annex of St. Marks Roman Catholic church in Harlem. The meeting was not a success. A majority of his audience who were mostly West Indians, were aware of the opposition Garvey had encountered in Jamaica and were hostile to his pan-African dream. And they made the evening hot for Garvey.

Garvey was not prepossessing in that first New York appearance. By purely Negroid standards he is an ugly man.

As a boy in Jamaica he had been nicknamed "Ugly Mug." He was short and ungainly, built something in the shape of a puncheon. He had not yet cultivated that stern domineering manner which later distinguished him. The audience listened attentively enough when he outlined his plan of establishing a school for the underprivileged children of Jamaica. But when he aired his pan-African ideas he was heckled and booed. In the confusion Garvey fell off the platform, hurting himself slightly, and the meeting broke up. Later, hostile critics said that his fall from the platform had been deliberate, to win the sympathy of the audience.

Subsequently Garvey was persuaded to join a group of street speakers of radical-racial ideas. And from 1916 onwards he harangued crowds on the sidewalks of Harlem.

A few persons who believed in him prevailed upon him to establish his Universal Negro organization in New York. They convinced him that New York was a world center, from which it would be possible for him to reach and influence more Negroes than anywhere else.

In 1917 Garvey organized in Harlem the Universal Negro Improvement Association. He had as a nucleus an intelligent group of men who belonged to a long established History Club, which specialized in the Negro people's ancient past. Auspiciously Garvey started off on a lecture tour, which covered a majority of the States that had a considerable Negro population. He was warmly welcomed and received large contributions of money.

Garvey was establishing himself. But he still faced serious opposition in Harlem. Towards the end of 1917 one of his opponents received a letter from Garvey's former associate in London, Duse Mohammed, which discredited Garvey and made serious charges against his character. The recipient of the letter read it at an open meeting. It exploded like a well-timed bomb and broke up the organization. But Garvey, determined, started again to build another organization. In the first month of 1918 the *Negro*

World, its weekly organ, was launched. Disseminating the pan-African ideas of Garvey, this newspaper in a few months established itself as the leading national Negro weekly.

Africa for the Africans! Renaissance of the Negro Race! Back to Africa! A Black Star Line! These were the slogans Garvey broadcast in a thousand different ways to move the mind of the Negro people. There was magic in his method. It worked miraculously. The Negro masses acclaimed the new leader. The black belts clamored to hear his voice and competed with one another for his lectures. Money poured in for subscriptions to the *Negro World,* money that would help establish the Black Star Line and set in motion the Redemption of Africa. Garvey struck African Redemption medals. A bronze cross was bestowed upon subscribers of from $50 to $100, a silver cross for subscribers of from $100 to $500 and a gold cross for donors of $500 to $1000.

Now, after many vicissitudes, Garvey was successfully launched on his career of world leadership of the Negroes. Evidently Garvey himself was astounded by the overwhelming acclaim he received in the United States. After extensive traveling he was convinced that the advance guard of the Negro race was in America. The Negroes, discovering in him the inspired prophet of their group, kept him here and lifted him to the dizzying pinnacle of fame.

There were other worthy organizations and leaders of the period. The National Association for the Advancement of Colored People and the Equal Rights League had fought for nearly a decade for the human and legal rights of Negroes. But Dr. DuBois and Monroe Trotter, the outstanding personalities of these organizations, respectively, were highly educated and refined men.

And the times were auspicious for a popular leader. The whole world was in the midst of war. Negroes from the United States, the West Indies and Africa were fighting the battle of Europe in France and the Near East. And there was no leader who was giving voice to the thoughts of these common Negro soldiers and their kinsfolk at home. Negroes were segregated as soldiers. In America there was a conflict raging within the group whether Negroes should participate in the war. Some held that Negroes should fight as other citizens: others maintained that Negroes were not as other citizens. In 1917, when America entered the war, there were frightful outbreaks and riots between whites and blacks, notably in Houston, Texas. A considerable body of Southern whites deplored the Negroes' participation in the war. The Negro minority lacked an authoritative voice of leadership.

The supply of cheap European labor was cut off by the World War. Southern Negro workers were available. The mills and factories of Northern industrialists were whirring with war orders. They dispatched agents to the South to round up Negro workers. The South was alarmed over losing the brawn and sinews of its mistreated minority. It didn't care to let the "unwanted" Negroes go. Every effort was used to restrain them. The Northern agents were intimidated. Negro migrants were pulled off trains and driven to the plantations with shotguns poking their backs. Still the Negroes contrived to elude their jailers and pour into the centers of Northern industry. The black migration increased industrial conflicts and race riots, of which the bloody massacre of East St. Louis was the most appalling.

The liberal spirit of the entire nation was outraged. Negro and white organizations demanded that the corrupt authorities of East St. Louis should protect the Negro citizens. But the American Federation of Labor president, Samuel Gompers, released a statement in which he justified the mob of white workers in their attacks upon the Negro workers, because the latter were imported to compete with the whites. Yet the Negroes were not strike-breakers. They were merely filling a gap that the United States war efforts had opened. The political horizon for the Negro was as full of foreboding as was the industrial horizon. The 1916 national election had returned another Democratic Administration. The men who controlled the destinies of the Republican Party were alarmed. There was a proposal to reform the electoral vote of the Southern States: either Negro citizens should vote, or their potential voting strength should not be misused to increase the power of the Southern political bloc. The entire block of Southern States and their sympathizers in the North were aroused to combat the idea. New York's leading Democratic organ came out flatly with this statement: "The white man will rule his land."

The statement was reprinted and commented upon by all the important Negro newspapers. Some of the most loyal meliorists of the Booker T. Washington political school were stirred to join up with the radicals. There was a general feeling abroad that the Negro, however loyal, would never be permitted to call America his land. However much property he acquired he would have no voice in the control of it and would remain at the mercy of white political sharks.

In the midst of this crisis Marcus Garvey appeared with his Negro Improvement and Back-to-Africa programme. He thundered phrases that were authoritative if not wise. But the Negro people were ripe for such a prophet. Girding for a supreme war effort, America had little time to devote to the growing problems of its large Negro minority. Harassed in the South and rebuffed in the North, the southern Negroes eagerly swallowed the sayings and the projects of Garvey.

Marcus Garvey became the mouthpiece of these southern and West Indian migrants to the northern centers of industry. Whether they worked in Jersey or Pennsylvania, Connecticut or Massachusetts, Harlem was their Mecca. They gave Garvey all the money he needed to institute his programme. But only an infinitesimal few of these people really desired to go—BACK TO AFRICA. And obviously Marcus Garvey himself had no intention of going back to live in some corner of the vast land of his ancestors. But Back-to-Africa on a Black Star Line was magical propaganda. American Negroes had never beheld a steamship with a Negro crew and owned and officered by Negroes. Even the smallest excursion boat chartered by a church for a summer's day vacation was owned and officered by whites. Garvey de-

clared that it could be otherwise. His disciples desired to
see.

Inspired by the response of the masses, Garvey outlined
a programme for a planned Negro economy. He exhorted
Negroes to trade among themselves, to make contacts for
trading with Negroes abroad, to start a real Negro Church
based upon African religion, build Negro schools and a
society of Negro people. He wanted to create a Negro
society according to the European plan, with royalty, nobility,
laity, priests, workers.

.   .   .   .

At first Garvey's mighty plans did not appeal to the
educated Negroes. Apparently they were no more than
grandiloquently spoken and printed words which could never
be translated into action. But certain individuals, leaders,
would-be leaders and practical politicians were disturbed by
the man's magnetic influence over the masses.

Just a few months after the founding of his organization,
Garvey was involved in disputes with his most prominent
officials. He ousted some of them. Already Garvey was
accused of misappropriation of funds which he had collected.
Early in 1919 he was nearly assassinated by one George
Tyler, who shot him three times in the arms and leg. He
was saved by his secretary, Miss Amy Ashwood, who threw
herself between him and his antagonist. The would-be
assassin committed suicide the following day by leaping from
the fourth-story window of the jail.

The attempt on Garvey's life, besides his arrest sky-rocketed
his stock. He incorporated the Black Star Line, capitalized
at ten million dollars. Shares sold at five dollars each. The
drive started for funds to purchase and launch that year the
first ship of the Black Star Line. "Up, you mighty race!"
cried Garvey. And the race rose up. Garvey spoke and the
Negro masses were transformed. "Negro, Black, and Africa,"
the magic words repeated again and again made Negroes
delirious with ecstasy. Wherever Garvey led they were

ready to follow. He was the modern Moses, the black savior. His message reached Negroes everywhere. From the plantation of the deep South, they hearkened to his voice, in the islands of the Caribbean they were moved as never before, now that the voice of Marcus Garvey was broadcast from New York. Across the Atlantic, in the heart of the Congo, Negroes talked of the black Messiah.

No wonder Garvey thought himself invested with godlike attributes. The Negro people pushed him up on a pedestal and seated him upon a throne. They were overwhelmed by waves of emotion, subterranean waves rising and sweeping over them, waves which might have frightened Garvey himself. Hitherto their enormous store of energy and emotion had swept along the channels of religion. But for the first time since Emancipation, they were touched by a momentous social awakening. Could Garvey rule this swelling ocean of enthusiasm? As it rolled along, carrying him on its heaving bosom, Garvey, in gaudy paraphernalia and with a symbolic sword, shouted gorgeous words, words spinning like bullets, words falling like bombs, sharp words, like poisoned daggers, thundering words and phrases lit with all the hues of the rainbow to match the wild approving roar of his people. And the words seemed sufficient, apparently of greater value even than the little action which resulted from them.

The pan-African empire which he builded in Harlem was a fantastic realm. But it flourished, extending its power over a mighty host. To the innumerable black subjects it was a real empire. The Garvey-created nobility were a serious ruling caste. The dukes and lords and ladies had special duties to perform as leaders of sections. They took precedence over the masses and were obliged to set an example of higher living. And it is interesting to observe that some of these titled personages of the dream empire came from the élite of Aframericans. The Duke of the Nile was Emmett J. Scott, a light mulatto, Registrar of Howard University, former Secretary of Tuskegee Institute, close associate of Booker T. Washington and friend of some high ranking leaders of the Republican Party. Lady Henrietta Vinton Davis was one of the finest elocutionists of the Negro group and a very sensitive interpreter of Shakespearean roles at home and abroad.

The Black Legion, in its dark-blue uniform and red stripes, was as imposing as the Black Guard of the Sultan of Morocco. The Black Cross nurse appeared as chic and competent as any one of the unit of colored girls in a New York hospital. The Black Star choristers chanted melodiously of the Empire land. Harlem became the provisional capital of the empire. And it carried an allure, a peacock pride at being the center of a colossal movement.

As thousands of dollars were rained down on Garvey for the founding of the Black Star Line and the glorification of his dream of African empire, other Negro leaders, less spectacular, showed serious concern about this waste of the earnings of the Negro masses. Standing aloof and extremely critical, few of the Negro intellectuals had any faith in the operation of a Black Star Line of ships.

A Negro ship! Master, officers and crew all Negro! Hostile Negro newspapers demanded to know where Marcus Garvey would find a Negro captain. If one could not be found in America, Garvey knew that specimens existed in the West Indies, where wealthy Negroids owned their own coastwise vessels, officered and manned by Negroes.

And so while leading Harlem Negroes were instigating an investigation of Garvey's financial ventures, he ran a series of articles in the *Negro World,* picturing the glories of the Black Star Line and the moral and material benefits that Negroes could get from running their own ships.

In the latter part of 1919, while the pundits of the Negro minority were still proving by mathematical manipulation that Negroes by themselves could not operate a line of ships, Marcus Garvey announced that the Black Star Line had acquired its first boat. There was consternation in the camp of his opponents, while the masses of Black Dixie shouted hosannas. Garvey also had the master of his ship in the person of Captain Joshua Cockburn, who had actually served with the British Merchant Fleet during the First

World War. Negro mates, first and second, and a Negro crew were also on hand.

There was a wild invasion of Harlem by Negroes from every black quarter of America. Hordes of disciples came with more dollars to buy more shares. The boat was moored at the pier with its all-Negro crew. And the common people gladly paid half a dollar to go aboard and look over the miracle. Loudly talking and gesturing, they inspected the ship, singing the praises of Marcus Garvey. Summer after summer most of them had taken excursion trips, organized by churches or clubs. But it was always a "white" boat and not always were they treated considerately and politely by officers and crew.

Now, in this first boat of the Black Star Line, owned by the Universal Negro Improvement Association, they saw something different. They saw themselves sailing without making any apology for being passengers. It was their own ship, a Negro ship. It was their money that had bought it. But it had required a black leader to show them how they could do it.

That night Liberty Hall was jammed with Negroes. Hundreds could not get in and the sidewalks overflowed with spectators between Lenox Avenue and Seventh Avenue. Marcus Garvey transformed the great audience into a waving, shouting, frenzied host as he cried: "Up, you mighty race, you can accomplish what you will."

The price of the boat was said to be $165,000. It was sent on goodwill trips to coastwise ports and enthusiastic supporters were sold hundreds of shares in the Negro line. Early in 1920 the boat sailed on its first voyage to the West Indies, carrying a cargo of liquor. It proved to be almost unseaworthy and foundered at Newport News. The trip did not enhance the prestige of the Black Star Line. The crew became undisciplined, raided the cargo and went on a boozers' holiday.

But if the Black Star did not shine so brilliantly at sea, Garvey's individual star, nevertheless, rose wonderfully. Towards the end of 1919, he married his secretary Miss Amy

Ashwood, who had flung herself between him and his would-be assassin. She too was from Jamaica, where she had graduated from the Westwood High School.

In 1920 Marcus Garvey staged the first Universal Negro Convention in Harlem. This was the dramatic occasion that made the City of New York fully aware of the movement in Harlem. The convention went over with theatrical éclat. During the hard years of organization, Garvey had lived simply and dressed modestly. His exuberant attitude toward life had been held under control in Jamaica. But in Harlem Garvey could let himself go. His speech could be as decorative as arabesques and his raiment as rich as an Eastern potentate's. The common people would pay him still greater homage, for Harlem adores colorful, colossal demonstrations. Garvey borrowed generously from cult manifestations and fraternal rituals in painting his political mission in gay colors.

And so a most gorgeous show was organized by Garvey in 1920. Delegates arrived from Africa, Brazil, Colombia, Panama and other Central American countries, and from the islands of the West Indies. Every State of the Union was represented. Harlem blinked at the dazzling splendor of that wonderful parade. Garvey wore a magnificent uniform of purple, green and black, and a plumed hat. He stood in his car and saluted the cheering crowds that jammed the sidewalks. Behind him in full regalia rode the nobility and the notables of the Universal Negro Association, brilliant sashes denoting their rank. The African Legion filed past, stiff, erect, left, right, left, right, and all the auxiliaries of the association and the enormous mass of the rank and file.

The following evening, Garvey packed Madison Square Garden with his followers and admirers. In a long speech he exhorted the Negroes to unite and work for the redemption of Africa. He recited the history of the organization, giving details of what had been accomplished. He told the people that they had done everything and could do greater things. Resolutions were passed and messages sent to United States government officials, to the Empress of

Ethiopia and the President of Liberia. Most significant of all was the message of sympathy and support sent to Eamon de Valera, Provisional President in Exile of the Irish Republic. That message was duly noted in certain London newspapers. The Irish struggle against Britain was most acute at that time. And if the British government had never heard of a British subject named Marcus Garvey in London and Jamaica, perhaps they became aware of him now in New York.

. . . .

In the fall of 1921 Garvey boldly took a position on the Negro's place in American politics, and thus arrayed against him the radical element of Negro leaders. President Harding had visited Birmingham, where he delivered a significant speech on the Negro's part in politics. There was an echo of Booker T. Washington's famous Atlanta speech in what the President had to say. He said that racial amalgamation there could not be, but partnership of the races there must be: "I wish that both the tradition of a solid Democratic South and the tradition of a solidly Republican black race might be broken up. . . . Let the black man vote when he is fit to vote, prohibit the white man from voting when he is unfit to vote."

The South was not too enthusiastic over the President's speech. And the northern Negroes were non-committal. Politically, the Negro minority was at that time in a dilemma. Dissatisfied with President Taft's administration and displeased with Theodore Roosevelt's stand on the Negroes in 1912, thousands had been led by their leaders to vote for President Wilson and The New Freedom. But politically the group had fared worse under the Democratic Administration than under any Republican Administration since Lincoln. The Negroes were demoralized, not knowing to which party they should turn. Booker T. Washington, although resident in the South, had always been a Republican and a strong influence among the conservative Negroes. But he had died during President Wilson's first term and no other Negro leader had forged forward to take his place.

Marcus Garvey sent a telegram of endorsement to President Harding, in which he said: "All true Negroes are against Social Equality, believing that all Negroes should develop along their own social lines. . . . The New Negro will join hands with those who are desirous of keeping the two opposite races socially pure and work together for the industrial, educational and political liberation of all peoples. The Negro peoples of the world expect the South to give the Negroes a fair chance. Long live America. Long live President Harding in his manly advocacy of Social Justice."

It is not recorded what effect this telegram had upon President Harding and his entourage. The Republicans were badly in need of a leader of national proportions, who could combine the shrewdness and sagacity of Booker T. Washington in dealing with the white North and the white South, while commanding the respect of the conservative majority of Negroes. Perhaps if Garvey were less bombastic and had apprenticed himself to learn more of the mechanism of American politics, he might have been that leader. There was no other Negro in sight for the job (there has not yet been one) and Garvey had the Negro masses in the hollow of his hand.

But Garvey had stumbled headlong into the hornet's nest of the Northern Negro intelligentsia. For 75 years "Social Equality" has been the red sign of danger between the white world and the Negro. Southern whites interpret it to mean, mainly, intimate social intercourse between whites and blacks, with resultant miscegenation. The Northern Negro intelligentsia challenge this interpretation. They interpret Social Equality to mean equal opportunity for Negro Americans under the American system of economy: equal opportunity in the industrial, educational, political and other avenues of American life.

In the West Indies, Social Equality is generally used in the careless way of the Southern whites. And so it meant the same thing to Marcus Garvey as it did to them. In his excessive group and racial pride Garvey held that social intercourse should not become an acute political issue be-

tween the colored minority and the whites in America. He
was too proud and self-confident to imagine that the Negro
was inferior. Garvey always preached to his followers the
potential equality of the Negro with the white person.

Garvey was a fervent admirer of Booker T. Washington's
marvellous skill in building up and holding together a
modern all-Negro institution. He was a partisan of the
Tuskegee school of politics. And this school was especially
detested by that northern Negro group led by the powerful
National Association for the Advancement of Colored People of New York and the Equal Rights Association of Boston.
They accused Garvey of advocating Segregation and of
pandering to the worst prejudices of Southern whites. Opposition was erected against him. This opposition was joined
by the small but intelligent and influential group of Negroes
affiliated with the Labor and Radical movements. And
doubtlessly it was this powerful combination of the Negro
intelligentsia, aided by wealthy white supporters, which
finally brought about Garvey's downfall.

The Negro masses throughout the nation backed Garvey.
And as the opposition of the Negro intelligentsia gained in
strength, the masses demonstrated their greater loyalty. At a
stupendous mass meeting in Harlem, Garvey was presented
with a new broom to sweep the opposition away. In every
State, loyalty meetings of the Universal Negro Improvement
Association were held. And resolutions were passed, pledging the loyalty of the Negro people to Garvey. He journeyed
triumphantly to the populous centers to show his appreciation
and stir the people with his magnetic oratory. Liberally
they contributed with donations or purchases of shares.

Garvey's invasion of the South, the acclamation of the
Black Belts and the attitude of the Southern whites presented a puzzle to northern Negro intellectuals. Garvey
had announced previously that he was going South to talk
to his own people and that the white man should leave him
alone.

Now many Northern blacks and whites had been manhandled and run out of the South for attempting to hold

peaceful meetings with colored people! A Mr. Shillady, the white Secretary of the National Association of Colored People, was obnoxiously insulted, beaten and driven out of the South, when he attempted to meet with colored persons. Booker T. Washington was always extremely cautious in his spoken and written words.

But in Louisiana and Alabama, notably, Garvey succeeded in holding some extremely boisterous and enthusiastic meetings and getting away without a scratch. Of course, he had his way of doing it. He employed a special technique. He thundered, "Africa for the Africans," and shouted at the white South in a semi-religious harangue, "Let my people go!"

The South permitted Marcus Garvey to talk that way to cheering multitudes of Negroes. Northern Negro critics maintained that the South gave Garvey leeway because he was not a challenge: the South wanted to get rid of the Negro and approved Garvey's slogan, "Let my people go." But Garvey *was* a challenge and the South did *not* want to get rid of its black serfs. During the World War and the years immediately following, when labor manpower was a problem, the South had desperately tried to keep its Negroes from migrating North.

Probably there was some truth in the report that Garvey had made a secret deal with the Ku Klux Klan that his meetings should not be molested. The Ku Klux Klan undoubtedly possessed the power and perhaps the Kleagle secretly admired a Negro who could organize the blacks on a grand scale, employing the same tactics by which the Klan had organized the whites.

Meanwhile, the Federal government had undertaken an investigation of Garvey. In January, 1922, he was arrested on a charge of using the mails to defraud. He was indicted with three high officials of his organization. The charge was that Garvey had used the mails to solicit funds for a Black Star Line which was not established. He was released on bail of $2500.

At the same time a vigorous campaign was launched

against Garvey by the Friends of Negro Freedom, a group composed of officials of the National Association for the Advancement of Colored People, and labor leaders, editors and ministers. But Garvey's loyal followers organized larger meetings and he received hundreds of telegrams pledging support. The Universal Negro Improvement Association released an open letter appealing to the White Race to let the Black Race manage its own affairs.

The prosecution of Marcus Garvey was not rushed. This delay aroused his opponents. Meetings were called and resolutions passed demanding his speedy prosecution. The resolutions were telegraphed to the Department of Justice. But it appeared as if the authorities were in no hurry to proceed. Perhaps Garvey had friends in high places of whom he was not even aware: he was too egotistic to care.

For the balance of the year he remained unmolested, and organized in Harlem one of his grandest conventions. From every State in the union, from the West Indies, from Central and South America, from Europe and Africa, an inspiring deputation of delegates converged upon Harlem. It was the greatest swarm since Garvey started his movement. They brought gifts to Garvey: special contributions to defend his case, sums for African Redemption and thousands of subscriptions to reorganize the Black Star Line. It was during this time that a delegate from Central America drafted a new will bequeathing to Garvey's organization his estate, valued at over $300,000. At that convention Garvey generously increased the strength of his nobility. Among the new titles were Duke of Nigeria and Overlord of Uganda. To the tremendous tributes he responded as befitted a grand potentate. The ribbons and braids of his gleaming satin robe were richer than ever, his plumes were as long as the leaves of the Guinea grass and as white as snow; seated in his car as upon a throne, he received the ovations and salutes of Harlem.

It was not until the following year, near the middle of 1923, that Garvey's trial began. It lasted a month. And it was a real show, one of the amusement features of the great

city of New York. The government's case was weak and
everything seemed in Garvey's favor. First, there was apparently official reluctance in prosecuting. The evidence
for prosecution was flimsy. There was no letter to prove that
the Black Star Line had directly sold shares through the
mails. Only an envelope was offered as evidence. Although
the Black Star Line was not actually in operation, since its
ships were old and broken down and lacked personnel, it
was not altogether bankrupt. Above all, the Garvey organization remained intact and its multitudes of members demonstrated implicit faith in their leader, supported him
morally and materially. Garvey also had an asset in the
Metropolitan press. It was always indulgent, perhaps because he provided such exciting and diverting items for the
edification of the reading public. Sometimes Garvey and his
antics crowded a lynching off the front page!

But as the trial progressed, it appeared as if Garvey was
determined to jail himself. This acknowledged leader of
millions of Negroes was extremely fond of litigation. Probably as a youth he had desired to become an attorney in
Jamaica, an ambition which might have remained. Here was
a chance to gratify this ambition. And upon such a stage!
A Federal courtroom in the great city of New York.

Garvey had in Mr. Henry Lincoln Johnson an able Negro
lawyer. But when the case started he dispensed with his
services and announced that he would be his own attorney.
For a month Garvey had a magnificent time indeed in that
Federal courtroom. In his role as attorney for the defendant,
he had such fun with the witnesses arrayed against him that
he appeared to forget entirely the gravity of the charge.
He corrected the witnesses' English, instructed them how
they should answer his question, declared that the British
government was behind his prosecution; he was frequently at
loggerheads with the judge. Yet he had some strong points
in his favor. He proved that his Black Star Line was not
merely a fabrication of his imagination. He had been
duped into buying rotten ships. The boat for which he
paid $165,000 had made only one trip before it fell apart.

It was sold as junk for $1650. But Joseph H. Philbin, sales-manager of the United States Shipping Board, testified that the Board held $22,500, which the Garvey organization had deposited on the purchase of a ship.

Garvey gloried in his day in court. He proved to his myriad of faithful followers that he was literally the Great Advocate. Perhaps in his self-conceit that was adequate consolation for his sentence of five years in prison and a fine of $1,000. The sentence was appealed. Garvey's prestige rose with his conviction. New recruits flocked to his African standard and he received strong support from West Africa. Africans were seriously listening to the words and pondering the plans of the American Negro Liberator. Consequently the *Negro World,* the organ of the Garvey movement, was banned in the colonies of British West Africa.

· · · · · · ·

Breaking away from the Roman Catholic Church, Garvey launched out in a new field. He established the African Orthodox Church as an adjunct to his organization. This was a bold stroke which excited the imagination of his followers. They would have their own church. But it was not so exciting to the Negro clergy. The majority of the Garvey following were members of ordinary Negro churches and the ministers were alarmed lest their flocks should desert them for the new church.

As protagonist of the new church, Garvey obtained a fine figure of a man. This was the Rev. George Alexander McGuire, a minister of the Episcopalian Church. Mr. Mc-Guire had served under Bishop Brown of Arkansas, who achieved national notoriety as a convert to and fearless advocate of Communism. But the Rev. McGuire had quarreled with his bishop, accusing him of race prejudice. Mr. McGuire was called to a church in Boston where he won the respect of the most influential white and colored people.

The Reverend McGuire was one of the many intellectuals of the Negro minority who joined the Garvey movement after the highly publicized maiden voyage of the first ship of the Black Star Line in 1920. His adherence to the movement was a sensational gesture. He had a marvelous voice for the tribune, much more cultured than Garvey's. His character was impeccable. His English education was excellent. He was a black gentleman who fiercely lived up to the high moral standard of the white world. Often in his sermons he tiraded against the laxity and shiftlessness of the Negroes. He denounced charlatans and buffoons who held up the Negro race to ridicule. And when he enlisted in the Garvey movement, he immeasurably increased its prestige among the skeptical intelligentsia and silenced many of its enemies. The Rev. George Alexander McGuire became the first archbishop of the African Orthodox Church. He was consecrated by an archbishop of the Greek church.

Garvey had established relationship with Liberia. His representatives there were two former high officials, ex-presidents Barclay and Howard. The Liberian government was almost without funds and unable to obtain more loans in Europe or America. Had Garvey been a little discreet and willing to make a secret deal with one of the major American political parties, he might have put over something concrete for the benefit of the post-war American Negro and the West African Negro. But Garvey was too self-confident and bombastic to understand practical hints. He did not even seem aware of the deep anxiety that his movement gave to certain European governments. He did not know that his contacts and understanding with Liberian officials were a matter of concern in European chancelleries. Yet it was public rumor that the Liberian government was using his movement to wring concessions out of European countries.

The annual convention of the Negro Improvement Association was attended by Gabriel Johnson, Mayor of Monrovia, capital of Liberia. The Mayor of Liberia was duly impressed. He saw with his own eyes that Marcus Garvey was indeed a mighty person not only in the Negro city of Harlem, but in New York at large. His meeting at

Madison Square Garden brought out a veritable army of white policemen to guard him. Why, the President of Liberia had no such honor accorded to him when he visited Paris and London. His visit would barely be chronicled in an obscure corner of the newspapers.

The Mayor of Monrovia, Liberia, was highly pleased to accept the grander title of High Potentate of Africa, conferred upon him by Marcus Garvey, Provisional President of the Empire of Africa. He was also voted a salary of $12,000 a year, almost as much as the salary of the President of Liberia. The Mayor of Monrovia returned to Liberia wearing his new Universal Improvement and Back-To-Africa regalia and insignia. The Mayor of Monrovia so seriously considered his new title of High Potentate of Africa that he demanded that he should take precedence over the President of Liberia at state functions! The black aristocracy of Liberia was outraged and the poor mayor was nearly lynched.

A delegation consisting of three members of the Universal Negro organization was dispatched to Liberia. Miss Henrietta Vinton Davis was a member of the delegation and its chairman was Robert L. Poston, the husband of the Negro sculptress, Augusta Savage. Marcus Garvey announced that $50,000 had been used in the purchase of materials towards establishing a colony in Liberia.

The Black Star Line was reorganized as the Black Cross, and the *General Goethals,* a boat of over four thousand tons, was purchased from the government. The first members of the colony were scheduled to sail in 1924. But trouble broke in Liberia. It was said that the Garvey party there was using the world-wide influence of the Universal Negro Organization to overthrow the government.

The opponents of Marcus Garvey were deeply troubled by the man's increasing power. Despite his romantic theory of an African empire, he was becoming more elastic in his methods. His plan for a ship of Negro officers and crew had failed. He had quarreled with his first Negro captain and there were not enough trained Negro officers to meet the demands of the Black Star Line. Therefore he put white

officers and a black crew on the new boat. He started flirt-
ing, too, with white politicians. At an overflow Madison
Square mass meeting held in March, 1924, one of the prominent speakers was Surrogate John P. O'Brien. At last
Marcus Garvey was taking his American lessons.

The common people humbly worshiped the man. They
bowed down when he passed by them in his Lord High
Potentate's robes. Wherever he went he was guarded by
his personal guard. At mass meetings members of the
African Legion lined the way in serried ranks as he strode
to the platform. His people believed that his enemies were
seeking to do him harm. His conviction had increased
his prestige a thousandfold. He wore his prison sentence
like a martyr's crown.

The August, 1924, convention of the Universal Negro
and Black Cross was designed as a monster farewell party to
the Negroes who were to leave for Liberia in the fall.
Bearing splendid gifts of household goods and special sums
of money, thousands of Universalites swarmed into Harlem.
Those who were chosen to go were religiously regarded as
angels of the New Heaven, Marcus Garvey's promised land,
the Negro Zion.

The Archbishop of the African Orthodox Church, the
Right Reverend C. A. McGuire, in his robes of state, pronounced a blessing upon the convention, said a special prayer
for Marcus Garvey and the Universal Negroes who were the
first to have elected to return to Africa. The Archbishop
discoursed on the past. He pictured the ruins of African
empires and of the dispersion of the Negro peoples. He
traced the beginning of the slave trade in America, described
the slave ship riding the Atlantic with the first cargo of
slaves. He told of the early lives of the slaves in the West
Indies and in the United States, of the rise of the Abolitionist
movement and the Emancipation. The Negroes came to
this land with bound hands and feet, he said. But their
children were returning with gifts to Africa and as brothers
of the children of Africa to build a new Africa. The children of the African Orthodox Church must return to the

bosom of the motherland. "You must forget the white gods," he said. "Erase the white gods from your hearts. We must go back to the native church, to our own true God."

Inspired, inflamed, the mighty assembly rose and cheered the Archbishop for many minutes, shouting, "Hallelujah, God save Africa, Hallelujah!"

Goodwill messages were sent to President King of Liberia, President Coolidge, the President of Haiti, the Empress of Ethiopia, the President of the Irish Free State, Kemal Pasha, Dictator of Turkey, Abdel Krim, the rebel leader of Spanish Morocco, Mahatma Gandhi and other internationally known personages who were more or less engaged in the battle of liberty.

But in the midst of the thirty-day convention, the Liberian government issued a statement repudiating the Universal Negro organization, and refusing to recognize its advance delegates. Some were actually arrested. It also protested to the American Administration against the activities of the Garvey organization in Liberia.

Marcus Garvey was stupefied—for a while. His followers were dismayed. He accused President King of treachery, declaring that the Universal Negro Association had already invested $50,000 in Liberia. He charged that European governments were intriguing in Africa against his organization. And the American Negro enemies of Africa were attempting again to sell the Negro race into slavery. He rallied his followers at mighty mass meetings, pledging his life to redeem the black man. He declared that with the secret magic of ancient Africa, he would reconquer the land for the Negro.

But while some of his obeah-minded and Voodoo-enchanted followers applauded, believing in Garvey's knowledge of deadly magic, he resorted to other means to discredit the Liberian government among the Negro peoples. In 1920 Garvey had sent Eli Garcia, his Secretary-General and formerly a Haitian official, to survey the Liberian field. Upon his return to the United States, Garcia presented a con-

fidential report to his chief, which contained a strong indictment of the Liberian governmental group.

Garcia said that the American-Liberians, because of their
"white" education, were vain, conceited and overbearing
toward the autochthonous people. The American-Liberians
called themselves "the Whites" and the tribes "the Natives."
All American-Liberians competed with one another for
government jobs, in which they are in a position to lord it
over the tribes. Yet, they did nothing to improve the standard of the natives, nothing to better their primitive standard
of living, nothing to exploit the vast, rich agricultural lands.

Rice, the staple food, was imported and sold so dearly
that the common people were undernourished. The primitive tribal economy was not sufficient to support the ruling
caste in the high European style of living. Therefore the
tribes were sullen and in some parts of the country revolted
against the government. Garcia charged that the ruling
Negroids countenanced the practice of slavery. Young native
girls were sold at from $20 to $30 per head.

Garcia said that by sounding out unofficial persons he was
convinced that the ruling clique of Liberians were opposed
to any considerable number of American Negroes emigrating
to Liberia to start a model colony. They were unprogressive
and opposed to any plan that would introduce new blood and
modern ideas into the so-called black republic.

Now Garvey released this grave report. And it certainly
injured the cause of the Liberians among the Negro peoples of the world. In the early nineteen thirties, the League
of Nations, notably Britain and France, presented sub-
stantially the same charges against Liberia during its border
troubles against the revolting tribes. And they were a
serious threat to the independence of the Monrovian administration.

Obviously Liberian officials had used the Marcus Garvey
colonization scheme to bargain with white governments and
capitalists for loans. They thought perhaps that the few
thousand dollars collected from the black folk could scarcely
compete with millions of white dollars. So the black vision-

ary lost his preliminary investments in Africa, and the golden faith of his myriad of disciples, even as he was doomed to lose in America.   Marcus Garvey had dreamed of a vast model colony in Liberia.   But it was Harvey Firestone who realized the dream with his extensive rubber plantations.

However, if Marcus Garvey felt his movement betrayed by the American-Liberian aristocracy, he and his following were inspirited and uplifted by a significant event.   That year the Prince Kogo Honeou Tovalou of Dahomey made his first voyage to America.   Prince Kogo, as a royal native potentate, was honored with a picturesque reception at Liberty Hall, where all the colors of God's fertile imagination were assembled in his honor.   He made a speech full of praise for the work of the Universal Negro Association and saluted Marcus Garvey as the leader of the Negro people of the world.   Prince Kogo was appointed representative of the Association for France and her colonies.

Probably Prince Kogo, overwhelmed by the wonderful reception, was not fully conscious of the political significance of his act.   He was no African clown prince.   He was an authentic member of the family of Behanzin, the deposed King of Dahomey.   Behanzin was exiled by the French to Algeria, where he had died and was buried.   His son, Prince Behanzin, lived in France and was in close touch with his cousin, Prince Kogo.

Kogo was a fine figure of an African, tall and as handsome and smooth and shiny as ebony.   He was educated in Europe and was fluent in French, English and German.   In Paris he was the mignon of bohemian artistic circles.   Among his friends there were titled French persons, officers of the navy and army, actors and actresses, painters, singers. Hitherto he had not identified himself with politics, especially African.   But these were early post-war years.   There were many changes in Africa and the African responds quickly to the influences of change.   Germany had lost her colonies.   There was friction in mandated colonies.   BATOUALA, *Prix Goncourt* novel by the Negro René Maran, had exploded like a bomb in intellectual and political circles, and had challenged new interest in Africa.

And above all there was Garvey's Universal Negro propaganda. Its repercussion in Africa was greater than the American Back-to-Africa devotees realized. In the interior of West Africa new legends arose of an African who had been lost in America, but would return to save his people. And there were sporadic demonstrations against the local administrations. In 1924 there was a countrywide strike of men and women in Nigeria against the administration. Stevedores in the ports refused to load the ships.

Kogo's princely act in acknowledging Garvey's leadership came as an inspiration to the movement at that critical time. But Kogo later paid dearly for it. In those days it was not considered good taste to mix political issues with smart bohemianism, at least not in Allied lands. It was the time when James Joyce and Marcel Proust and T. S. Eliot were the intellectual gods. It was ten years before the Popular Front brought about a democratic marriage between Dilettantism and Bolshevism. And so when Prince Kogo returned to Paris as representative of the Universal Negro, he was no more *persona grata* in ultra-chic circles. Later he was ignominiously humiliated. One of the largest Paris dailies published a report on his personal affairs. It stated that Kogo was a swindler and a faker. He was not truly a prince. Posing as a prince of Dahomey he had borrowed large sums of money from people which had never been repaid. Gallant as he was, and certainly spoiled by the sophisticated Parisian circles, to whom an educated and suave African like Kogo was something like a rare piece of primitive African sculpture, perhaps Kogo was no worse than the whites of that same circle. But he *was* a prince of Dahomey, recognized by Behanzin, the son of the dethroned king. And when the latter died a few years later, his South American wife put herself under the protection of Kogo as the next of kin in France.

•　　•　　•　　•　　•　　•

Enemies black and white were constantly badgering Garvey and reminding the authorities of his menacing existence. His appeal slowly dragged along its course. The following Negroes, in a signed petition to the Department of Justice, demanded his imprisonment and deportation: George W. Harris, prominent politician, editor of New York (Harlem) *News,* Robert S. Abbott, editor-publisher of the Chicago *Defender,* John E. Nail, wealthy realtor, William Pickens and Robert W. Bagnall, officials of the National Association for the Advancement of Colored People; Chandler Owen, editor of the *Messenger* magazine, Harry H. Price and Dr. Julia P. Coleman. Finally, in 1925, the appeal was rejected by the United States Supreme Court. In February, 1925, Marcus Garvey entered Atlanta Federal Penitentiary to serve a five-year term of imprisonment.

But in prison he was perhaps as powerful as he was when free. His message to his followers appeared every week on the front page of the *Negro World.* Often it read like an epistle of one of the Apostles. While he was on trial, the prosecuting attorney referred to him as "The Tiger." And when he was at last convicted, his former editor and countryman, now turned enemy, Mr. W. A. Domingo, telegraphed congratulations to the United States Attorney-General that the Tiger was caged. The Garvey people delighted in the phrase and said, "They put our Tiger in the cage, but we will never rest until we get him out." They fought hard to free Garvey. His lawyer released a memorandum showing that the chief count upon which Garvey was convicted was untenable. Petitions were sent to the President of the United States. The jury that convicted him came out with a statement in favor of his release. Metropolitan newspapers, such as the *Daily News,* which has a large circulation in Harlem, demanded that Garvey be pardoned. He was turned loose in November, 1927, and deported to Jamaica.

Delegations of his increased multitude of followers made the pilgrimage to New Orleans to bid him farewell. Garvey was profoundly moved by the unflagging demonstration of loyalty. His people declared that they would follow him wherever he went, in spirit at least, if it were impossible in the flesh. And Garvey promised that he would always fight for them. He declared that wherever he was, his one aim in life would be the welfare of the Universal Negroes. His address to them from the deck of the SS. Saramacca, just before sailing, is one of the finest episodes of his life.

Thus Garvey was returned to the island of Jamaica. It was over a decade since he had sailed away to the United States unheralded. But a vast multitude was awaiting his return. The Jamaica natives, disciplined in British reserve and restraint, let themselves go to welcome the man. From the plains and the hills the peasants swarmed along the roads to join the city folk and hail the leader who had lifted up the Negro race with his voice and carried it round the world. Even if he had wanted to, Garvey could not escape from the movement that he had started. The man had that magic in him by which the Negro masses were bewitched.

From Jamaica he continued to conduct his world-wide propaganda. Every week his message cabled to New York was printed in large type on the front page of the *Negro World*. His family (second wife and two children) had joined him there with a staff of workers from the New York office. The program of the Universal Negro Association remained the same.

Marcus Garvey had promised his people to take his propaganda in person to Europe. And he was only a few months in Jamaica before he made his plans to go. He arrived in England in May, 1928. He rented Albert Hall in London for a mass meeting, but merely a handful of people attended. The English press was not so indulgent to him as had been the American.

Garvey had better luck in Paris. He addressed the French intellectuals at the Club du Faubourg and received a remarkable reception. His style was something that the French could appreciate more than the English. He visited the League of Nations, to which he had previously sent delegations from the Universal Negro Association. But there was very little he could do in Europe. He yearned to see something of that African land to the redemption of which he had dedicated his life, but British authority kept him out. He was never to see the Promised Land.

In the fall he landed in Canada. It was the year of the Hoover election. Garvey sent out an appeal to Negroes advising them to vote for Governor Smith. The Canadian authorities objected to his political activities and he was ordered to leave the country.

Back he went to the suffocating island prison. The members of the organization had to decide upon the vexing issue as to whether New York or the island of Jamaica should be their headquarters. Many preferred New York because it was a great world center, but Garvey felt that the center of the world was wherever Garvey resided. He announced that "the Greatest Assembly of Negroes Since Creation," would meet in Jamaica in 1929. And the future of the Universal Negro organization would be decided at that convention. In his enthusiasm, Garvey acted the part of a tourist barker for the island of Jamaica. He invited the delegates to "come and see the beautiful tropics: make a tour of Jamaica, the most beautiful island in the world."

And indeed it was a gigantic convention, the greatest international group of visitors that ever landed in Jamaica. Speaking English, Spanish, French and Portuguese and coming from Africa, Central and South America, the other West Indies and the United States, the delegates, accompanied by relatives and friends, descended on Jamaica. These delegates from abroad were incomparably superior, socially and intellectually, to the majority of the peasant followers of Garvey in Jamaica. And so Garvey received the coveted homage of the Jamaica élite, who honored the delegates. The mayor, members of the Legislature and other politicians and leading citizens attended the great reception. At last the King, Garvey the Great, was fully honored in his own country.

The Garvey folk staged a monster parade through the

streets of Kingston. Over 25,000 people were estimated to be in the procession. Garvey and his delegates in uniform and costume captured the tropical scene. More than a hundred and twenty-five of the delegates came from the United States. They were nearly all American Negroes. Some were students, others were in business. The Madame C. J. Walker Manufacturing Company sent a special New York representative. Doctors and lawyers were there. At least two of the student delegates are at present responsible Federal employees. The Communist Party sent its international carpet-bagger, Otto Huiswoud, who challenged Garvey to debate whether Negroes should join the Comintern. Garvey took up the challenge and, speaking on the negative side, won overwhelmingly.

Marcus Garvey became the most popular personage in Jamaica. But the British government was vigilantly watching him. During the first week of the convention (it lasted a month) he was humiliated with arrest for contempt of court, because he had said uncomplimentary things against Jamaica justice and judges in his daily newspaper. The Chief Justice fined him $500. The delegates paid the fine. The convention projected a grand plan for the rehabilitation of the movement. Millions of dollars were to be raised to start the Black Star Line again and carry trade forward between the Negro peoples. As the West Indies and Africa were entirely agricultural lands, the delegates agreed that the United States should be the industrial center of the Negro movement. But Garvey was determined to reorganize the Universal Association with Jamaica as Chief Headquarters. This plan hurt the pride of the American delegates. They held that as the association was founded in New York and had there grown to international fame, the headquarters should there abide. Garvey curried favor with the delegates and played them against one another. Finally he won and organized the Parent Body of the Association in Jamaica. But that stratagem split the movement and a rival group was started in the United States with headquarters in New York. That was the beginning of the breakup of Garvey's vast organization. Eventually Garvey's highhandedness resulted in his forfeiting a $300,000 estate, which, although bequeathed by a wealthy Central American Negro to the Universal Negro Association, was primarily intended to be at his disposal. In the long, exciting litigation which ensued, it was finally ruled by the highest English court that Garvey's claim to the estate as the head of the "Parent Body" in Jamaica was illegal, and it was allocated to the original New York organization.

Garvey soon lost much of his popularity in Jamaica. Not contented with living as an exalted exiled ruler, he became active in local politics. Again he attacked the Jamaica courts and again he was fined and this time sentenced to three months in prison by three judges of the High Court. Dramatically Garvey declared in court: "I will be an everlasting flea in the collar of my enemies."

Jamaica, the more-English-than-the-English little England of the West Indies, was gradually subduing and demoralizing the great Garvey. When a man is sent to prison in a British colony, even for a political offense, he loses prestige among the common people. It is not like going to prison for a political offense in America. While Garvey was in prison the people elected him to the City Council. His seat was voided by the municipal government. But immediately upon his release the people re-elected him by popular vote.

Garvey served for a year. But he was naturally uncomfortable in a city councillor's little seat in the tight island of Jamaica. He organized a People's Party. But the local politicians united to block his way to power. They told Garvey that they would make it harder for him in Jamaica than in America. At one of his mass meetings a heckler baited him and said Garvey thought he was a great man, but he could make him look like a foolish boy. Immediately Garvey challenged him to do it. Advising Garvey's American bodyguard to stand aside, the strapping peasant rushed Garvey, knocked him down on the platform and ripped his pants off. There was no more meeting. Deprived of his pants, Garvey was hastily wrapped in a blanket, hurried to his car and quickly driven away.

Shortly afterwards he left Jamaica for Europe. He took up residence in London. Intermittently he published a magazine entitled *The Black Man*. But, broken into disunited fragments, the Universal Negro Association lost its irresistible international appeal.

His leadership was finally eclipsed by the Ethiopian conflict. In the early days of the Italian invasion he made the cause of the Emperor of Ethiopia his own and exhorted the remnants of his followers to organize to help Ethiopia. He denounced Mussolini. He turned to exercise his hand at a Martin Tupper-like kind of didactic verse. And one of his contributions to *The Black Man* was a poem entitled "The Smell of Mussolini," and one couplet ran:

> We hate the smell of Mussolini,
> We'll lay quite low the violent Roman hog.

But the Emperor of Ethiopia was forced to flee his country, leaving it in the hands of Mussolini, to seek refuge in Europe.

When the Emperor of Ethiopia and Lion of Judah arrived in London he avoided all contact with Marcus Garvey, "Highest Potentate of the Negro World and Lion of Numidia." A delegation of colored folk in London attempted to present the Emperor of Ethiopia with an address when he arrived, but could not come near his high person. It had been published abroad that the emperor did not desire any contact with "Negroes."

All during the Ethiopian crisis such rumors had persisted. As soon as agitation over Italy's designs on Ethiopia began stirring the Africans and Aframericans, the English-speaking press took to publishing articles which said that the Ethiopians were not Negroes. So American Negroes queried whether the Ethiopians were Europeans and white. Aframericans are not generally aware that many other Africans besides Ethiopians object to being called Negroes, because they regard it as a name fit for black slaves. The Ethiopians will not even allow themselves to be designated as Abyssinians, because it is Arabic for slave. Yet because of this propaganda against the Ethiopians, many Aframericans refused to identify themselves with the Help Ethiopia movement.

Garvey struck out in his magazine, *The Blackman*, and bluntly denounced the emperor as a coward and a traitor to desert his people and run away from his country. Garvey said the emperor was prouder of being the descendant of Solomon than the ruler of a black land, that he had played a "white" game all during his reign and trusted white advisors only, and that they had betrayed him in his hour of need. Garvey wrote: "Haile Selassie is the ruler of a country where black men are chained and flogged. . . . He proved the incompetence of the Negro for political authority. . . . The emperor's usefulness is at an end. He will go down in history as a great coward who ran away from his country."

But Garvey's denunciation did not swing his people. To the emotional masses of the American Negro church the Ethiopia of today is the wonderful Ethiopia of the Bible. In a religious sense it is far more real to them than the West African lands, from which it is assumed that most of the ancestors of Aframericans came. They were happy that the emperor had escaped alive. As an ex-ruler he remained a symbol of authority over the Negro state of their imagination.

Ex-Emperor Haile Selassie wisely sent his personal emissary, the native Ethiopian, Dr. Malaku Bayen,* to represent him in Harlem. In Dr. Bayen's charming presence Aframericans could be convinced that Ethiopians are not white or Mongolians, but authentic native Africans, even if, like thousands of educated Aframericans, they reject the word "Negro."

When Dr. Malaku Bayen arrived here in 1936, Harlem gave him a grand welcome. On the day of his arrival with his Aframerican wife, Dorothy, and their young son, he attempted to establish temporary residence in a modest downtown hotel (there is not one decent family hotel in Harlem) but owing

* Recently deceased.

Photos by M. and M. Smith

Types of Harlem Women.

Photo by Chidnoff

The late James Weldon Johnson, poet and writer, former United States Consul, Secretary of the National Association of Colored People, Professor of Literature at Fisk University and lecturer on Negro Culture at New York University.

to the conspicuousness of his Ethiopian skin, he was unceremoniously shunted up to the inconvenience of Harlem.

The direction of the Harlem United Aid to Ethiopia was turned over to Dr. Bayen and the name was changed to the "Ethiopian World Federation." The Federation established a weekly organ, the *Voice of Ethiopia* (in which the word "Negro" is proscribed), and conducts propaganda meetings in New York and other cities. It draws its supporters from the same common people that gave power to the Garvey movement. Many were once members of the Garvey Universal Negro organization. One of the principal animators, Mr. Rudolph Smith, was formerly a top figure and sparkling orator of the Back-To-Africa movement.

Marcus Garvey's influence over Aframericans, native Africans and people of African descent everywhere was vast. Whether that influence was positive or pervasive and indirect, Negroes of all classes were stirred to a finer feeling of racial consciousness. The intellectual Negro's hostility to and criticism of Garvey were also motivated by a spirit of resentment that the amazing energy and will to uplift awakened in the Negroes by Garvey were not harnessed to the purpose of a practical, constructive industrial project.

Garvey assembled an exhibition of Negro accomplishment in all the skilled crafts, and art work produced by exhibitors from all the Americas and Africa, which were revelations to Harlem of what the Negro people were capable of achieving.

The vivid, albeit crude, paintings of the Black Christ and the Black Virgin of the African Orthodox Church were startling omens of the Negro Renaissance movement of the nineteen twenties, which whipped up the appetite of literary and artistic America for a season. The flowering of Harlem's creative life came in the Garvey era. The anthology, THE NEW NEGRO, which orientated the debut of the Renaissance writers, was printed in 1925. If Marcus Garvey did not originate the phrase, New Negro, he at least made it popular. First novels by Harlem writers were published in that period: Jessie Fauset's THERE IS CONFUSION, Walter White's THE FIRE IN THE FLINT, Nella Larsen's QUICKSAND, Rudolph Fisher's

THE WALLS OF JERICHO and Wallace Thurman's THE BLACKER THE BERRY. Eric Walrond, who was author of TROPIC DEATH, was the literary editor of the Garvey organ, the *Negro World*.

The sweet singer of Harlem, Countee Cullen, plaintively cried in *Heritage*:*

> What is Africa to me:
> Copper sun or scarlet sea,
> Jungle star or jungle track,
> Strong bronzed men, or regal black . . .
> *One three centuries removed*
> *From the scenes his fathers loved,*
> *Spicy grove, cinnamon tree.*
> *What is Africa to me?*

Another contemporary poet, Langston Hughes,† chanted:

> All the tom-toms of the jungle beat in my blood,
> And all the wild hot moons of the jungles shine
>   in my soul.
> I am afraid of this civilization—
>   So hard,
>   So strong,
>   So cold.

The "Black Tiger" and "President-General" of the Negro World, Marcus Garvey, died in London on June 10, 1940. At the time of his death he still was revered as their greatest leader by the American Negro masses. His prestige remains higher among Americans than among West Indian Negroes. No ordinary Negro, and only a few intellectual Negroes, believe that Garvey appropriated to his personal use the enormous sums which were dissipated by his Universal Negro-Back-To-Africa movement. And the hostility of the intellectuals has undergone a striking change since the Great Depression. They say now that Garvey's ideas were sounder

---

* (Abridgment of first stanza) "Heritage" from *On These I Stand* by Countee Cullen. Copyright 1925 by Harper & Row, Publishers, Inc.; renewed, 1953 by Ida M. Cullen. Reprinted by permission.

†Reprinted from *The Weary Blues*. Copyright 1926 by Alfred A. Knopf; renewed, 1954 by Langston Hughes. Reprinted by permission.

than his methods. The Communists again tried to woo him during their Popular Front Five-Year plan. But even though they were formidably powerful, operating under the good will of the democratic forces of Europe and America, Garvey, poor and in exile, still rejected them. Although something of a dictator himself, to the last he preferred government under Democracy to government under Fascism. Many of the Garveyites compare Garvey with Hitler, to the latter's disadvantage. They say that Hitler's torrential flood of rhetoric, with its direct appeal to primitive mass emotions, is similar to the Garvey oratory, but that Hitler perverted Garvey's racial philosophy and proclaimed the superiority of the German over all other races, while Garvey tried to lift up and convince the Negro that it was basically the equal of other races.

Editorially commenting upon his death, the New York *Times* estimates: "He no more represented the Negro race in this country than Mr. Capone or Mr. Hauptmann the white race." This is a strange and cryptic comparison to Negro readers, for although Marcus Garvey was a demagogue, he was not a common criminal, a bandit ambushing and blackmailing the unwary wealthy, or a kidnaper and murderer of babies. Garvey was no violator of the flower of the human spirit; he was more obsessed with the idea that the spirit of humanity should flower more universally.

The late James Weldon Johnson, who was the most diplomatic and distinguished representative of the Negro élite, and also endowed with the shrewdest mind among contemporary Negroes, has this penetrating estimate of Garvey in BLACK MANHATTAN,* published in 1930. "Garvey failed; yet he might have succeeded with more than moderate success. He had energy and daring. . . . He stirred the imagination of the Negro masses as no Negro ever had. He raised more money in a few years than any other Negro organization ever dreamed of. He had great power and great possibilities within his grasp. But his deficiencies as a leader outweighed his abilities. . . . Garvey made several vital blunders, which,

---

*Reprinted by permission of Grace Nail Johnson.

with any intelligent advice, he might have avoided. . . . He made the mistake of ignoring or looking with disdain upon the technique of the American Negro in dealing with his problems of race. . . . To this man came an opportunity such as comes to few men, and he clutched greedily at the glitter and let the substance slip from his fingers."

Sufi Abdul Hamid and Organized Labor

The effort of Negro Harlem to shed its swaddling clothes and grow up and adjust its community life to the American standard is a drama unfolding from the depths of the grim and lugubrious to the heights of the fantastic. In the early period the all-absorbing problem of the Negro nucleus was to plant its feet firmly and expand. In the years that have ensued it has been a long, unrelenting struggle—against members of the group and against exterior forces—for cultural, political and economic adjustment.

Religious, political and industrial factors are intricately jumbled in Negro life and the indiscriminate mix-up is not only appalling, but also paralyzing to Negro progress. In the white man's world these different elements are correlated and benefit from autonomous status. Labor has forged its special instrument to bargain with capital. Political leaders consult with labor leaders and recognize the special prerogatives of labor. Religious leaders have their special functions to perform. They may criticize capitalists and laborites and politicians, but they do not attempt to usurp their powers.

There is no such order in the Negro world. Negro labor exists on a much lower level than white labor and, with rare exceptions, does not enjoy the privileges of the latter. It is overwhelmingly unskilled and largely unorganized. Negro business, such as there is, stands in a category of its own. It remains unharassed by labor troubles. The Negro businessman imagines that he has rendered service enough to the community, when he has established a business and made it succeed against white competition. He regards the idea of the Negro worker organizing against *him* as an affront. Why, workers should organize only against white bosses! Negro preachers intervene in labor disputes. As they lack the "white" knowledge of the social problems of modern labor their action is often disastrous.

Organized Negro workers in New York number about 50,000. But more than half are out of work. The largest numbers are in the Seamen's Union, the Clothing Workers' Union, the Building Service Union, and the Laundry Workers' Union. But whether it is in the privileged realm of craft unionism or in the more democratic atmosphere of industrial unionism, the problem of Negro workers remains acute.

The majority of Negro workers have been traditionally herded into the despised domestic depths of the labor world. And all labor men agree that the domestic world is the most difficult to organize. There are few Negroes, even the most intellectual among them, such as college and professional persons, who are unfamiliar with domestic toil. Negro students must work to help finance their higher education. Many white students also work. But while many of the latter may obtain clerical or salesmen's work during vacation, the Negro student is limited to the job of porter or waiter.

Naturally Negroes are agitated by the universal American urge to improve one's position. Those who become skilled or semi-skilled members of labor unions are inordinately proud of it. For it is a privilege from which the majority are automatically barred. A score of American Federation of Labor crafts exclude Negroes by special clauses. Thousands of skilled Negro workers can work at their trades only by surreptitious bootlegging of their labor. When as individuals they break into the ranks of white organized labor it is almost like being initiated into a secret society.

This may explain somewhat the romantic academic attitude of the few Negro labor leaders toward organized labor. Catholics, Jews, Italians and other minority groups are realistically aware that the labor game is an eternally grim one, not merely of workers against employers, but of workers among themselves.   Because of this, the aforementioned groups have fashioned effective instruments to protect the special interests of each group in the world of labor.

But Negroes in the trade unions have never had any group organization to protect their special interests.   The first outstanding effort of Negroes for effective group organization was effected when A. Phillip Randolph began the organization of the Pullman Porters.   After eleven years of hard, gruelling work he obtained an international charter from the American Federation of Labor.   Mr. Randolph had to face and fight the criticism of his own group.   Negro intellectuals charged that he was endorsing and increasing the segregation of Negroes by the organization of a Negro union.   White radicals criticized and obstructed his efforts on the same grounds.   But apparently the real reason was their fear of the growth of independent Negro organization, which they could not control.   By steadfastly following the plan he had charted, Mr. Randolph won out and thus was the first Negro to become a national leader in the American Federation of Labor.

This issue of Segregation is a formidable specter, paralyzing to the progress of the Negro community in every aspect of its life: in politics, in culture, in business and labor.   The Negro community is feverishly agitated and divided by it. And in this respect it is unlike any other American community.   Negroes realize that they are segregated and thus hate their community.   A white person in Little Rock, Arkansas or Davenport, Iowa, may dislike his town and prefer to live in Chicago or New York.   But compelled from industrial or political reasons to be a small town resident he does his bit to help make his town as fine as possible.   He works to obtain maximum sanitary and social services, for if an epidemic or a fire sweeps the town, he and his family may be victims.

But in a Negro community the élite will refuse the building of a hospital for Negroes, because they believe that it may result in the exclusion of Negro doctors and patients from the white hospital. They may even object to play-grounds and pools and model houses for similar reasons. Such objections would be flouted in an Italian, Irish or Jewish community. Yet the masses of these minorities are as effectively "segregated" among themselves as are Negroes.

Thus in Negro communities there is a tacit evasion of direct social responsibility that is peculiar to them. The Negro accepts the substance of segregation and remains fixedly frightened by the shadow of it. And every aspect of his life suffers therefrom. Possibly in northern Negro communities there could be found whites who will function in secondary places in Negro institutions, as symbols to demonstrate that there is no segregation between the races. But what ambitious, intelligent white person will readily assume second place in a Negro institution? Such a white person will not want to take second place within a group that is in an inferior social status, unless he is a Communist or some such type who is willing to immolate himself to promote propaganda.

Undoubtedly the chaotic defeatist mentality of the Negro community is responsible for the phenomenal increase of supernatural agencies, cults, numbers games, dream books and other mumbo-jumbo, and the maze of abortive movements among the masses.

Even white-collar movements, which naturally should have been promoted by the professional strata of Negroes, were initiated by the common people. Unlike the Negro intelligentsia ineffectually fretting its soul away over a symbolic gesture, the inarticulate Negro masses realize that they have special community rights.

Perhaps there is nothing more significant in the social history of the United States than the spectacle of the common black folk in overalls and sweaters agitating and parading for jobs for apathetic white-collar Negroes. Ninety-five per cent of the worth-while businesses in Negro communities are operated by white merchants. In all American communities, department and chain stores and other businesses have recognized their responsibility to give employment locally. But

Negro communities were precluded from benefiting from this procedure. Negro youth, graduating from grade and high school, had no opportunity to qualify for an ordinary community job, such as white youth might expect. Many such Negroes could not attend college. Prior to 1929 they had little difficulty obtaining jobs in the white business districts as messengers in stores and switchboard operators and even as workers in small factories. But the industrial crisis had created strong competition among whites in the building services. Negroes out of school could find nothing to do with their hands. The condition created an appalling sickness within the Negro community. It was like a body with head and feet, but no belly.

The movement for community jobs started in Chicago, in 1930. Its outstanding animator was one Sufi Abdul Hamid. He was a powerfully built black man and he dressed himself up in a bright-colored cape, Russian long boots and Hindu-type turban. His slogan was, "More Jobs for Negroes: Buy Where You Can Work." Sponsored by Editor Bibbs of the Chicago *Whip*, a Negro weekly, and ably supported by the Rev. J. C. Austin of the Pilgrim Baptist Church and a group of Chicago's Negro youth, the Sufi's campaign was a signal success. The merchants were soon persuaded that the demands of the Negro community were legitimate. They capitulated. Chain and department stores and other businesses in the Black Belt employed Negro clerks. The experiment resulted in better social relationship between white employers and colored consumers in Chicago.

It was odd that a man of the Sufi's type should have been prominent in such a campaign. Prior to that time he was known as Bishop Conshankin and a mystic. He delved into the mysteries of occultism and, mixing together a hash of Hindoo, Persian and Chinese religions, he promoted himself as an Oriental philosopher. But his agitating brought him into acquaintance with a group of Negro Moslems in Chicago. They convinced him that the magic racket was a hindrance to the more serious work of job campaigning.

Then Sufi heard the cry of Harlem. He had accomplished what he had set himself to do in Chicago. And he decided to transfer his attention to New York. Chicago's Negroes often voice criticism of Harlem as a backward community, falling far below the standard of what should be expected of a locality situated in the heart of the great American metropolis. Now that they had won recognition of their right to more and better work their criticism was louder. Endorsing the criticism of colored Chicagoans, the Sufi announced his intention of going to New York to start a similar campaign in Harlem.

Quick at apprehending new ideas, the Sufi buried the name of Bishop Conshankin in Chicago, added Islam to his repertory of religions and started out in Harlem in 1932 as Sufi Abdul Hamid. As a mystic consoling ignorant members of his race with magical words and revelations, the Sufi led a fairly comfortable existence. When he was attracted to the Jobs-for-Negroes campaign in Chicago, he had no real awareness of the organized labor movement and of the Negroes' relationship to it. His was a rather quixotic disposition heightened by a considerable amount of vanity. The street meetings served to show off his gorgeous oriental outfit. His clothes made him the main attraction and his strong, deep-sounding voice won the admiration of the people. The Sufi was avid of admiration. He perceived that he was reaching the large masses of his people and articulating their hidden thoughts better than by deceiving a few psychic-twisted souls with mumbo-jumbo.

Starting his campaign in New York early in 1933, the Sufi soon discovered that the Harlem nut was not so easy to crack as Chicago's South Side. Whereas in Chicago the Sufi won the support and cooperation of an influential Negro newspaper and a leading minister, in Harlem the Church and the Press were against him.

But, haranguing the Harlem crowds on Lenox and Seventh Avenues in the neighborhood of 135th Street, he convinced thousands. There is no exaggerating the acute misery existing among the entire people of Harlem. In pre-depression

years the Negro laborer landed his job easily as longshore-
man, hod-carrier, janitor, husky helper in store or hotel
downtown; and as helper too to the many bootleg painters,
carpenters and other tradesmen who hired Negroes at cut-
rate.   The colored female worker could find her job even
more readily than the male.   Doing house-cleaning tasks by
the hour, she made from $4 to $6 a day.   The cleaning
women had worked out a plan by which one woman might
have a number of employers on her list and a certain day
to work for each one.   Thus she was never idle, and had no
difficulty earning a total wage of $25 weekly.   For those
domestics who were willing to sleep in their employer's
homes, there were always jobs.   But now there was little
work for the casual Negro worker.   His white brother had
been pushed to compete with him in that unorganized field of
labor which he formerly held so lightly.   And the very large
middle stratum of white folk who employed the day-by-day
colored woman worker were now in financial straits.   The
Harlem women went to the Bronx, gladly offering themselves
to work for a dollar a day.   The places where they waited to
be hired became notorious to Harlemites as the Bronx Slave
Market.

The educated Negro was in grave difficulty.   Scores of
professional persons, doctors, dentists and salesmen had nothing to do.   Their clients were all members of their own race,
now jobless, and for the first time an economic law was
revealed to these Negro professionals.   They realized that
their prosperity was bound up with the welfare of the common Negroes.

Harlem was the backwash of New York's economic crisis.
Its sickness was chronic, its plight appalling.   Social agencies
such as the Urban League were swamped with applications
for help.   In this grim crisis there was no sympathetic contact between the white business people of Harlem and the
colored community.   Harlem was the only community in
which the youth of good appearance, educated in American
schools and able to figure and write correctly, could not approach the business men for decent jobs, because they were

dark-hued. From all over New York white workers came
to Harlem and found jobs writing and figuring, and selling
to black customers. Meanwhile the black white-collars, cut
off from narrow avenues of employment downtown, sul-
lenly watched their white brothers coming into the black
belt to find jobs, when they could not find work anywhere.

The Sufi had something there to agitate upon and he
exploited it to the utmost. Soon he had an impressive following among the jobless Harlem youth with high school
and college education. It was the first time on record of
young members of the Negro intelligentsia following the
leadership of a vulgar street agitator. And it was ominous.
Circumstances and conditions were transforming the former
occultist of Chicago into a labor leader.

Harlem was overrun with white Communists who promoted themselves as the only leaders of the Negroes. They
were converting a few Negroes into Bolshevik propagandists,
but they were actually doing nothing to help alleviate the
social misery of Negroes. The Socialists too were represented
in Harlem by Frank Crosswaith and the symbol of a black-
and-white hand clasped in fellowship. But while they all
insisted on the misery of Harlem, and fraternized and
frolicked with their Negro comrades, they did nothing to
better economic conditions. Did they really want to do
anything?

The Sufi and his black white-collars organized the Negro
Industrial and Clerical Alliance. In middle Harlem above
125th Street they canvassed grocers, druggists and owners of
other small white establishments, soliciting jobs for Negro
clerks. Mostly unsuccessful in their demands, they picketed
the stores, carrying placards exhorting Negroes to "Buy from
Stores in Which Negroes Can Work." They won the immediate support of the poorer housewives of Harlem. The
intellectuals, newspapers and social leaders remained blindly
opposed to the movement, but the common people quickly
apprehended its import. The small white businessmen in
the solid heart of the black belt also understood its significance and for the first time some establishments employed

THIS SIDE OF CARD IS FOR ADDRESS

BOARD OF EDUCATION

PARK AVENUE & 59th STREET

NEW YORK, N. Y.

As a taxpayer, beg to draw the attention of the Board of Education to the continuous, viscious Political slanders, issued weekly through the Negro Press by Professor Willis N. Huggins, 1890 7th Avenue, of Wadleigh High School, against the cause of Ethiopia and the Negro People.

The recent decision in the case of Laura Leibman who was kept out of the Public School system because of Radical activities should be brought to bear against the Professor for Fascist activities.

Name ....

Address ....

Sample of Communist attack upon the assistant principal of Harlem Evening High School, Dr. Willis N. Huggins, who opposed the Communists in the Aid-to-Ethiopia Campaign. Hundreds of these cards were mailed to the Board of Education, signed by people rounded up by the Communists and who were not aware of the real issues involved.

Negro grocery clerks, in 1933. Now the sophisticated white reader may smile at this "triumph." Educated Negroes getting jobs as grocery clerks! But the white world's industrial standard is so high that the white person has no adequate conception of the black world's dilemma. A job as a grocery clerk means as much to the pride of a young Negro as the job of junior clerk in a large corporation means to the white youth.

The Sufi and his followers dominated the street corners; night and day they picketed stores for jobs. Headquarters for the movement was established in the Hotel Dumas in 135th Street, near Seventh Avenue. At first, for the reasons given previously, it was not so spectacular as the Chicago drive. It was ignored by the Church, ridiculed by the Press and cold-shouldered by the oldsters of the Harlem intelligentsia. The Sufi's activities were denounced by the pastor of Abyssinia Baptist Church, the largest Negro church in the world, having 14,000 members. The Sufi answered back by standing his step ladder at the corner of the street in which the church stood. With a vast crowd milling around him, he denounced the young pastor as a drunken fool and damned Abyssinia to hell.

Surrounded by young men of a higher education than himself the Sufi pretended that he was a product of institutions of higher learning. He highly appreciated education and intelligence. He said that he was born in the Egyptian Sudan and had studied at the Islamic University of Cairo and graduated from the University of Athens. He did possess some knowledge of Greek, less Arabic and a smattering of the Romance languages. But his intimates knew that he was born in the South and had gone to sea as a lad and voyaged all over the world. He had an excellent ear and was quick to acquire some command of a new language.

With a modicum of success in the small stores in middle Harlem, the Sufi and his men were determined to accomplish as much in New York as they had in Chicago, where chain and department stores, milk wagons and bread and beer trucks had recognized the special rights of Negroes to obtain more and better jobs in the predominantly Negro districts.

.   .   .   .

The hub of Harlem had shifted from 135th Street to the animated shopping center of 125th Street. And Harlem's dark folk did their biggest shopping there. There was a time when the same types of people preferred to shop in 14th Street. But 125th Street had superseded 14th Street as a bargain spot and it was just in their midst. The Sufists went into caucus and planned to carry into 125th Street the campaign for jobs. They started early in 1934. First delegates of the Negro Industrial Alliance were sent into 125th Street's largest stores and the managers were asked to employ a certain percentage of colored clerks. Every store refused. The demands were ridiculed as preposterous. The manager of one of the large 5 & 10 cent stores declared that he was born in the South, where Negroes were not permitted even to buy goods in first class stores and that as long as he was manager, "not a damned 'nigger' " would serve anything over his counter, even if his customers were "niggers."

The Sufi turned to action and this "5 & 10" was the first store he picketed on 125th Street. Harlem was startled by the daring gesture. Just a few years previous, Negro customers were not so warmly welcomed in 125th Street, and that was why so many trekked to 14th Street. At eventide the Sufi would place his step-ladder at the corner of Seventh Avenue and 125th Street and exhort Harlemites to support his campaign. He informed them about the campaign in Chicago. He taunted them by saying that Chicago's Negroes were better fighters and more race-conscious. He said that the Harlem Negroes were folding their arms, waiting for the white folk to do something, but that white folk could not help them if they did not help themselves.

The Sufi became the most picturesque and appealing figure in 125th Street and his movement was full of "ginger." He won many recruits. The colored white-collars were grateful to this man who had boldly stepped out of the black mass to become their advocate. "We are only asking the white merchants to give the colored community a fighting chance," the Sufi cried. "Live and let live. Share the jobs!"

The Sufi called for volunteers to make speeches. And some of Harlem's young intellectuals responded. They mounted the step-ladder and talked to their people, telling them to stay out of stores which, while they did not disdain to take their money, yet despised their starving, unemployed children. That was no easy feat for an educated young Harlemite to perform. For the soap-boxers of Harlem were rough men of the people, whom educated Harlemites considered amusing or dangerous, according to the speakers' choices of subject. One night I heard a passing woman say to another, "Good God, look at my son P—— making an exhibition of himself on the street."

Slowly the consumers of Harlem began to wake up to an understanding of the Sufi's message. And business was less cheerful in 125th Street. Finally one of the big merchants, Koch, was seized with an idea. He thought the employment of colored clerks might effect not only better relations between white employers and colored consumers, but also bigger business. And so an agreement was concluded in June of 1934 for this establishment to employ a fair percentage of colored clerks. Although it was never admitted by either side, it was understood that there was a secret agreement that the Negro Industrial and Clerical Alliance should boost this business among the people of Harlem.

But the other merchants had agreed not to set a precedent of hiring colored clerks, and the isolated action of one of them threw a scare into the ranks of the rest. And it also disturbed the more respectable leaders of Harlem: ministers, newspaper editors and writers, politicians, radicals and others. Harlemites were hopelessly divided over the dilemma of Harlem. One of the leading ministers, the Rev. John H. Johnson, supported the idea of giving Negro youth a chance at decent jobs in the community. But he wanted the thing accomplished in a spirit of Christian kindliness. Harlem had achieved much unsavory notoriety in recent

Sculpture by Augusta Savage, evocative of Negro music; commissioned by the New York World's Fair.

Mother bathing her child in apartment without bath.

years. He and other ministers were anxious to uphold the good name of the community.

Led by the Reverend John H. Johnson, Rector of St. Martin's Episcopal Church, and Miss Effa Manley, a Harlem Citizens' League for Fair Play was organized to negotiate with 125th Street's intransigeant merchants. The first mass meeting was held in St. Martin's Church. Sixty-two of Harlem's social, religious and business groups, comprising eighteen of the leading churches, responded to the call. The prominent agitators represented a cross section of the most influential of Harlem's residents. Besides the Rev. William Lloyd Imes, of sophisticated St. James Presbyterian Church, there were Attorney William Pickens, son of an executive of the National Association for the Advancement of Colored People, Mrs. Florence Richardson, representing Harlem's actors, Bishop Collins, Rudolph Smith, former "star" promoter of the Garvey Movement, Arthur Reid, President of the African Patriotic League, Editor Fred R. Moore of the New York *Age*, Curator Arthur A. Schomburg, of the Negro Division of the 135th Street Public Library, Mrs. Bessy Bearden, social chronicler of the affairs of Harlem's smart set, and others who were none the less outstanding because their names are not recorded here. The Sufists sent an observer of their own.

The Citizens' League created various committees for special work and named a delegation to approach the merchants. The Rev. John H. Johnson was chairman. The delegation's method was to deal with one store at a time, and it picked first the large Blumstein store. The Rev. Johnson tried this system: He collected the sales receipts of Harlemites who made purchases at the Blumstein store and accumulated a total representing $5,000. Armed with these, he sought to convince Mr. Blumstein that he should cooperate with the community in the crisis of depression and employ some of the jobless educated Negroes. Mr. Blumstein said that he had already cooperated in the manner he considered best for the Negro group and for the interests of his business. He had employed Negroes as maids, porters and elevator operators. (One of Mr. Blumstein's elevator operators was a graduate of the College of the City of New York.) Also he was a sponsor of the charitable Negro organization, The Urban League, to which he donated money for social work. He steadfastly refused to employ Negroes in better positions.

It was the first time that Rev. John Johnson had had to negotiate with practical business men in the interests of those that labor, and he learned now that his conception of Christian gentleness was inadequate. Crestfallen, he reported back to the Citizens' League. After many conferences the League decided that its only effective weapon for 125th Street was that which the Sufi had fashioned—picketing. In the spectacular picketing which took place at Blumstein's, when Harlem's ministers, professional men and smartest matrons carried signs, the Sufi and his followers participated. Business declined seriously for the big store after a month of mass picketing. Mr. Blumstein changed his views about positions for Negroes. He called in the Rev. Johnson and signed an agreement to hire 35 "colored clerical and sales help."

And here dissension started between the Citizens' League and the Sufi's Clerical and Industrial Alliance. The Sufi maintained that his organization as a labor agency should have jurisdiction over the clerks. The "Citizens" opposed the idea. The Sufi was a crude giant of a rough-neck. It was said that there was an odor of racketeering in his methods, even though all traces of it were hidden. Harlem's nose is wonderfully keen for scandal: The colored men who were to be given a chance as clerks were coming from the highest types of Harlem families. Here is an excellent example of the vast difference between the standards of the white and of the Negro world. The average salesgirl at Macy's, Gimbel's or Wanamaker's comes from the working class or from a family given to small business. Her father and brothers may be members of a trade union and she has no snobbish attitude towards labor organization. But in the Negro world the field of sales clerk is especially privileged, and the girl breaking into it may be a Harlem debutante.

She is sure to belong to a professional family that looks askance at organized labor. Becoming a saleslady in a "white" store is a novelty. It is a "nice" position, an item which will make the news column or even the headlines of the local Negro paper.

The Citizens' League, glad to avail themselves of the Sufists experience in picketing, did not wish that the maidens of Harlem, who were to be chosen as the vanguard to represent Negro Harlem in 125th Street, should be members of the Negro Industrial and Clerical Alliance. The Employment Committee of the Citizens' League also objected to the Sufi's charging dues. The Sufi retorted that a labor organization must have dues-paying members. He resented the attempt of the League to usurp the function of a labor union. The Sufi insisted that merely getting employment for colored clerks was not enough: they should have an organization to protect their interests. He failed to reach an agreement with the Citizens' League and withdrew from the organization.

The sensibilities of the Citizens' League were shocked when the Sufists continued their aggressive picketing in 125th Street. Meanwhile, the bigger merchants of Harlem became seriously alarmed at the manifestation of social and racial consciousness in the campaign for jobs among the Harlem community. Hastily they formed a Harlem Merchants' Association. None of the few Negro merchants was asked to join. The white merchants exploited the division among the Negroes. As the Sufi was their most formidable opponent, he became the target of their antagonism. They promoted an interracial banquet to which they invited representative Negroes, who made good-will speeches and denounced the activities of irresponsible trouble-makers in Harlem. On the Negro side there was a deplorable exhibition of cross-purpose. Of the three Harlem newspapers, the *Age* and the *News* supported the Citizens' League. The *Amsterdam News* was hostile. Criticizing in an editorial the Urban League's attitude, the *News* said: "Blumstein refuses to employ Harlem clerks. Blumstein is thereby committing a crime against the community. The Urban League has for its motto, "Not Alms but Opportunity." At its annual meeting, in willful and reckless disregard of this community's welfare, it boosted William Blumstein as a "benefactor of the community." "Those publications and institutions in Harlem that condone economic crimes against the community because of puny advertising and contribution bribes are Judases and traitors to this community."

But leading Negro scribes and Negro radicals were extremely bitter in their denunciation of the movement. Among them were the loudest professional opponents of Negro Segregation. Some declared that Harlemites should not bring pressure upon the merchants to obtain community jobs! Negroes should open their own stores to employ Negroes!

.   .   .   .

The Communists were savage in their opposition. At that time they had been waging a national and international campaign for the recognition of the Negro's right to life. The Scottsboro and Angelo Herndon cases were the flaming stars around which their campaign revolved. The Communists fixed their eyes on the stars and refused to look down upon the common ground of community life, where the Negroes were carrying on a practical struggle for bread and shelter. Their primary aim has been radically to exploit the Negro's grievances. Therefore they use their influence to destroy any movement which might make for a practical amelioration of the Negro's problems. In their Harlem *Liberator,* the Communists launched a bitter attack against the Sufi and his followers.

Suddenly, the Sufi's campaign was denounced as anti-Semitic, and articles describing the Sufi as a "Harlem Hitler" or a "Black Hitler" appeared simultaneously in the Harlem *Liberator,* the Jewish *Day* and the Jewish *Bulletin.* Each day the onslaught against the Sufi was intensified in savagery and fury. The Negro Clerical and Industrial Alliance was publicised as a Fascist organization, with a Nazi set-up. The Sufi's chief aide, Francis Minor, was dubbed Hermann Goering.

Now the Communists had valid Communistic reasons for hating and baiting the Sufi. They were on the warpath to gather up the Negro masses under the standard of Communism. And they employed the most reprehensible means to discredit bonafide Negro organizations and any Negro leader enjoying a popular support which they, the Communists, could not control. For years they had fought against A. Phillip Randolph and striven to wreck his organization of the Pullman Porters. They seized the case of the Scottsboro boys and wielded it as a club to beat the National Association for the Advancement of Colored People. They aimed to destroy this organization and substitute International Labor Defense as the national legal defender of the Negro minority. In like manner they worked strenuously to disrupt the Universal Negro Improvement Association which, faithful to the dogma of its exiled leader, Marcus Garvey, was unswervingly opposed to the Communists. The huge street meetings of this group were often sabotaged by the Communists, who sent their thugs up on the roof tops to hurl down bricks and create panic among the crowd.

Perhaps it was the shrewd instinct of an oppressed group, that sixth sense of understanding, which caused the Negro masses to resist the Communists. They sensed their dishonesty of motives and insincerity of purpose, where intellectual persons were easily deceived.

Out in Chicago the Sufi had opposed the Communists when they tried to bore their way into his campaign. And in Harlem he was more adamant and outspoken in his opposition to them. Communists and Socialists have always been evasive on the issue of employment for the Negro minority and integrating it with American industry. They prefer to agitate about Segregation and Race Prejudice in general, and avoid the fundamental issue. They write reams of stuff and parade with placards demanding that Negroes be employed in industry and damning the Capitalists. But actually, the colored workers as a group are confronted with the self interests of white workers. The white workers are conservative about holding down their jobs. They

naturally regard the colored workers as a threat to their own
security. It is not primarily a racial antagonism. One group
of white workers is just as intolerant towards another group
of white workers who threaten their security. It is this fear
that prompted the leaders of regular organized workers to
demand a special status for W. P. A. workers, which should
not undermine their standards.

If Communists and Socialists were to demand of the
white workers whom they influence that they make places
for colored workers, they would precipitate a revolt. Faced
with this dilemma, their propaganda among Negroes remains an abstract crusade against Segregation and Race
Prejudice, with fraternal contact as a proof of their sincerity.
The one true solution of this problem would be the stupendous task of engineering new jobs for Negroes. Practical-minded Negroes realize this. And it is this realization
that has given form and drive to the comparatively recent
movement of the Negro people towards greater self-develop-
ment and community autonomy. Negro intellectuals and
white radicals describe it by such delectable phrases as Negro
Nationalism, Black Fascism and Color Chauvinism.

But the Negro people have never been dazzled by the
grand picture of the Communist Utopia's solving their social
problems. Perhaps, because they are kept down so close to
earth, they have learned too much of its simple wisdom to
be fooled by showy pretense.

No one was more astonished than the Sufi himself when
he was accused of organizing an anti-Semitic movement.
Of all the newssheets, Negro, Communist and Jewish, which
joined in the drive against him, the Jewish Daily *Bulletin* of
the Fall of 1934 contains the most complete picture of what
actually occurred. The subject is of real importance, because it highlights the differences which might arise between
various minority groups in this country. Again, it illuminates
the obscure aspects of indecent propaganda.

The idea has been spread abroad that there is a growth of
anti-Semitism among Negroes. National publications have
identified the Sufi movement with anti-Semitism. The

special New York City number of *Fortune* has an article
on Negro Harlem and stresses "the wave of anti-Semitism in
Harlem . . . of which the first preacher was Sufi Abdul
Hamid." Mr. Stanley High stated in the *Saturday Evening
Post* that the Sufi movement was anti-Semitic. The W. P. A.
New York *Panorama* printed a similar lie. The radical
leaders, Communist James W. Ford and Socialist Frank
Crosswaith, were the black barkers of the slander. It is a
question whether the incessant drumming up of a non-
existent anti-Semitism among Negroes was designed, for
obscure purposes, further to alarm the Jews, or to injure the
Negroes. It has certainly created, between both minority
groups, great controversy and friction of a special kind not
previously in evidence!

Now to examination of the facts. It was on September 25,
1934, that the emergence of a "Black Fuehrer" in Harlem
named Sufi Abdul Hamid was headlined by the Jewish
Daily *Bulletin*. This newspaper stated that the Sufi had
been summoned to the office of Assistant District Attorney
Pelley for an investigation into his activities against the
merchants of Harlem. It said also that an association of
Anti-Nazi Minute Men, headed by Edgar Berman, brother
of the Commander-in-Chief of the Jewish War Veterans,
had recorded the remarks of a speech by the Harlem agitator
in which he said, "Hitler don't want the damn Jews in
Germany and we don't want them in Harlem . . . etc. . . ."
The same *Bulletin* describes the Sufi as a man "mild of mien
and cultured in tone with a sleek long mustache, which
coupled with his thick Van Dyke, gave him the appearance
of an Oriental potentate, who indignantly denied the con-
tents of the speech and said, 'We are not against the Jews.
To us here in Harlem it is an economic problem. We have
between 11,000 and 14,000 members in the Negro Industrial
and Clerical Alliance. We are out to get jobs for them!' "
It also quotes the Sufi as saying that the true Jerusalem was
in Abyssinia, where the Jews originated, and that the real
Yehudim was in Abyssinia.

In spite of his denial of being anti-Semitic, there was no

let-up in the campaign against the Sufi. The *Bulletin* was joined by the *Day*, the Communist Harlem *Liberator* and the leading Negro weeklies. The Sufi was described as "Harlem Hitler," "Dusky Hitler," "Black Hitler." The nation was treated to a fantastically exaggerated idea of the growth of an organized Nazi and anti-Semitic movement among Negroes.

Aside from the Press campaign, the Harlem merchants organized, three hundred strong, to combat the Sufi campaign. A delegation waited upon Aldermanic President Deutsch, and a protest was sent to Mayor La Guardia. An appeal for aid was sent to the American Jewish Congress. On October 8, 1934, the Sufi was brought before Magistrate Overton Harris on a charge of disorderly conduct, which specified that he was conducting a race war against the Jews. The charge was pressed by Edgar Berman, head of the Anti-Nazi Minute Men. The Sufi categorically denied the charges. He had an array of witnesses to testify in his favor. The Sufi said that there were many non-Jews among the merchants of Harlem who also were opposing his organization. He was agitating against all the merchants and it was unfair and unjust to say that his movement was anti-Semitic. The police did not support the charges that the Sufi's meeting and his conduct were disorderly. As he himself denied being anti-Semitic, and as the evidence of invective against Jews was considered untrustworthy, he was therefore discharged.

It is interesting to observe that one of the witnesses who testified that the Sufi was anti-Semitic was an Italian named Carmelo Odovardi, who said that the Sufi had also described the Italians as "spaghetti-slingers." It is interesting because anti-Jewish, if not anti-Semitic, feeling in Negro Harlem prevails among the Italian businessmen in the Negro district. The Sufi's campaign did not differentiate among the several groups of white businessmen in the colored district, who were mainly Jews, Italians and Greeks. The Italians control over seventy-five per cent of the saloons and cabarets in Harlem, which in the beginning of the movement almost entirely employed Italian bartenders.

Their patronage was 95 per cent Negro and there was a movement under way to compel the Italians to employ Negro bartenders.

In the early stages of his campaign the Sufi had had his greatest success with the Greeks, who were the first of the whites in Harlem to employ Negroes, perhaps because he was so glibly adept at exhibiting his smattering of Greek. The Greeks were a little amused at this huge American Negro, who styled himself an Egyptian, talking to them in their native language. There is a larger number than is generally known, because the people mistake the Greeks for Jews—they look so much alike! When the Sufi organization made a survey of the white grocery stores in Negro Harlem it was discovered that there were one hundred and fifty-one Greek places as against two hundred and forty-one Jewish. There was an organization of the Greek grocers, so also of Jewish grocers. Among the smaller dry goods merchants the independent ones a Merchants' Association. The downtown stores which had branches in 125th Street were represented by the Uptown Chamber of Commerce.

Meanwhile, the Citizens' League had secured the services of two other street agitators, Arthur Reid and Ira Kemp, to carry on with the rough job of picketing while it conducted negotiations with the merchants. The Picket Committee of the League received a major set-back in court on October 31, 1934. The Beck Shoe Corporation, at 264 West 125th Street, sought an injunction to restrain it from picketing its stores. The complainant maintained that the League was not a labor union and that its action tended to "incite race riots, instil race prejudice, to foster racial strife and to foment racial dispute."

The case was argued before Justice Samuel I. Rosenman, who decided in favor of the complainant. The Citizens' League was enjoined from picketing, boycotting or taking other action to obtain jobs for Negroes. The militant Harlem soap-boxer and Chairman of the Picket Committee, Ira Kemp, remarked that such a decision would only stir up further trouble in Harlem.

The plaintiff in the case had explicitly stated that the Citizens' League was repudiated by the Negro Press, which, solicitous for its advertisements, had denounced a movement that had the support of the entire Harlem community.

But it was amazing that such a decision should have been handed down by an American court at a time when a nation-wide boycott, involving business and trade relations, was being maintained against the German nation for its unjust treatment of a racial minority.

The attitude of the Communists during this struggle is enlightening and may be taken as a test, an indication, of the real motives of the Communists towards the Negro minority. To divert attention from the larger interest of the community's jobs-for-Negroes campaign, the Communists started another to obtain jobs for Negroes as conductors and drivers on the Fifth Avenue Bus Company. Now the majority of Negroes patronized the Fifth Avenue busses only when they went through the Harlem district. And it was obvious that the Communist campaign could not be effective, because they made no attempt to picket the downown offices of the bus company. The Communists obtained jobs for Negroes as countermen and busboys in the large Empire cafeteria at Lenox Avenue and 125th Street and announced that as a triumph for jobs!

Evidently the Communists could not imagine Negroes and whites working together in clerical positions in 125th Street! Through their stooge organ, the Harlem *Liberator,* run by a board of White and Negro Communists, they denounced the movement and Sufi's "pernicious doctrine of anti-Semitism and Jew-baiting campaign." They also frightened the Harlem community with the fear of retaliation, by suggesting that white employers would discharge their Negro workers if the agitators did not cease their tactics. Almost jubilantly the *Liberator* headlined the news that a Jewish garage owner of the Bronx had "fired fifteen Negro cab drivers and another is reported ready to release twenty-five more as retaliatory measures" against the Harlem agitators.

Exactly at that time the Communists were conducting their

high-pressure campaign in Harlem with huge parades and meetings for the Scottsboro boys and Angelo Herndon, and against Southern injustice.

To the thinking Negro it was too obvious that the Communists were out to exploit all the social disadvantages of the Negro minority for propaganda effect, but that they were little interested in practical efforts to ameliorate the social conditions of that minority. The reaction of such organs as the *Day* and the *Bulletin* was more understandable, if deplorable. Inside Germany the vicious Nazi proscription against the Jewish minority was in effect. There were riotous outbreaks against it in North Africa and Palestine. It was almost unwittingly that the Harlem agitator had purloined an Arab name and adopted a costume half-Indian, half-Arabian, hoping thus to enhance his influence among a people avid of color and show. Little idea had he of the hornets he was drawing to buzz around his head when he put on that Oriental turban!

It was only after the wide publicity given him as a "Harlem Hitler" that the Sufi had his first contact with American Nazis. It happened that I was at his office one day trying to get some facts for an article when two Germans or German-Americans called on him. They invited him to a meeting in Yorkville. Later he told me that he had gone with his chief aide, Francis Minor (now President of the Harlem Labor Union) whom the *Bulletin* had called "Hermann Goering." "I was curious," he said "to find out what the pure blond Nordicans could have to offer to the pure black Africans when their Hitler says we are no better than monkeys. But I couldn't imagine cooperating with the Nazis any more than with the Ku Klux Klan."

After the injunction against picketing and boycotting was handed down, Sufi organized the Afro-American Federation of Labor. The Picket Committee of the Citizens' League could no longer operate. Under the new name the Sufi continued activities, and now trouble arose in the rank of the Citizens' Leaguers over the type of girls to be placed. The rough-necks of the Picket Committee charged that the more refined members of the Citizens' League were recommending light-complexioned colored girls from the Y. W. C. A. and other institutions who had scorned picketing, while the dark girls who had marched in the picket line were ignored.

A real battle was fought over the perennially sore point of the shades of color within the Negro group. It is a notorious fact that on the stage and in clerical work Negro men always show a preference for the light-complexioned girls. Yet these strange little prejudices within the group are never publicly aired.

But the Communist *Liberator* was on the warpath to destroy the Citizens' League which it called "The Boycott Mis-leaders." Said the *Liberator:* "The boycott misleaders incite dark-skinned and light-skinned Negroes against each other. Fred R. Moore (Editor of the [Harlem] *Age*) advocated that, 'Light Negroes should be given employment first while the black ones should wait their chance later.' Dark skinned girls who had actually participated in the picketing of the stores were left out in the cold, while relatives and friends of the 'leaders' who had taken part in the struggles were given employment on recommendation of the reformist leaders. . . ."

The *Liberator's* stand was a most titillating thing to Harlemites, who are acquainted with the exemplary lives of the Communists. For in practice the Negro Communist leaders (in Harlem at least) leave not only the dark-skinned girls in the cold, but also the light-skinned ones. They are all married to white women. The practice became such a scandal that it created a revolt of the colored women among the Communists. This subject will be treated elsewhere.

The *Liberator's* article served its purpose. Evening after evening the rival step-ladder orators of Harlem harangued the crowds on the subject of color discrimination within the Negro group. But the Sufi in his broadside declared that the Communists had a cheek to criticise the Citizens' Leaguers, who were at least married to colored women while the Negro Communist leaders had married white.

Because of the confusion within the Negro group, most of the gains of the campaign were lost.   The stores that had hired Negro clerical help before the injunction, discharged many of them.   All kinds of excuses were given.   Many managers maintained that most of the girls did not measure up to the standards.   What the Sufi had predicted happened. The colored clerks had no union to protect their positions.

In January, 1935, the law caught up with the Sufi at last. He had escaped conviction for disorderly conduct and anti-Semitism.   But he had compiled a pamphlet on the Black Race.   The frontispiece contained a photograph of the turbaned Sufi and under it this verse from Omar Khayyam:

> Oh! my beloved, fill the cup that clears
> Today of past Regret and future Fears:
> Tomorrow:— Why tomorrow I may be
> Myself with yesterday's Seven Thousand Years.

The thin pamphlet of 24 pages purports to be a history of the Negro race and ranges through the ancient world of Egypt.   It extols Hermes Trismegistus as the greatest black man—he had discovered and created the "immortal works known as the 'Caballah' which is now in the hands of the Jewish Race and considered one of the world's greatest philosophical achievements."   Strangely enough, this is the one reference to the Jews that was made by the man who was thought to be an anti-Semite.

The Sufi was arrested and charged with preaching atheism and peddling his pamphlet without a license.   But apparently the real reason was his "Black Hitler" record.   For Magistrate Thomas Aurelio demanded: "Do you regard yourself as a Harlem Hitler?"   The Sufi said he was so persecuted he did not know what he was, but he had never titled himself a "Harlem Hitler."   He was sentenced to 10 days in jail for making a public speech without a license and 10 days for selling a pamphlet without a license.

With all the agitators effectively checked by legal action, the campaign for jobs was discontinued in Harlem.   And

there was peace in 125th Street. That blessed word "Peace!"
—like the Peace of Father Divine and his followers. The
Negro press, lauded by the merchants, could now devote its
precious columns to the recording of petty criminal acts of
switch-blade slashers and muggers, the highlights of Sugar
Hill society and the abstract denunciation of Race Prejudice.

And now, dominating the Harlem scene, Father Divine
herded thousands of bewildered, helpless Negroes into his
kingdoms and made them contented with singing and dancing and ten-cent meals. The Sufi appeared envious of the
almost miraculous Divine success and announced that he
too would return to the black magic of mysticism, where he
could always make a comfortable living.

But the youth of Harlem that he had stirred and led on
the picket lines for jobs could not go back to mysticism with
the Sufi nor acknowledge Father Divine as God. Recently
graduated from the DeWitt Clinton High School, one of
the Sufi's brightest lieutenants, Mr. Phillip Arundel, joined
the Communist Party and soon became educational director
of the Young Communists. Many others followed him.
Still others swelled the rank of the Unemployment Council
and Workers Alliance.

That winter of 1934-35 was an unforgettable desperate one
for Harlem. And on March 19, 1935, Harlem broke loose.
The Black Belt ran amok along Fifth, Lenox, Seventh and
Eighth Avenues, from 116th to 145th Street, and smashed
and looted the stores. The storm broke in the afternoon
and lasted all night long. It was a spontaneous community
protest against social and legal injustice. Stirred out of
their somber apathy, forgetting the differences within the
group between black and brown, the humble and the high,
the bad and the good got together in a frenzied orgy of
destruction. Those who were angry vented their wrath by
smashing the stores; those who were hungry looted them.

That night, while I was dashing from one point to the
other, I met many prominent Harlemites participating in the
party. One of the most unusual was a Harlem playgirl and
relative of one of the most conservative of Harlem's ministers.

Under her coat she was carrying a bag full of bricks and was taxied from place to place hurling them through the plate glass.

The riot started when a Puerto Rican boy tried to steal a pocket knife in Kress's department store on 125th Street. He was grabbed by guards, who attempted to take him to the basement, probably to give him a "whacking." That procedure is often resorted to, even by the police, when a case is too trivial for the courts. But the boy resisted stubbornly. The struggle attracted the crowd of colored shoppers, who tried to rescue him. The guards dragged him below.

The rumor started that they were beating a colored boy in the basement. A crowd gathered and rushed the store to rescue him. The boy wasn't found, for the guards had wisely let him go. But the rumor grew that he was so badly beaten that an ambulance was called to take him to the hospital. Some declared that the boy was dead. And the trouble was on.

125th Street had been the center of many incidents. The boycott campaign had multiplied them. The police contingent had been considerably reinforced. There were so many in evidence everywhere that Harlem appeared like an occupied territory. When the white policeman is sent to Harlem from another district, he regards it as a punishment. Until he is acclimatized his attitude is hostile—at least the majority of Harlemites believe so. There were innumerable provocative police incidents during the campaign. The people had remained calm and docile as Negroes naturally are. But the incident of March 19, more inconsequential than many, finally "blew the lid off." However, it must be recorded that the police handled the riot situation with exceptional tact; otherwise Harlem might have been reduced to a shambles.

A group of scared merchants implored Governor Lehman to dispatch the National Guard to Harlem. But the blow-up was not a race riot at all. White persons as such were not molested. Here and there a few were jostled, but not nearly to the extent they might be during the celebration of a Joe Louis victory. The wrath of the populace was entirely directed against the stores. That was the striking feature about the rioting. All the recent trouble in Harlem had centered in the stores.

If Negroes were anti-Semitic, as the merchants and their friends and stooges were trying to prove, it would have been manifest during the riot. But there was never any anti-Semitism in Harlem and there still is none, in spite of the stupid and vicious propaganda which endeavored to create an anti-Semitic issue out of the legitimate movement of Negroes to improve their social condition. That reactionary attitude has created a certain anti-Jewish feeling, which is strongest among the white-collar blacks, and specially those who were formerly Communists and Socialists!

Nowhere have I seen Jews doing business more peaceably than among Negroes in Harlem. And I have seen Jews among other peoples in Europe and Africa. The Negroes certainly draw no line between the Jews and other whites. The only time that one of the white groups in Harlem was singled out for special attention was during the Italo-Ethiopian War, when Italian business in Harlem was effectively boycotted.

What then is the real situation? The Negro minority nurses resentment against the white majority as such, because against them it maintains a barrier of social and economic discrimination. It is sound Americanism that the Negro minority should voice its protest and exercise its constitutional right to agitate and strive to ameliorate its social status.

Then why accuse Negroes of race hatred against whites, when the truth is exactly the other way around? Communists and radical sophisticates have made much of this, accusing certain Negroes of chauvinism and nationalism, because they so often oppose their methods and decline to associate with them. But what is really behind this attitude? It is that these radicals, mouthing the shibboleths of fraternity and equality between all peoples, actually consider themselves superior to Negroes. This is manifest in their resentment of Negroes who think for themselves. Those who raised against Negroes an indecent hue and cry of anti-Semitism were aiding the forces of reaction. It did not help the cause of Jewry when it was falsely published abroad that even the most oppressed American minority was anti-Semitic.

The Harlem riots brought home to New York the tragedy of the Negro district, a sprawling, menacing, malignant growth in the heart of New York. Mayor La Guardia appointed a commission to investigate. The commission sat in Washington Heights Municipal Court building for many weeks. And it uncovered a stinking manure heap of destitution and starvation, tumble-down firetrap tenements, black rats and white rent sharks, prostitution and crime, police brutality and civic neglect. Five years have passed. A group of low-rent model houses has been erected and occupied, a fine pool constructed and playgrounds built. But fundamentally conditions remain the same. The vast majority of tenements and living conditions in Harlem are horrible.

In the days following the riot Harlem looked like a hurricane-blasted place. When the external wreckage was cleaned up, all thoughts were turned to the Mayor's investigating committee. Clergymen, eminent professional men and women, high-placed social workers, Citizens' Leaguers, trade unionists, Communists and their Young Liberators—all appeared on the witness stand to testify to the intolerable conditions prevailing in Harlem.

But the Sufi did not appear. In fact his picturesque figure had not been seen all during the big disturbance. Now the Black Belt was quiet again. All agitation subsided. The merchants were demanding payment from the city for the destruction of their property. The Negro élite hoped that some solution of Harlem's problem would come out of the investigation.

Then the Sufi startled black aristocrats and white merchants by starting again in the same old way. He did not even wait for the outcome of the investigation. From his step-ladder above the pavement the Sufi thundered: "The investigation will not solve your problem. Harlem is expecting a miracle, but nothing can save Negroes but themselves. The Communists and Socialists cannot; Republicans, Democrats cannot save Negroes." It was odd to listen to him all tricked out in his Oriental toggery. When I challenged him about it and his recent reversion to the practice of mysticism, he said that there was so much religion and regalia in the soul of the Negroes one could do nothing with them without some show of it.

At this time the Sufi's headquarters was in a dilapidated old store at Fifth Avenue and 135th Street. He divided it, holding union meetings in one part and in the other attempting to run a combination grocery-and-butcher store for his followers. New adherents had sold him the idea of cooperative business among Negroes. It had split his intelligent student group off from him. They thought the Sufi had all he could handle in trying to organize Negroes and get jobs for them, and should not confuse the movement by mixing it up with a dubious business enterprise. The Sufi could not see the sense of their objection, for he himself was an unusually strange mixture of opposing elements.

Under the banner of the Afro-American Federation he led the non-intellectual remnant of his following on the picket line. The Harlem Press began pecking at him again and declared that Sufi was a danger to Harlem. His activities were stopped by court action in July, 1935. The Manhattan Lerner Company instituted suit for an injunction against the Sufi's Afro-American union. Again the court action was based upon the issue of race. The Sufi could not escape his race, whether he wore a Hindu turban, or British officer's belt, or Russian high boots. Since he had laid hold of his first conviction, he had ingeniously changed his propaganda method and always began with a proemial statement that Africa was the cradle of religion, that the original Semites are Ethiopians, who are the true Negroes, and that therefore there can be no fundamental conflict of race between Negroes and Jews. The Sufi failed to understand that such conciliatory statements could not help him at a time when the mighty Nordic Nazis were raining propaganda upon the world in an effort to differentiate the Jewish people from the rest of the white world!

Bernard J. Axelrod, attorney for the Lerner Company, said the aim of the Sufi was to drive the whites and particularly the white Jews out of Harlem. Also for the plaintiff, Fred R. Moore, Harlem's hoariest politician, and the editor of the (Negro) *Age,* deponed that Sufi's presence in Harlem and his activities were deplored by all law-abiding citizens. Sufi said that if it were his intention to drive the whites out of Harlem, he would not be demanding that they give jobs to Negroes. He was only asking the white merchants to cooperate with the colored community. An important witness in his favor was Dr. Charles A. Petioni, who stated: "The ideals of and the principles of Hamid and his organization are for benefit of the community of Harlem and organized society." Supreme Court Justice Cotillo ruled that the Sufi's organization was not a labor union, and handed down an injunction against its activities. Thus the remnant of the Sufists was disbanded. And the Sufi again retired to the mumbo-jumbo of African fetishism and Oriental philosophy.

Many Negroes could not understand why they were debarred from organizing as a racial group in the field of labor. Negroes are barred from membership in 21 American Federation of Labor unions. And even in those unions which admitted them there were complaints that Negro members suffered from discrimination—and not only from white workers. Sometimes white employers objected to having a Negro worker. Besides, there were other labor organizations which were founded on a racial or national basis, such as the United Hebrew Trades and the Italian Chamber of Labor.

The new spirit that the Sufi had kindled in Harlem remained alive. With the passing of the Afro-American Federation of Labor, the leaders of the Picket Committee of the Citizens' League, Ira Kemp and Arthur Reid, organized the Harlem Labor Union and applied for a state charter. By eliminating the word Negro or Afro-American or Colored they avoided being challenged as "a labor organization based on race."

About that time also the Socialist Negro Labor Committee was formed in Harlem. Its chairman was Frank Crosswaith, Negro Socialist lecturer and organizer for the International Ladies Garment Workers Union. The working committee was composed of twenty-five colored and white trade unionists of New York. There were representatives from the Clothing Workers Unions, the Brotherhood of Sleeping Car Porters, the Taxi Chauffeurs, the Laundry Workers, the Bricklayers, the American Federation of Musicians, the Newspaper Guild, and the Building Service Employees. Congratulatory messages were received from A. F. of L. President William Green and David Dubinsky, President of the Ladies' Garment Workers Union.

The Committee maintains, in 125th Street, a Harlem Labor Center. It is a meeting place for Harlem's trade unionists. One of its principal aims is to iron out difficulties arising between colored and white workers and employers; also to educate Negroes in trade union consciousness, to support the existing bona fide trade unions, to work and fight for elimination of the color bar and to bring all Negroes into the American Federation of Labor.

From its inception the Socialist Negro Committee was in open conflict with the independent Harlem Labor Union. The Negro Trade Union Committee was extremely conservative, while the Harlem Union's avowed purpose was legimately to carry on in the tradition of the Sufists and the Citizens' League for Fairplay. The Negro Labor Committee charged that the independent union was a gang of racketeers. The independent union replied that its opponent was racketeering on the weakness of the Negro in the organized labor movement. It cited the exclusion of Negroes from major American Federation unions and said it was the white workers who needed education in fair play towards Negro workers, and not the Negro workers who re-

quired education in a trade union movement that was
traditionally hostile to them.

The Socialist Negro Labor Committee had no adequate
reply to the issues raised by the roughneck Harlem Labor
Union. Frank Crosswaith, the Chairman of the Committee,
is a former Rand School student and a Marxist of many years
standing. But the problem facing Negroes could not be
solved by Marxian theory any more than could the acute
social problems of the world at large.

.   .   .   .

Then an epochal event stirred up a hurly-burly of labor
action in Harlem, greater and more bitter than anything
that ever agitated the tranquillity of the merchants. The
C. I. O. was organized and started its irresistible national
drive for industrial unionism. Religiously supported by the
Communists, who hated the Socialist Negro Labor Committee as much as they did the independent Harlem Labor
Union, the C. I. O. soon had Harlem humming with its
organizers and pickets.

The C. I. O. declared its primary aim to organize the
disinherited among American workers, the semi-skilled and
unskilled, regardless of nationality, race and color, Norman
or Brahmin birth or previous state of servitude, and most of
Harlem's leaders and former members of the Citizens' League
hailed it as a solution of the dilemma of the Negro worker.
Many were sick and tired of the employment problems, which
were harsher than they had imagined when they linked up
with the movement. And now they thought that as the
C. I. O. was ready to kick race and color line in the face
and organize black and white workers together, there was
no necessity for independent Negro action.

But the leaders and members of the independent Harlem
Labor Union did not fall in with the ideas of the professional
Negro leaders. Fooled and kicked around so much by
politicians and fakers of the whites and of their own group,
they had become chary of promises. Hard experience had
tempered their social attitude. Now that they had formed
their own union, they wanted to keep it.

The battle that raged in the long neglected bootleg labor jungle of Harlem was the strangest and wildest in the history of labor in New York. It started in 1936 with the full-fledged support of the C. I. O., and there were strikes and picketing all over New York. But Harlem was the scene of infernal confusion. The C. I. O. was embattled with the A. F. of L. It was a pell-mell conflict of whites against whites, blacks against whites and blacks against blacks. The Communists, under the banner of the C. I. O., fought the A. F. of L. and the Socialist Negro Labor Committee. And the A. F. of L. and C. I. O., together with the Communists and Socialists, turned like tigers on the independent Negro Harlem Labor Union. But they hated one another so much that they could not agree on a program to combat the Negro union, which they all regarded as the greatest possible menace.

Pressed from different sides, the pickets of the Harlem Labor Union actually fisted for position against the pickets of the A. F. of L. and the C. I. O. And the Negro union possessed one invaluable asset which the others lacked. At night, Arthur Reid and Ira Kemp, the Harlem Labor Union leaders, mounted step ladders and appealed to the people for support. They told of the long struggle against employers in Harlem to get a few decent jobs for Negroes, of battling in the courts and doggedly carrying on in the face of court decrees until finally they had received a state charter. Now the white unions were trying to rob them of their victory. They said that the Communists and the C. I. O. were not interested in placing Negroes in better jobs, that they operated under the slogan, "Black and White Workers Unite," but actually were organizing the whites as clerks and the blacks as menials. *"They* say, 'Black and white workers unite!' *We* say, 'Share the jobs!' "

Although backing the C. I. O., Harlem's harassed intellectuals could not answer the indictment of the independent leaders. The latter were even gaining prestige at last among the merchants. The fight among the whites of the A. F. of L. and the C. I. O. was so brutal, bitter and unscrupulous that it disgusted many of the merchants, perhaps made them ashamed of their earlier intransigeance, and they preferred to give the Negro union a chance.

Despite the formidable funds at the disposal of the A. F. of L., the C. I. O. and the Communists, the independent Negro union was able to hold out against them. Certain local factors worked in its favor. The C. I. O. was organizing the shops without thought of the community's aspiration for better positions. Its few Negro organizers were all in minor positions. The common people said they were selling out the race for a little white favor. The Harlem Labor Union would not organize a store that did not employ some colored clerks.

It was a scandalous fact that the slogan, "Black and White Workers Unite," was not always advantageous to the Negro when it was put into effect. Many employers who hired Negro help would fire them and take on white when their shops were organized and paid a higher wage scale. These employers refused to pay Negroes "white men's wages." And the white workers not only did not fight to keep Negroes in employment, but they took their jobs.

When the Building Service Employees' Union was organized at a higher wage scale, most of the better buildings formerly operated by Negroes were taken by white employees. The Negro employees of this union, with few exceptions, were limited to the Harlem district, where wages are infinitely lower. As it was economically impracticable for the Harlem employers to pay the union scale of wages, or for the employees to contribute the union scale of dues, they were shunted off into a Jim-Crow local known as Building Service Employees Local 32B. Yet so overwhelmingly large was the percentage of Negroes in the Building Service just a few years ago that the initial organization of this group of workers started among Negroes.

Taking the Jim-Crow Building Service local as an example of black-and-white-unite cooperation, the independent labor leaders made effective propaganda against the Communist and Negro radicals who were forever touting it. The C. I. O. charged with fanfare into fields from which they quietly withdrew later on. They tried to organize the moving van workers, of which there are hundreds in Harlem. But they were compelled to drop them, too, because they could not put into application the wages and dues scale of the whites. The economy of Harlem is so lean that the people could not afford to pay for moving. Owners of trucks could not pay their helpers the union scale. Indeed they did not get the business at all, for the poorer class of Harlemites moved their belongings in pushcarts. The C. I. O. dropped like a hot potato the attempt to organize and the Harlem Labor Union took over.

Conditions in Harlem are indicative of what obtains in other Negro districts. Thousands work for whites (and Negroes too) for sweatshop wages. They simply cannot be organized with whites who have a higher standard of wages. But their condition demands something be done to lift these black thousands up to share in the American standard of human dignity and decency. It would benefit the Negro community and the entire American nation.

Once I mentioned to Mr. Manning Johnson the fact of hundreds of Negroes working in the innumerable coffee shops, sandwich shops, fish-and-potato shops, Southern-cooking restaurants, etc., in Harlem. Mr. Johnson is a college graduate, an efficient organizer of the Cafeteria Union and prominent in the Communist hierarchy. I said I thought it would help the community if those workers were welded together in a General Union of Negroes or some such organization. But at the places I mentioned Mr. Johnson sneered as stink-pots.

He was right. These Harlem places cannot be compared to cafeterias downtown. But after all, the whites whom we envy—beating our brains out against the walls of their prejudice—they too began at the bottom. White trade unions did not spring up suddenly as great organizations with huge bank accounts and highly paid officials.

During the year I stayed in Great Britain just after the First World War, I gave much of my time to acquiring information about the trade union movement. One of the unions which interested me most was the General Union of Workers, of which Mr. J. R. Clynes was president. This union was composed of the most despised and neglected group of persons in Britain: the so-called "boots," the charwomen, kitchen workers, porters, errand boys, ditch diggers. It was an unwieldy conglomeration of workers rejected by the craft unions. But that union did not only ameliorate the condition of its members, it radically changed the outlook of the public on the servant problem. It became one of the most influential unions in England. And when the Labor Government took power, its president Mr. J. R. Clynes was made Home Secretary and a member of the cabinet.

Here in America the preponderantly Jewish unions began in the same humble way. They were created out of stark necessity. The Jewish sweatshops were a reproach to New York. Forty years ago a nice Negro girl would consider herself in a better position as a maid in a comfortable family than to be employed as needle worker. Today the order is exactly reversed. And Negro college graduates would feel proud to obtain positions with any of the Clothing Workers unions.

Idealistic yet practical Jewish intellectuals were the original organizers of these unions. They saw the unconscionable suffering and economic disadvantage of the members of their own group. They were part of it and understood the situation more than outsiders. So they helped their people and found an outlet for their own talents. They went to their own people and helped to organize them into unions. They found places for them to meet. They published newspapers in their interest.

Jews were not barred from existing trade unions. At that time the President of the American Federation of Labor was the Jewish Samuel Gompers. And unlike Negroes, Jews as individuals were members of exclusive craft unions. But here was a special situation that the Federation could not handle. Most of the sweatshop Jews were Russian. Miss Henrietta Izold said of them: "The Russian Jews are looked upon by their patrons and by their own leaders as the most unorganizable material among the Jews." Their social welfare was in the hands of the United Hebrew Charities, which was administered by German Jews. It did not always meet the test of acute unemployment and sickness. It was to eliminate the need for cold charity that the educated young Jews assisted their less fortunate brothers to organize mutual benefit associations. Out of that pioneer spade work grew the powerful Jewish unions of today. Some are independent, some affiliated with the American Federation of Labor, but all of them are in the vanguard of the labor movement.

Negro intellectuals who are interested in the labor and radical movements show little understanding of the special needs of their group. They imagine they can escape the problems of their group by joining the whites as individuals. Their approach is academic. And the attitude of the whites is to regard them as novelties. Every radical sect in New York has its Negro exhibit. Socialists and Communists; Lovestonites, Trotskyites, Stalinists. The Stalinists have attracted the largest number, but to them Negroes are mere exhibits: "Negro leaders" hand-picked by the white comrades, foisted on the Negro group and touted as their leaders. Of course the Negroes get the treatment they deserve.

I know some of them in Harlem: such excellent types as Mr. Edward Welsh of the Lovestonites, Mr. Harold Williams, former circulation manager of the *Daily Worker*, Mr. George Streator, former assistant editor of the *Crisis,* who has been an organizer of the International Ladies' Garment Workers' Union, Mr. Charles White, who spilled the black beans before the Dies Committee, Mr. George Schuyler, of the *Pittsburgh Courier,* Mr. Herman Mackawain, who denounced Russia during the Ethiopian war, Mr. Richard Moore, who said he would rather have his right hand chopped off than lose membership in the C. P., Miss Grace Campbell, who said, when I asked her to denounce the red assassins, "I am afraid of getting shot myself." Then there are Mr. Simon Williamson, who has been a member of all the sects, Mr. George Padmore, an exile in Britain, and many others who joined the

Communists during the years when they made hay behind the façade of the Popular Front.

They are all disillusioned, cynical, bitter. They gave the best of themselves to the leftists. They thought that they could belong to the left, where they imagined that race and color were unimportant. At last they discovered that such things were important, that they were *colored* comrades. And because they were not closely identified with their group they had no group influence in the radical movement, such as the Finns, the Russians, the Poles and the Jews enjoy. Some of them have turned away from the left in bitterness to find that they have little in common with the feelings and aspirations of their own folk. Having lost contact and sympathy with the whites, they remain more or less forlorn unattached souls.

Of the many educated Negroes who have felt the powerful pull of the modern movement of the worker, A. Phillip Randolph is one of the few who made it serve the interests of the Negro group. He is perhaps the only one who has attempted to do for his people what the Jewish intellectuals did for theirs. For many years Mr. Randolph was an academic Socialist. Possessing a fine presence and a grand voice, he was a high light of the Socialist tribune. He was one of the editors of the most brilliant radical Negro magazine, *The Messenger*.

Then, back in 1925, he became interested in a movement for organization among the Pullman porters. It was a natural interest; many educated Negroes have worked as Pullman porters to obtain a college education. Mr. Randolph gave up active work as an academic Socialist to devote his time to organizing of the Pullman Porters. He accepted the presidency of the porters' organization. Ably assisted by Secretary-Treasurer Ashley L. Totten, former Pullman porter, he worked to organize the porters and to win recognition from the powerful Pullman Company, which was supporting a company union of the porters.

It was a desperately hard struggle. Often the organizers could not meet the bill for their dilapidated office and hall.

Sometimes Randolph took no salary. He received tempting offers in other fields and bribes to quit. But he had a vision of a national Negro union of Negro workers, competently officered and intelligently led, a union that could demonstrate that colored people were also organizable. And he followed the light.

The members of the Brotherhood of Pullman Porters were continually spied upon and victimized. Randolph worked out a plan by which the membership roll was kept secret and known only to himself and the secretary. But it was not a struggle only against the Pullman Company. It was also one against other labor unions. The A. F. of L. International Hotel and Restaurant Employees' Alliance, the International Bartenders' League and the Pullman Car Conductors endeavored to block the American Federation of Labor from granting a charter. They had never lifted a finger to help organize the Negroes, but now that they were organized they claimed jurisdiction over them. Randolph defeated the "chiselers" and the A. F. of L. granted a Federal charter in 1929.

But the meanest enemy of the Pullman porters' union was the American Communist Party. In press and on platform the Communists engineered a bitter campaign of denunciation against Randolph. They trotted out the eternal scarecrow of Segregation and made it look as terrifying as a lynching victim. They depicted Randolph in alliance with the makers of the national Jim Crow policy. In Harlem they attempted to break up his meetings. They sent Negro Communists to them with chains on their hands and feet to demonstrate that Randolph was enslaving the Negroes again. The Negro Communist leader, James W. Ford, put Randolph among the fakers and betrayers of the Negro people for having "brought the Brotherhood of Sleeping Car Porters into the Jim Crow American Federation of Labor."

But when at last Mr. Randolph triumphed over all opposition in 1935 and became the national president of a union with the right to sit in the highest council of the

A. F. of L. to plead the cause of the Negro worker, the Communists made a rapid about-face to chant his praises.

The Communist International had just launched the ambitious movement of the Popular Front to fool the world and take Democracy for a grand ride. Concomitantly the American Communists created the National Negro Congress in the beginning of 1936. This was a grandiose and purely fluid organization, which brought together hundreds of Negro organizations, little and big, to represent the Negroes nationally and internationally. It received extensive publicity and consideration from public officials and prominent persons that was far in excess of its actual significance. But the Communists are experts in the publicity business.

Affiliated more or less under the Negro Congress were the leading Negro organizations, which the Communists had formerly done their best to bedevil and disrupt: the National Association for the Advancement of Colored People, The National Urban League, the Garvey rump of the Universal Negro Improvement Association, and the leading Negro churches. The Popular Front against War, Fascism, Nazism and anti-Semitism appeared to be of such urgent and vast significance for all of humanity that no liberal or humane organization seemed able to abstain without compromising itself with large numbers of its supporters. Apt students of the Russian method and a ruthless pressure group with a perfect technique of overt and covert propaganda, the Communists could put any opposing organization in an unfavorable and untenable position. Then there is the fact that the Communists can stage some of the most spectacular affairs and could bring obscure Negroes into the spotlight to speak in splendid halls before huge audiences.

Undoubtedly Mr. Randolph's prestige contributed immensely to the success of the Negro Congress. Mr. Randolph is not a vain man, nor can he be intimidated. He is perhaps the most honest and incorruptible of Negro leaders. His record as a young radical lecturer, magazine editor and subsequently labor organizer is the most exemplary in the history of the Negro. A Socialist of the Debs school, he is quite aware of the unscrupulous, intriguing and destructive tactics of the Communists, for he has combated them over a number of years. It must be presumed, therefore, that he headed the Negro Congress because he believed that the Communists were really sincere when they adapted a neo-liberal style of clothing and promoted the Popular Front in the interests of Democracy.

Operating through organizations like the National Negro Congress, the Communists have exerted wide influence over the Negro minority. This is especially true of educated Negro youth, who are more easily swayed by resolutions and slogans denouncing social injustice than are the working masses who are interested in practical action. This does not mean that educated Negroes are all Communists. Perhaps only a small part of a faction are actually members of the Communist Party. But they have been largely influenced by the Communist policy of the last five years in its domination of the Popular Front. Even literary, artistic and cultural Negro organizations of that Front, or Façade, were promoted and controlled by Communist units.

To maintain the social exactions of the Popular Front, the Communists plunged gaily into respectability, aided by dollars without stint, tails, white tie instead of red, caviar and champagne. And the degree of their rapid social transformation may explain their implacable hostility to the organizations of humble working people, like Negroes, who instinctively opposed them. Since they failed to make any headway among the Negro masses during many years of propaganda, the new Communist scheme was to corral them through the agency of the organizations of educated Negroes.

The jobs-for-Negroes campaign was especially anathema to the Communists. It was like pins in their hides, because it unmasked them before the colored community as hypocritical enemies who opposed its realistic demands, while parading under the symbol of unity among black-and-white workers.

.   .   .   .

James S. Allen, the white Communist expert on Negro

affairs (that same expert who authored the plan of a Negro nation within the nation, carved out of the black belts of the South), and Communist Negro leader James W. Ford denounced the danger of the movement towards race segregation and singled out for special attack Sufi Abdul Hamid and Ira Kemp of the Picket Committee. In collaboration they wrote: "Among the new movements . . . are those which aim to obtain 'jobs for Negroes'. . . . These movements confine their activities to establishments in the Negro communities. So small and few are these business houses that it is clear they could only provide a limited number of jobs for Negro workers and would in no way help solve the problem of mass unemployment. These movements have the effect of hindering the struggle for unemployment insurance for all workers and for adequate relief."

But the will of the common people to promote some practical undertaking that might help them in their economic distress was so patiently persevering that even some of the theorists among the Negro Communists were moved by it. Thus Miss Grace Campbell, city employee and oldest Negro member of the Party, organized a group to found a co-operative business. Following the new party line Miss Campbell had chosen competent persons from the professional group of Negroes to help her.

Miss Campbell believed that co-operative enterprises would help the Negro masses, if they were educated to appreciate them. She said that besides picketing the white stores for jobs, the Negroes should build their own little stores. Her group opened one co-operative grocery store, but it received no support from the Communists. As a pioneer Communist Miss Campbell expected more support from her comrades in the initial phase of her enterprise.

She delivered many speeches to explain the co-operative idea. She was an old friend of mine and once I accompanied her to one of these meetings. It was well attended. The Negro Communist leader James W. Ford presided. Miss Campbell appealed for Communist support and new members to join the first store that was opened. She said she believed that the Communists should do something other than simply agitate to help the community, for the people's grievances were just. She pointed out that the white merchants made their profits in the Harlem community and spent it all in other communities. None of them lived in Harlem or spent their money there. She said she had made a study of the English and Scandinavian co-operatives, which began in a small way and grew considerably.

Miss Campbell made a simple, earnest speech and the audience was moved. But when she had finished speaking, Comrade leader James W. Ford took the floor and declared that real Communists could not support their own comrade Campbell's scheme because it was not Communist! The black-red leader said that the time had passed when Negroes could consider establishing co-operatives. The English and Scandinavian co-operatives were founded in the heyday of Capitalism. Then co-operatives were a middle way. But now that Capitalism was undergoing a rapid decline, its inevitable successor was Communism, and Negroes therefore should not tinker with co-operatives. Comrade-leader Ford again cracked down on the jobs-for-Negroes campaign. Said he, "It is dangerous to the real interests of the Negro masses for the leaders to advocate the replacement of white workers employed in Negro neighborhoods."

It is of interest to record that not long after the white directors of the Uptown Chamber of Commerce had convinced the Negroes that they had not a chance to compete with whites in other districts, they conceded the Negroes' right to replace "white workers in Negro neighborhoods" and announced that one-third of clerical jobs in Harlem would be given to Negroes.

Meanwhile the feeble infant of the Sufists and the Citizens' Committee, the Harlem Labor Union, struggled for existence. But its nourishment was poor, its nurses incompetent, its enemies formidable. Besides the defeatist Communists there were powerful forces in the A. F. of L. and the C. I. O., who were apparently alarmed at the prospects of the development of an independent Negro union.

They enlisted the aid of the educated Negroes to fight the union. The Communists have made a careful study of the educated Negro and are aware of his weakest points. They know that Segregation is the delicate, sensitive issue about which few educated Negroes are sane and logical. They know that by professing a belief in social equality without actually practicing it, they can rip the clothes off an educated Negro and leave him naked but contented. Their Negro fronts were all too eager to fight the independent union as a segregated organization.

Adam Powell, Jr. cleric of that gargantuan church, Abyssinia Baptist, with a vast army of domestics as members, denounced the independent movement as nationalistic and a danger to the race. The opponents of the Harlem union were plentifully supplied with dollars. They hired Negro mercenaries to steal the members of the Harlem union and bring them into the A. F. of L. and the C. I. O.

The Harlem union organizers went out into the field that the A. F. of L. and the C. I. O. had ignored: grocery stores, butcher shops, pawnshops, shoe repair shops and bars (for Negro bartenders were not let into the real A. F. of L union). But as soon as the Harlem union organized the men, the black spies of the A. F. of L. and the C. I. O. enticed them away with a promise of higher wages and fellowship with white workers. It was obvious that the enemies of the Harlem union were not interested in organizing the Negro workers but only in preventing them from getting organized among themselves.

With no help from those educated Negroes who had a knowledge of the labor movements, the survival of the Harlem union appeared miraculous. It was haled before New York's district attorney and the Labor Relations Board, and accused of racketeering, but somehow it pulled through. Its members could not be confused by propaganda. They had faith in it. Caught between the forces of the A. F. of L. and the C. I. O., scabbing and picketing one against the other, denounced as advocates of racial segregation by the

Negro élite, bombarded by Communist defeatist propaganda, they needed faith indeed in something of their own.

All through 1937 Harlem was a hectic scene of conflict between the opposing racial forces. Representing the A. F. of L. and the C. I. O. and supported by some of the best citizens of Harlem, the Socialist Harlem Labor Center declared war on the independent Harlem Labor Union. The chief charge was that the independent union was not a union but a petty racket. Now it appears that the Negro opponents of the independents were not so greatly aroused about the big white racket of the trade unions. Just when they were denouncing the independent Harlem union because it was said that a couple of unscrupulous members had "shaken down" store owners for small sums, it was disclosed that one of the large waiters' unions was in the hands of notorious crooks. And recently it has come to light that the Building Service Employees' Union, with its segregated Negro local, was presided over by a racketeer no better than the white overlords who blackjacked the black numbers operators into submission.

If the Communists became less open in their opposition than previously, it was because they desired to bring the entire Negro minority into the Popular Front. They had secretly adopted a new policy to refrain from an open attack on *any* Negroes. So they obtained stooges instead to carry out the "dirty work." Also, serious defections had taken place among the Negro comrades. The Communists were in the front ranks of the Negro protest against Italian aggression in Ethiopia. They had made effective propaganda of the fact that Russia, through Foreign Secretary Litvinoff, had opposed the Fascists at Geneva.

But when it was uncovered that Russia, while spouting idealistic froth about the rights of small, weak nations and colonial peoples, was actually delivering oil, manganese and other war material to Italy to wage war against Ethiopia, there was a bitter reaction among the Negroes. Herman Mackawain, a prominent member, quit the Party and took with him many more members to form an all-Negro group.

Naturally he also gave his support to the independent Harlem union. Mackawain was rebuked by his former comrades for black chauvinism.

There were defections also when Senator Black was nominated to become a justice of the Supreme Court in 1937. The Communists endorsed the nomination, so also did the Communist-controlled National Negro Congress. The endorsement by the Negro Congress was a scandal because many prominent Negro leaders and organizations were opposed to the nomination when it became known that Senator Black had been a member of the Ku Klux Klan. His endorsement by the Negro Congress gave the nation the impression that the Negroes were not aroused over the senator's Ku Klux Klan background.

Had it been proved that the senator was a secret Nazi agent, would Communists and other Leftists have supported his nomination? That was the question that many Negroes asked. They did not think, as did the Communists and Leftists, that the senator's admirable record on social legislation was qualification enough. Moreover, when the senator broadcast his speech to apologize about his former membership in the Ku Klux Klan, he said specifically that he was not anti-Semitic, but never mentioned the Negro at all. Negroes wondered if their group was so negligible that it did not require special mention. For they know that although the platform of the Ku Klux Klan is also against Catholics and Jews, the program of the Ku Klux Klan in the South is directed primarily against the Negroes, supporting the denial to them of civic rights and economic opportunity and intimidating their lives.

Negro Communists wrote to the *Daily Worker,* protesting the appointment of Justice Black to the Supreme Court and his endorsement by the Communists. The letters were not published. Instead, the editor invited the writers to that newspaper's office for a verbal discussion of the issue. Thus the Negro comrades could not get their dissenting view before the public.

·   ·   ·   ·   ·   ·   ·

The struggle for independent Negro unions and for the right of Negroes to organize and seek employment as a racial group was recognized by a Supreme Court decision of March, 1938, when it was ruled that as discrimination against Negroes in terms and conditions of employment was based upon difference of race and color they possessed the right to make special demands for employment upon that basis.

The decision was a stinging rebuke to the Communists, Socialists and the defeatist horde of the Negro intelligentsia who had opposed the crude yet constructive efforts of the black masses to organize themselves. Many of them now rushed into the arena to take advantage of the situation. In Harlem, the foremost opponent of the independent Negro movement was the young minister of the Abyssinia Baptist Church, Adam Powell, Jr. He set up a Coordinating Committee to seek jobs for Negroes which had the support of the Communist Party. The *Daily Worker* gave the Communists credit for promoting it. A rival organization was sponsored by the *Amsterdam News*.

Sufi Abdul Hamid, who had startled Harlem with his foreign make-up and his spectacular picketing, boycotting and parading, lived long enough to rejoice in the Supreme Court's decision. But he no longer was surveying the uncharted territory of labor, for he had retreated into the jungle of the occult; merchants and law officers do not invade these precincts, in which members of the black élite are submissive. He had increased his store of the wisdom of the Orient by marrying a high priestess of neo-African fetishism. Together they had just thrown open the door of an elaborate Buddhist Temple of Tranquillity, which they hoped would outshine the kingdom of Father Divine. A few weeks later the Sufi went aloft in an airplane in which he intended to demonstrate his mystic powers. It crashed, and ended his career.

But Ira Kemp, militant president of the independent Harlem Labor Union, was not destined to know that his rough-and-tumble struggle for the right of Negroes as such to organize was supported by the highest authority in the country. He had continued the fight where the Sufi had left off. But he died suddenly in December, 1937. He was able to gauge his popularity among the people of Harlem the summer before, when he ran as assemblyman on the Republican ticket in a Democratic New Deal stronghold and failed of election by only a few score votes. It was the first time that an ordinary, uneducated Negro of the common people was put up as candidate for such a position. The large number of votes for Kemp showed which way the community was drifting.

Kemp was given a grand funeral in the Abyssinia Baptist Church. Vast numbers overflowed the church and filled the streets to pay him their last tribute. The Rev. Adam Powell, Jr., who had opposed the work of the man, delivered a marvelous display of eulogy over his corpse.

The independent Negro union struggles and struggles along. Between the A. F. of L. and the C. I. O. on the one hand, and the District Attorney and the Labor Relations Board on the other, it has a hectic time. Its membership is loyal and persevering, but its leadership, which originally excelled in the rough, pioneering tactics of picketing and boycotting, lacks organizational ability and a clear conception of the labor movement in its relationship to the Negro minority. In December, 1939, all its officers were compelled through pressure from the District Attorney's office to resign. The present president is Mr. Francis Minor, who was formerly the chief aide of Sufi Abdul Hamid in his job campaign.

Perhaps the one person who is intellectually and practically equipped to make this union a shining success is Mr. Phillip Randolph, the President of the Brotherhood of Pullman Porters. But even if he were willing, the job might overtax his physical resources. Fifteen years of strenuous work among the porters have sapped his robustness and left him in poor health. Besides, the porters' organization requires all his attention.

The transformation of Mr. Randolph from a Socialist theorist and lecturer into a constructive organizer and leader in the labor movement is a significant augury of the future role of the Negro minority in the national scheme. Mr. Randolph, more than any other Negro leader, has a comprehensive understanding of the vast conquests of modern industry and the grand movement of labor to keep abreast of it. And he is aware that the Negro group is in a special position and has a special force. His outlook remains unblurred by passion and prejudice. He takes a long-balanced view of men and affairs. He could not be tagged with radical, chauvinist, nationalist, or reactionary labels, or with any other slanderous names such as the Communists and the other labor henchmen attach to those colored people who oppose their unscrupulous exploitation of Negro organizations in the interests of Soviet Russia.

Mr. Randolph believes that the Negro group must cooperate, but only with other American groups. He believes that the mainspring of the Negro minority lies within itself.

When the C. I. O. was launched he did not rashly remove the Brotherhood of Pullman Porters from the A. F. of L. and into the new organization. He preferred to watch developments. His attitude was criticised. Yet he envisaged industrial unionism as labor's goal in place of the craft unionism of the A. F. of L. Also he was a friend of John L. Lewis, who had nobly aided him in his fight to bring the Pullman Porters into full membership in the A. F. of L.

Although the National Negro Congress, from its inception in 1936, was manifestly controlled by the Communists, Mr. Randolph, just elected president, released this statement: "The National Negro Congress, as its name plainly expresses, is a Negro movement, and it has been projected to fight for Negro rights. It was not, is not and will not be dominated by either Communists, Republicans, Socialists or Democrats. Being a Negro movement, it naturally includes Negroes of all political faiths as well as Negroes of various religious creeds and denominations."

But as president of the Negro Congress he had little control over and knowledge of the activities of Secretary John P. Davis. At the conclusion of the second annual meeting of the Congress in October, 1937, Mr. Secretary Davis rushed off to Moscow, there to give an account of the American Negro, while the members of the Congress were left without any report of the proceedings. Engrossed in the executive work of his union, Randolph was not aware that the Communists had complete control of the apparatus of the Negro Congress.

But at last he arrived at a realization of the fact. He also discovered that the Communist Party was contributing $100 monthly to the secretariat of the Congress. When he resigned the presidency at the annual Congress meeting held in Washington in April, 1940, Randolph declared: "I am convinced that the National Negro Congress has not succeeded in removing from the mind of the public the idea . . . that the National Negro Congress is a Communist Front and a transmission belt for Communist propaganda. . . .

"American Negroes will not long follow any organization which accepts dictation and control from the Communist Party. The American Negro will not long follow any organization which accepts dictation and control from any white organization. . . .

"Whatever is the source of the money with which the Congress is run, that will also be the source of its ideas, policies and control. . . . I am opposed to the National Negro Congress depending upon the Communists or the C. I. O. for its financial maintenance. The Congress should be uncontrolled and responsible to no one but the Negro people. . . . When the National Negro Congress loses its independence, it loses its soul and has no further reason for being. It also forfeits and betrays the faith of the Negro masses. . . .

"I am not only opposed to domination of the Congress by the Communists, but I consider the Communists a definite menace and a danger to the Negro people and labor, because of their disruptive tactics in the interest of the Soviet Union. . . .

"The Congress is not truly a Negro Congress. Out of some 1200 delegates assembled at the 1940 Washington convention 300 are whites, which made the Congress look like a joke. It is unthinkable that the Jewish Congress would have gentiles in it or that a Catholic Congress would have Protestants in it. . . . Why should a Negro Congress have white people in it?"

President A. Phillip Randolph was isolated among the members of the mammoth Negro Congress, over which he had presided with great skill and distinction for five years. He carried no group of delegates with him when he made his speech and resigned. Effective Communist maneuver took care of that. Yet he had said exactly what the Negro in the street had long been discussing. During the days of tribulation of Sufi Abdul Hamid, the National Negro Congress was often discussed by common groups of Negroes, who thought that if the Sufi were to take his case to the tribunal of the Negro Congress, he would only discover that its higher-ups were white and red and against him and his works.

.   .   .   .

The Harlem aggregate of the Workers' Alliance was one of the finest units of that organization. It comprised over a thousand members and was in charge of a West Indian Negro, Louis Campbell, and an American, Mrs. Frank Duty.

Mrs. Duty is an interesting example of the radical colored woman. She is a brown woman of mixed strains, practical-minded and with a flavor of Gallic realism. The Negro men among the Communists appear romantic and confused. But the Negro women, who are not the artistic, bohemian type, are different. When Mrs. Duty broke away from the Communists in the fall of 1938 she said something publicly which the many colored women members of the party had been discussing privately for a long time.

Mrs. Duty said the Communist Party was hurting instead of helping Negro life, for all the bright Negro men and all the leaders were connected legitimately or otherwise with white women, while the Negro women remained wallflowers. There were a few instances of insignificant white comrades who were married to or keeping company with Negro women. But no white party leader had a Negro wife, while all the Negro leaders had white wives.

In Negro circles, this is a frequent topic of conversation, especially among the women. They assert that the Communists get Negro men to join by seducing them with white women. This interesting subject has never been discussed in Negro publications. It is one of those subjects of exciting gossip which are considered unprintable. Negroes won't air it, because intermarriage is one of the sorest problems agitating the group. The white world overwhelmingly disapproves of it. The average white man loses all sense of logic when he discusses it and the intellectual develops a neurosis. Yet the mulattoes increase and the Negro minority is growing lighter.

Negro leaders and intellectuals believe that this is one issue on which the Communists are correct. They believe that any man under a democracy should reserve the right to choose his mate. Yet, however much they may be fascinated by one of the opposite type, rarely does one of them marry out of his group. This is not because of the white taboo, but because the white wife will be ostracized by all the "high-toned" Negro women. The white wives of Harlem have had such a rough time from the Negro matrons that recently there was organized an Association of White Wives of Negro Men to promote friendly social intercourse among themselves.

Negro intellectuals are becoming as neurotic as the whites about this matter, albeit in a different way. To them, the white taboo, especially in the South, is unreasonably objectionable. Negro men bitterly assert that only two types of persons are really free—sexually free—in the South: white men and colored women. However keenly the Negro men may resent that state of things in the South, they are not much happier in the North, for the Negro women are right there, keeping them in line.

The Communists, in trying to break down that taboo, discover that their most formidable enemy is the Negro woman. She remains the bulwark against the Communist penetration of the Negro minority. I remember visiting in 1938 the pioneer Negro member of the Party, Grace Campbell, and finding a group of women assembled at her hotel. They had come together to discuss the subject of all the Negro party leaders' being married to white women. They were a bitter lot. They argued that it was an insult to Negro woman-hood that their radical leaders should take white wives, especially as the Negro woman is nationally regarded as being on a lower social and moral level than the white woman. They felt that the Negro Communist leaders were supporting the general national attitude by marrying white wives. The thing was not reciprocal in the Communist Party, for the white Communist leaders were not marrying colored women. The Communist Party therefore was not truly an uplift organization trying to solve the Negro prob-lem, for it was creating an altogether new social problem.

The assembled women were emphatic in objecting to Negro Communist leader James W. Ford's having a white wife. Because, said they, she cannot be *our* leader, she does not understand the problems of Negro women. They drew up a resolution to forward to Comrade Stalin and the Executive of the Communist International in Moscow, pro-testing against Communist Negro leaders marrying white women.

I have never been informed of the outcome of this resolu-tion. For I was soon regarded in Harlem as an enemy of the Communist fake Popular Front and a Potential Fascist and my dear friend of many long years, Grace Campbell, decided that I could no longer be her friend because I was "the enemy of her class and her spiritual Fatherland."

When Mrs. Frank Duty quit the party she made a public issue of the hitherto unmentioned subject. She declared that the Communists were demoralizing the Negro group by seducing its men with white women. She said they were not interested in helping Negroes to a better life. They paid the white supervisor of the Harlem Branch of the Workers' Alliance thirty-five dollars a week and gave the Negro or-ganizer who did all the spade work five dollars a week. Mrs.

Duty and Louis Campbell withdrew from the Workers' Alliance, taking with them seventy-five per cent of the membership to form a non-Communist group. Nearly all the dissidents were members of the Communist Party. Many were relief recipients. The Communists employed subterfuge to have them cut off relief. But as a group they fought back.

Mrs. Duty gave evidence before the Dies Committee. Another interesting witness was Mr. Charles White, a Communist-made writer, who told about his military training in Moscow. But more extraordinary from the aspect of race and intermarriage is Mr. White's private story of his marriage to a white comrade. It focuses fresh light upon a subject which no ordinary white or colored person will discuss logically.

Mr. White is an imposing tower of a black Negro. He was born in Georgia and grew up in Ohio. His father was a preacher. He joined the Communist Party in 1930 and in 1931 was sent to Moscow. There he was indoctrinated with Bolshevism and received a year's practical training as a red volunteer. Upon his return he married a white comrade. His wife's parents were orthodox Jews and disapproved of the marriage. This is not unusual: Negro parents are as much opposed as are white parents to mixed marriages. (In one case in Harlem a Negro refused to see his daughter after her marriage to a white comrade. And he believes that because of his attitude, the hidden hand of the Communists lost him his job.)

Charles White, like most Negro Communists who are not paid functionaries, was more interested in the progress of his race in America than in the defense of Soviet Russia. That is to say he was more race-conscious than class-conscious. He came into contact with a group of Negroes who were concerned about the welfare of their race and were not convinced that it could be improved through the cathartic progress of the Soviet system. Some of these Negroes were former members of the Communist Party and expelled for over-emphasis on racial consciousness.

Mr. White carried on a lively secret correspondence with the anti-Communist Negroes. His white wife discovered the letters. She turned them in to officers of the Communist Party. At a convention in Chicago, some of these letters were read to the assembly. Mr. White was reprimanded for his action and warned to revise his ideas in order to qualify as a real Communist. But the Ethiopian conflict was under way and Mr. White became even more chauvinistically African in outlook. He was one of those who openly criticized Russia for selling war materials to Italy to wage war on Ethiopia. Because he refused to heed the warning of the Party he was expelled. His wife left him, taking their baby. Mr. White had become attached to his child and desired a reconciliation. He states that his wife refused to see him and said that *she married him as a duty to the Communist Party and she could be reconciled to him only if he confessed his error and begged to be readmitted to the Party.*

His wife, refusing to let him see the child, wrote: "First make your peace with the Communist Party. It is a hard turn, but it's the only turn that will give you life and aspiration. Let the intellectuals and petty bourgeoisie have sympathy with the anti-Communist groups. You belong with us."

Perplexed by the sentiment of home and family life (such as it was), of loyalty to the Communist Party and to his racial group, Mr. White still remained unconvinced that the Communists held the solution of the problem. However, the young father's heart hankered after the five-year-old fledgling of misalliance. One afternoon he visited the place where the mother was living. He found the child with a friend of the mother and took it to a nearby shop to buy it candy. The mother returned and discovered the child "missing." She telephoned a description of White to the police and had him apprehended for "kidnaping." The case was finally adjudicated in the Domestic Relations Court. Mr. White produced a witness who stated that he overheard his wife say, "I will get Charles White and put him in jail for the things he did against the Communist Party, for anybody who does as he did to the party deserves to be in jail."

There has been considerable aimless talk among white and colored folk about sexual relations between colored and white Communists, talk that suggests an orgy of looseness and immorality. But so far as I have been able to gauge, there is far less social happiness and physical enjoyment in the mixed alliances than is conjured up by prurient persons. The Communists appear to be as disciplined, as realistic and objective in the adjustment of their private lives to party needs as in their politics.

As the White case illustrates, it seems that the Communist whites who marry Negroes make the sacrifice solely in the interest of the Party. They are more like missionaries, or spies, whose primary purpose is holding Negroes to the party line.

The following letter was written jointly by Mrs. Frank Duty and Louis Campbell, erstwhile Communists and organizers of the Workers' Alliance. It is illuminating and interesting as evidence, and as the opinion of two intelligent Negroes who were placed in a position to estimate from the inside the demoralizing result of the work of the Communist Party among Negroes.

EDITOR OF THE NEW YORK AGE:

Some of our confidential friends inside the Harlem Division of the Communist Party, whose names we cannot expose at this time, have informed us that Mr. Ford, Mr. Berry and Mr. Basset, the leading Negro stooges of Mr. Browder in Harlem, are circulating a report that Duty and Campbell, who broke from the Communist Party some time ago and formed the Afro-American Union of Unemployed and W. P. A. with Negroes dissatisfied with the policy of the Workers' Alliance, are seeking re-admittance into Mr. Stalin's organization.

Positively no. We are out of the Communist Party and we intend to stay out. We have organized the Afro-Amer-

ican Union of Unemployed and W. P. A. workers as an all-
Negro group to defend the rights and to take up the grievances of our indigent people, and we are determined to keep
it as it is, free from subversive influences.

But in going about the task of organizing the destitute of
our race, we realize that there are obstacles in our way. We
are acquainted with the subtlety of Jas. W. Ford and his
Communist cohorts. We passed through their school of
thought and are aware of the trickery used by them and their
white Communist masters to discredit every independent
effort of Negroes to organize and become strong and self-
reliant. We know that the white Communists fear the organized national and international might of the Negro more
than they fear the capitalist system. And, moreover, we
have learned how they develop and use Negro weaklings (the
so-called radical intellectuals of the race, as Peeping Toms
to disrupt independent Negro business and spread malcon-
tent among the ranks of their own radical organization).
And because of our awareness of the corruptness of the "Communist movement" (sic!) as we have so often-times stated,
we see in it one of the worst enemies that our people can
have.

We have no intention of changing our position on organized Russian Communism. We wish the public to know
that we regard it as another brand of totalitarian dictatorship
analogous to Hitlerism in Germany and Fascism in Italy.
We believe that the economic and social structure of those
three states are similar in every detail, and that when sufficient moves have been made on the political checker board
of Europe and America, the world will find the Three
Musketeers, Russia, Italy and Germany, allied, each killing
his share of Jews and advocating racial inferiority of all
weaker and darker races.

(Mrs.) *Frankie Duty*
Louis Campbell

New York, N. Y.
    January 21, 1939

Louis Campbell was a West Indian immigrant who had lived in this country about fifteen years. He was formerly a seaman, but had taken French leave of his banana boat to enter the United States without benefit of legal declaration. This fact was known for many years among his Communist comrades. But nothing ever happened to him. However, when he quit the Party it was not long before his secret was known to the proper authorities. He was recently arrested and deported for illegal entry.

·   ·   ·   ·   ·   ·   ·

The launching of the Popular Front simultaneously with the setting up of the New Deal's W. P. A. gave the Communists that vast influence among colored professional groups which they could not succeed in wielding among the masses. The W. P. A. gave hundreds of college-bred Negroes their first opportunity at clerical jobs. And their attitude was different from that of many white workers who had held better positions before the depression and regarded W. P. A. as a stop-gap only. As the Communists were the most efficient organizers of the W. P. A. workers it was natural that they should make headway among the Negro white-collars who, unlike many whites, had no previous radical affiliations.

Under the aegis of the Popular Front, the Help Ethiopia and the Negro Aid for Spanish Democracy groups enlisted leading Negro ministers, doctors, nurses, teachers, actors and the rest of the Negro intelligentsia. The black bohemians of the pre-depression era were influenced by white friends, many of whom became seriously social-minded after 1929, visited Soviet Russia and were enlisted under the banner of the Popular Front.

The Communists actively organized the Emergency Relief Bureau Workers. But soon a militant nucleus of colored workers generated opposition to the Communists. They complained that the white comrades, while mouthing fraternity and equality and promoting interracial affairs, were taking all the best jobs for themselves. The discontented nucleus organized a majority of Negro workers of the ERB into an association called the Metropolitan Guild. It proposed to take steps directly to protect the members against Communist intrigue and to win promotions. The Communists were opposed to the Guild and denounced it as a segregated group whose aim was to separate the Negroes from their white comrades. But the Guild was supported by non-Communist whites. Father Mulvoy of St. Mark's Roman Catholic Church was one of its most active supporters.

An almost similar situation arose among Negroes on the Federal Writers' Project. The New York Project set up groups of several nationalities—Italian, Jewish, Negro and others—who were engaged in special work pertaining to these groups. But as soon as the writers became organized the Communists started a whispering campaign to the effect that the Negro writers were segregated on the project. There was no truth in the accusation. Many Negroes on the project were engaged on other assignments and were working with white writers. But the Negro group was doing special research work and some of us preferred it, because the facts we unearthed were of intrinsic value to those of us who were writing about Negro life in our off-project time.

All of us went in at the same door, used the same sanitary conveniences and signed the same time sheets, and there was friendly contact between these white and colored workers, who felt they had something in common. Into this atmosphere the Communists injected the poison of Segregation. Then, strangely enough, a Negro Writers' Guild was organized in Harlem. Most of its members were little known in Harlem as writers, but they were on the project and were putty in the hands of the Communists. None of us who had any reputation as writers was asked to join, but the assistant director of the New York Federal Writers' Project and the white supervisor of the Negro group were invited to their meeting. The assistant director was said to be a former Communist Party member who had resigned when he was appointed to the high administrative post. But those who understood the inside methods of the Communists asserted that the resignation was not real but a blind, as the Communists did not want members who held important positions to be known as party members.

Two of Harlem's most expert journalists were on the project—Mr. Henry Lee Moon, who contributed occasional articles to the New York *Times* and Mr. Theodore Poston, the New York *Post's* Harlem reporter. They had recently lost their jobs on a Harlem weekly because of their Newspaper Guild and strike activities. I spoke to them about the Negro Writers' Guild and said we ought to join and checkmate the Communists. But Moon and Poston refused because they were jealous of their craft standards and did not rate the members of the Guild as first-class journalists. I joined up.

Soon afterwards the famous Federal writers' sit-down strike was sprung. It had been whispered for some two weeks that a strike was due. Certain of the Communists said they had "inside information" from Washington. That "inside information" trick was played by the comrades to the extreme note. They always knew before the rest of us when administrative changes were going to occur, when there was to be a lay-off of workers (even the names of those who would be laid off), when promotions would take place and who would be promoted. Naturally, then, it appeared to everyone that the Communists controlled the Writers' Project, and all the motley gang of careerists who wanted advancement or some consideration were submissive to and fawned upon them.

When we learned about the strike, we who were not on the inside called it a "company" strike. And it certainly was. It was a strike in which the rank and file paraded and starved for the benefit of the little bosses. It was a kind of strike that any real labor leader would be ashamed of and of which only Communists could be proud. It lasted a week. On the second day all the supervisors passed through the picket line and signed the time sheets. We of the rank and file were amazed. Why should the supervisors, whose wages were double and treble our own, be allowed to scab on the rank and file? Yet the few members of the rank and file who decided to pass through the picket line and sign in were booed and pilloried.

We demanded to know why this was, and were told that the supervisors were being organized and the Communists desired to placate them so that they might be easier to organize! Thus they were allowed to break through the picket line, and each supervisor agreed to contribute a day's pay to the strike fund. A meeting of the supervisors was held to discuss the issue. Some of the members belonged to the Newspaper Guild unit. At this meeting the Harlem journalists Moon and Poston were the only persons who protested against the supervisors' passing the picket line. They contended that this practice was having a bad effect on the rank and file workers, that, if anything, the supervisors should be setting an example of solidarity with these workers by staying away from the office. A few of the supervisors who had not shed all ideas of manly decency, despite contact with Communists, were sympathetic. But soon it was whispered around that the supervisors' action was entirely approved by the Communist Party unit, and Moon and Poston were squelched.

The supervisors received their week's salary and donated a day's pay to the strike fund, most of which, it was rumored, found its way to the coffers of the Communist Party. The Administration tried to soften the effects of the strike for the rank and file and sent out forms for the workers to sign in place of the time sheets. It was a purely nominal thing, which would have insured the payment of the week's wages lost. But the Communist leaders of the strike advised all the employees not to sign. And they posted pickets to spy upon all who did. It was all right for the rank and file to lose a week's wages and tighten their belts in the interest of Communist Party discipline. But not the supervisors! It was a heyday for the Popular Front when the Communists were so careful not to offend the sensibilities of the better people.

The two strange creatures of backward Harlem who tried to teach the Communists a lesson in human decency, Henry

Moon and Theodore Poston, paid the penalty of their audacity. The Communists, active in supporting and financing Harlem's *Amsterdam News* strike, had expected that Moon and Poston would show gratitude at least and become good "fellow travellers." For these two Harlemites had been chalked up on the Communist blacklist for over five years—ever since they did their part in exposing the ruthless opportunism of the red apostles of idealism!

It all happened in that historic period of 1932-33, when Franklin Delano Roosevelt and Adolf Hitler rose to the leadership of two great nations. Up until then the Kremlin was still ostensibly the pretended champion of the working people, suppressed minorities and the rest. And as a part of its world program, a group of American Negroes were summoned to Moscow to make a documentary film of Negro life in the United States. The idea first took form in the Scottsboro year of 1931. The group of some twenty persons was headed by the poet and storyteller, Langston Hughes, and Moon, Poston and other prominent persons of the outmoded Negro Renaissance set were members. They arrived in Moscow towards the end of 1932.

But before anything could be done on the film project, Hitler, now at the helm of the German nation, was already directing his flaming threats against the mighty seat of Bolshevism. And the Kremlin, seeking allies, was hastily editing its idea of white America towards its black minority. Among other things of major importance, so infinitesimal an item as the Russian projection of a film of American Negro life was abandoned.

Limited and confined to the provincial theater of Harlem, few of the members of the troupe were aware that they were minor actors in a vast drama in which the idea of a red film of black oppression in America was less than a blade of seaweed washed up on the shore of the mighty ocean.

The Negro Film Group was extravagantly entertained in a series of receptions by Moscow politicians and cultural groups. They met big men of the Russian Film industry and there were perfunctory conversations about the Negro picture. But weeks petered out and there was no action preparatory to the making of the film. At last the Negro troupe was informed that because of inadequate material and technical difficulties the decision was taken to scrap the project.

Nearly all the members of the company accepted the decision without protest. They had had a fine trip and the Russians had given them a good time in the lavish Russian manner, as they do when they desire to woo people. But the newspapermen, Moon and Poston, remained dissatisfied. Attracted to the Communists mainly by the Scottsboro case, they had given up their positions on the Harlem weekly to go to Moscow with the one purpose of making a Negro film. Ferreting out the real reasons why the film was not to be made, they discovered that the Kremlin was already angling for United States recognition of the Soviet government. And the Negro picture which Moscow intended to make was such a trenchant indictment of American civilization that it could not have contributed to friendly relations between the two nations. Moon and Poston released their findings to foreign correspondents in Moscow and the story was sent around the world.

It enraged not only the Moscow Communist hierarchy, but the entire Comintern. They denied the assertions and declared that the Negro picture was abandoned for purely cultural and technical reasons, which were non-political. As if there is anything in the Communist conception of life that is not political! Through its leading Negro spokesman, James W. Ford, the American Communist Party published a refutation of the accusation and castigated the two obstreperous Negro journalists. Speaking for the rest of the company, Mr. Langston Hughes said that "the newspaper reports of the Film group are absolutely untrue," and that the film would be made in the spring. But that spring Moscow was busy baiting its hook for much bigger fish than the Negro. And in the spring the Kremlin shed its proletarian red shirt and donned a stiff white front to enter the democratic League of Nations.

Following this incident, Moon and Poston were having a hard time among the "redskins" of Moscow and were glad to get away and back to America with their black skins intact. Reprimanding Mr. Moon for releasing private Communist items to bourgeois newspapers, a big red official said: "You would not be so bold if you were in Georgia."   Mr. Moon replied that when he published the facts, he had not imagined that a Negro should feel afraid in the utopian metropolis of Moscow.   If it were not for the publicity they obtained through the bourgeois press, Moon and Poston might have landed in an "utopian" jail.

Thus the two Harlem journalists earned themselves a place on the red blacklist.   And when they returned to America, many Communist-inspired innuendoes were printed about their character.   Indeed, the Harlem comrades were hostile to almost the entire film group.   They were often referred to as "moral degenerates"—that delectable phrase which Moscow reserves for "the enemies of the Soviets."

However Moon and Poston were the most capable newspapermen in Harlem, and with the launching of the Popular Front and the National Negro Congress their friendly cooperation might have been invaluable to the Communists. But the young journalists would respond to no more blandishments.   And now again, during the Federal Writers' strike, they had dared to expose the Communist double-crossing of the rank-and-file writers.   The result was that immediately after the strike they were summarily expelled from the company of the supervisors and reduced to rank-and-file status. The administrative excuse for this act was that the junior assistant supervisorship, or master writer's rank, which they held, had been abolished.   But for many succeeding months other writers of that rank were carried on the payroll.

The Negro Writers' Guild had received front-page notice as one of the units.   At the first meeting that was held after the strike, I told the members that such front-page publicity was of no material benefit to the Negro group on the project.   And since the guild was recognized as representing the Negroes among the Federal Writers, they should demand something concrete from the union. I submitted that the guild should ask the union to recommend the promotion of capable Negro writers to the post of supervisor. The three supervisors of the Negro group were all white, enjoying nice salaries. I thought that if the fraternity-and-solidarity always flaunted by the comrades in the union was something real, it should be translated into something substantial.

But instead of acting on the question of Negro supervisors, the Communists again agitated against the segregation of Negroes within the group. Nothing was said about segregation of the other racial groups in the project. The red heart was bleeding for the poor Negro. Why not? If there were no Negro group, the Harlem Guild might not be demanding Negro supervisors! The next step in the comedy was to plant a number of white writers among the Negro group. Down at the union hall and at Communist meetings there always were notices drawing the attention of members to the Negro minority as a special field in which to gather material for literary and theatrical innovations. But there never was any appeal to Negro writers and artists to explore the white field.

When the Negro Writers' Guild convened again, a Negro Communist came with a white woman whom he proposed for membership. For many years this woman had been interested in Negro uplift and she devoted much of her time to the cause. She had undertaken special investigations for the National Association for the Advancement of Colored People and acquitted herself brilliantly. She published articles about the Negro in distinguished magazines. Her work in the interest of fairness and justice to the Negro minority was purely unselfish and so ardent and incautious that she had paid dearly for it. She was a staff worker on one of our great charitable organizations which, although considered to be above all prejudice, had followed a secret policy of discrimination against the Negro. She divulged the fact that it cost her her job.

The Negro Communist brought this woman to our Guild

meeting and sprang her candidacy on the members without previously consulting them.   She desired to join because she considered herself a friend of the Negro minority.   That was her qualification for joining a Negro guild.   The situation was embarrassing, just the kind that intriguing Communists delight in.   None of us there who were opposed to a white person's joining a Negro guild had any desire to wound the sensibilities of this fine-spirited woman.   But the unpleasant thing had to be done and we had to inform her that we wanted the guild to remain Negro.

She could not understand this.   She taunted us with condoning the Jim Crow policy and segregating ourselves.   The Negro Communists sided with her.   A non-Communist member said the Communists were trying to break up the guild by forcing in a white person as member.   The white woman informed the meeting that she was not a Communist and was opposed to some Communist measures.   But it was precisely because she was not a Communist that the situation was so confused.   She was a left liberal of Abolitionist tradition.   Perhaps she was not even aware that the Communists were using her to disrupt our group, precisely as they had done with liberal groups in promoting their innumerable "front" organizations.   The very thing we feared now occurred.   The Communists got enough of their members to swing the vote in favor of admitting a white person as member.   However, the officers of our organization were opposed to a white person's becoming a member of a Negro Guild.   They quit with the records, and left the rump of the Negro Guild to the Communists.   It died.   In releasing the incident to the Negro newspapers, those who opposed the candidacy of the white woman were made to appear as advocates of Negro Segregation.

A few of us tried to bring the Negro writers together in an organization with the late James Weldon Johnson as President.   There are about twelve creative writers of some distinction in Harlem and an equal number of journalists.   No one could accuse James Weldon Johnson of believing in any kind of Segregation.   He was a member of numerous

white cultural and artistic organizations, and his prestige
then meant much in setting up a group, especially as he was
a lecturer on Negro culture at New York University. He
was the perfect person around whom we could organize—
well balanced, a meliorist in his attitude towards race relations.

A representative group of us came together: Miss Zora
Neale Hurston, Mrs. Jessie Fauset Harris, novelist of the
Negro intelligentsia and teacher of French at DeWitt Clinton
High School, Mrs. Regina Andrews, Head Librarian of the
115th Street Library, Mrs. Catherine Latimer, Reference
Librarian at the 135th Street Library, Miss Marcia Prender-
gast, the late Arthur Schomburg, curator of the Negro Division at the 135th Street Library, Mr. Earl Brown, Editor of
the *Amsterdam News,* Henry Lee Moon, Theodore Poston,
Bruce Nugent, M. Casseus, a Haitian writer, Countee Cullen
and myself.

At an initial meeting James Weldon Johnson pointed
out that he could see no segregation in Negroes having their
own all-Negro groups. It was something like a man organizing his own household and running it in his own way. He
could have his neighbors in as guests, and they could cooperate on general lines, but they could not be members.
Negroes had the same larger human interests as white people,
but also they had peculiar interests which could be worked
out only among themselves. For example, any group of
Negroes who are freely discussing relations between colored
and white persons will say things they never would if a white
person were present, unless they intended to be rude.

However, Negro intellectuals among themselves, even more
than the masses, are hard to organize. The Harlem renaissance movement of the antic nineteen twenties was really
inspired and kept alive by the interest and presence of white
bohemians. It faded out when they became tired of the
new plaything. And so even the prestige of James Weldon
Johnson was of no avail. Most of the Negro intellectuals
were directly or indirectly hypnotized by the propaganda of
the Popular Front. Anathema to them was any idea of an

exclusive Negro organization.   It was not merely segregationist: a new label was made, isolationist.   The League
of American Writers was open to every Negro who professed
to be a writer, and its propaganda was active in Harlem.
Any insignificant coterie of whites could get the proudest of
the Harlem élite scampering downtown to a meeting.   Suddenly, tragically, James Weldon Johnson was killed in the
spring of 1938.   And the group of Negro writers came together for the last time at his funeral.

.   .   .   .

The Harlem artists encountered difficulties similar to
those of the writers and other cultural Harlem groups.
The graphic arts have the largest numbers of students among
those young Harlemites who are spurred by the creative
spirit.   Through the agency of Adult Education two art
schools for youngsters were established in Harlem.   Harlem artists, like other American artists, were groping under
the pall of Depression.

They were youngsters compared to the writers.   Five of
the more mature decided to organize as a group in 1935.
They were Charles Alston, Henry Bannarn, Romare Bearden,
Aaron Douglas and Augusta Savage.   Their purpose was to
band all the Harlem artists together in a cultural group.
Their immediate object was to obtain jobs and relief for
artists of the Negro Belt.   There were over 50 of them.   The
Y. M. C. A. provided a meeting place.

Perhaps there were only three Communists in the midst
of them.   But even one Communist in a group of a hundred
can be as annoying as a blue fly if he hews to the Party line
and takes the lead in all discussions to promote the Party's
point of view.   And this was exactly what happened to
the Harlem Artists' Guild.   None of the founding members
was a Communist.   They were interested in the details of
placing their members on art projects and discussing constructive phases of art work.   The small Communist faction
tried to make a Communist tribune of all the meetings.

Nor were the founding members rabidly anti-Communist.
Some were previously with the Vanguard Group—one of the

first of the "Front" organization in Harlem, which was created to bring professional and artistic Harlemites together in a propaganda group. Since the Communists had promoted themselves as the champions of Negro rights, few intelligent Negroes could oppose their ideas without being placed on the defensive as opponents of Negro progress.

The Harlem Artists' Guild was kept in a constant state of irritation by matters having little to do with their material and cultural interests. Above all other things the Communists wished to get white members into the guild. And so they started agitation against the Negro artists' segregating themselves. They brought white artists from downtown and proposed them for membership. The founding group objected. Theirs was a Harlem Guild; there were regional problems peculiar to Negro artists living in Harlem. They did not want as members white artists from downtown who did not understand the needs of Harlem. In fact they had organized among themselves precisely because they were dissatisfied with conditions under the downtown College Arts setup.

The Communist zealots adopted ridiculous subterfuges to obtain their ends. They sent up white artists from downtown to reside in Harlem and qualify as members. Events came about which unfortunately are not suitable for these pages, because they would appear better in the form of fiction than of fact. Still the artists preferred to keep their organization as it originally was.

However, the intrigue had its effect upon the body of the membership. The Communists got around the youngsters who were pupils of the founding artists. And the founding members were voted out of all executive positions. The guild became an adjunct of the American Artists' Union and lost its effectiveness as a social force and instrument of inspirational contact among the artists of Harlem.

One afternoon I was visiting a studio and nearly all the founding artists were present. They were discussing the crisis which had resulted in their elimination from the guild. Said one of them, who was an artist of the Harlem renaissance period: "I realize now that the Communists are powerful and it's no use Negroes trying to fight them. For Negroes are weak, but the Communists are strong. They have some of the most powerful people in this country behind them. And although I dislike them, I am going to play ball. I've got to live."

Not long afterwards, this artist was receiving favorable mention in the *Daily Worker*. Soon he was the happy recipient of a scholarship. He traveled abroad. Upon his return a fine reception was given to him downtown and his pictures exhibited. Many notabilities among "fellow travelers" of the Communists were present. And also the most exclusive of the Harlem élite.

It is not my intention to insinuate that the source from which this artist received pecuniary assistance was controlled by Communists. In fact I know that the president of one of the foundations which helped him is emphatically anti-Communist. But the Communists, as the artist said, have captured a vast, limitless field of influence under the aegis of the Popular Front.

Is it to be wondered at that all the Harlem people who wanted to eat and live above the gutter should, as did that artist, stop fighting when the odds were against them? What happened to writers and artists happened also in the fields of religion, amusement, education, journalism and social work. To tell about each one individually, I should have to entitle this book, "The Reds among the Blacks."

What took place in Negro Harlem must have occurred in different degree among white groups. But among Negroes the crisis was probably more acute. The white world is wide and complex and its boundaries are elastic. A savage onslaught of propaganda is not so powerful and effective as it may be in the Negro world, where all strata are close-packed and the propagandists can leap to action like wolves in an overcrowded sheepfold.

Manipulating poison letters, having the local news agencies feature canards and hoaxes, sending pressure letters to politicians and other notables and picketing individuals

and establishments, the Communists have used every imaginable weapon to blackmail those Negroes who, believing in
the larger interest of their group, have had the courage to
withstand their pressure.

In floating a colossal fraud to snare one of the largest American minorities, the Communists have succeeded in making
Negroes more internationally conscious than ever before in
their history. The Garvey movement stirred the group emotion of the Negro masses to a high pitch of Negro Zionism—
so that they sought some vague place in Africa as a spiritual
refuge. The Communists promoted among the educated
groups the notion of Soviet Russia as the one political state
which stands for social justice for oppressed peoples. Despite the blood purges, the wholesale uprooting of peasant
populations and Soviet Russia's aggressions against small
countries, this idea remains fixed in gullible minds.

Yet perhaps the greatest danger of the new orientation of
the Negro intelligentsia is internal—within the group itself.
It is the danger of demoralization. Educated Negroes say
among themselves that *no* Negro is really Communistic.
The late Kelly Miller, shrewd professor at Howard University, once remarked that the Negro radical is an educated
West Indian without a job. That may have been true
enough in the pioneering period of Communism. But when
Moscow ordered the Party to Americanize itself prior to setting up the Popular Front, the leading West Indians were
eliminated as Garvey nationalists or Trotskyites, and the
large numbers of native-born Negroes from the colleges who
paraded with the red flag must have amazed Kelly Miller.

But if the Negro intelligentsia who march with the Communists are not sincerely Communist-minded, why then do
they rally to the Communists? I believe it is because they
imagine they can use the threat of Communism among
Negroes to wring concessions from the major political parties.
And it is this attitude which makes the Communist philosophy
such a grave internal danger to the Negro minority. Other
minority groups and weak and subject nations have invited
disaster by pursuing such a policy. There were the Ar-

menians in Turkey, the Chinese being bandied between the
Japanese and European Powers, the Poles, the Czechs and
the Ethiopians.   They were the footballs of foreign nations
who agitated and protested in their behalf.   But when they
were faced with a supreme crisis, they had to stand and fight
alone.

Even while the Communists here were corralling Negroes
into the Popular Front in 1936, they were at that time
cruelly deceiving the natives of North Africa (Algeria, Tunis
and Morocco) who became victims of Imperialist reaction.
For many years the native organizations, mildly reformist in
character, had the support of the Radical and Socialist parties
in France.   The Communists, outlawed from the colonies
by the Metropolitan government, had no influence among
the native intellectuals until the launching of the Popular
Front and the advent of the Blum Government gave them
their chance.   But soon the native organizations became the
first casualties.   In 1935 the Socialists vociferously welcomed
them to the Popular Front.   And the Communists, who were
affiliated with the Socialists, egged them on to increase their
demands for native reforms.   When the Blum Socialist government came to power and rushed through special laws
providing higher wages and shorter hours for the French
workers, the North African native workers naturally expected that they too would be beneficiaries of the new social
legislation.   Their status as colonials compared with that of
the French workers as the status of the cotton pickers of
the deep South compared with that of the skilled workers of
the North.

As nothing was done for them, they agitated.   The big
colonists were aroused.   The colonial administrations took
action.   The Communists were the loudest in denouncing
the native agitators, declaring that they were Fascists and
under the influence of German and Italian propaganda.
The Socialists of the home country were embarrassed.   The
Popular Front included not only workers, but the influential
middle class and all the liberal intellectuals.   To grant the
native demands they would have alienated the vast army of

functionaries and middling colonists whose support was necessary. The problem was solved by denouncing the native organizations as Fascist and expelling them from the Popular Front. Thus the radical ideas fostered by Socialists and Communists among the natives became Fascist ideas—when they were inconvenient to the radicals. The native organizations were suppressed by the colonial administrations and their leaders arrested and imprisoned.

With a fair knowledge of the situation in North Africa and with supplementary information from American and native friends in Morocco, I wrote an article about the actual conditions which was published in "Commonsense," of March, 1938. The *Daily Worker* must surely have been informed of the true facts about the native unrest in North Africa. But it preferred to suppress them. It carried nothing about the progressive native movements. It was too busy depicting Moroccans as savage pagans engaged in a holy war against Christian Spain.

The Communists would just as readily betray the Negro minority here in America if it suited their purpose. It should be plain why they are seeking to penetrate every Negro organization. The Negro intellectual, apparently becoming neurotic and therefore confused on the issue of Segregation, may not perceive that the Communist maneuver is to make an appendage of his race—a red Uncle Tom of Communism. They are striving for control of the political mind of the Negro so that they may do his thinking for him.

But now, more than ever, Negroes should think for themselves. It is hurting their cause when any organization not truly representative sets itself up as their national and international spokesman. Wild-eyed, panic-stricken neurotic whites who cannot think how to save themselves from the bankruptcy of their own isms, certainly cannot think for the Negro people.

Marcus Garvey said: "The Negro intellectual is the greatest fraud and stumbling block to the progress of the race." In this severe indictment Garvey was undoubtedly justified by his own experience.   The implacable opponents of his abortive attempt to lead the great body of his people were intellectuals who themselves lacked the magnetism of popular leadership.   Popular movements of another era, such as Sufi Abdul Hamid's, encountered similar misunderstanding and destructive opposition.

Yet the popular, as well as the intellectual, movements of the Negro people are based on the same fundamental of racial consciousness.   What then, is the real difference between these two forces which have split the Negro minority and neutralized its potentialities ever since its emancipation? The difference lies in the Negro people's instinctive urge to group themselves, to distinguish themselves as a responsible, integral part of the American commonwealth as against the intellectuals' resistance to this effort, which they combat as a measure of Segregation.

Both groups nourish the same grievances against white Society as such.   But instinctively the commonalty of colored people seek some practical way of compromise and adjustment to this white society, because no individual or group can be happy living under an eternal grievance.   On the other hand, the intellectuals apparently find psychic satisfaction in a tangle of race problems and in resistance to the sane measures which may eventually untangle them.   Thus the practical body of the Negro group and its romantic intellectuals are locked in a long internecine struggle on major and minor issues.   And the conflict is intensified, perhaps, because the white society which they resent is beyond their reach.

While the Negro masses seek to promote responsible Negro leadership as a means of normal adjustment to the American way of life, the Negro intellectuals balk their aspirations by supinely abdicating their prerogatives to white leaders, who have no deep understanding of the Negro people.   The Negro intelligentsia's flirtation with the Communist hierarchy is illuminating.   Some critics imagine that the professional classes—preachers and teachers, social workers, stage personalities and artists and writers of the National Negro Congress —are not aware that it is Communist led.   But such critics are fooling themselves. The Communist-minded Negro intellectuals of today are as aware of their position as the Republican-minded Negro intellectuals of yesterday. For decades the Negro minority was the pliable ward of the Republican Party. But in the larger interest of the Nation and the ward itself such an arrangement could not continue· forever. Some day wards must grow up and assume responsibility. I believe that the Negro intellectuals turn to the Left (if there is anything "left" to the Communists but their betrayal of the spirit of human progress) out of resentment of the treatment accorded them by the Republican Party.

But as Communist policy is determined by Soviet Russia, which is mainly influenced by political events in Europe and Asia, I fail to understand the American Negro intellectuals, who imagine that they will eventually obtain great social advantages by aligning themselves with Soviet policy rather than by fighting forthrightly a hard battle with American parties on the American continent.

Because of its unconstructivism and defeatism, the Communist and even the Socialist philosophy of life is inimical to the interests of the Negro people. Upon the platform and in print, Negro Communists and Socialists have preached that Negroes should not support Negro business, because it is an incipient rash of the Capitalism which class-conscious workers are pledged to destroy.

Less quixotic members of the other minorities have not scrupled in using Radicalism as an instrument to serve the interests of their particular group. But in their zeal for a chimerical Utopia, Negro radicals have done their utmost to starve the Negro belly. The Negro radicals have come finally to find themselves on the same platform with the more conservative race-radical wing of the group, who scent Segregation in every serious attempt of Negroes to adjust themselves to the American pattern of life.

The Communists have put over the Defense of Soviet Russia on the National Negro Congress: Soviet Russia right or wrong. The black Marxists are apparently unable to think out to its logical premise the importance of having the Negroes defend America first even if under its social system they are a minority without advantages. They cannot answer the question, why should not the Negro first defend America and fight to make it a better place for himself to live? Instead they religiously endeavor to promote Russia as the sacred, the holy land.

They cannot answer the criticism that Soviet Russia, founded upon the principle of Karl Marx's conception of industrial society, is a failure. Marx's ideology of the Class Struggle enjoyed a universal popular appeal because it buoyed up the people with hope that injustices and prejudices between different classes and races would be eliminated from society and humanity benefit from a classless world. But the Russian Soviets simply set up a proletarian Dictatorship to persecute all other classes. The Communists destroyed Royalty, Nobility, Aristocracy. They exterminated the Capitalist class. Ruthlessly they fell upon the middling class of engineers and technicians who were essential to their gigantic job of post-revolution construction. Finally they turned viciously upon one another, suppressed free Trade Unionism, terrorized unorthodox members of the proletariat and uprooted millions of peasants for labor in concentration camps.

Some Communist critics place the catastrophic débacle of Communism on Stalin's doorstep. But upon analysis it is apparent that they really blame Stalin for not being more extremist. Yet Stalin is no more than an instrument of the perverted idea of the Class Struggle. Some of us saw the system at work in Russia under Lenin, before there appeared the faintest sign of Stalin becoming the Russian Dictator. We saw the remnants of the middle classes existing without hope, even though they were partisans of the Revolution and worked loyally for the Communists. There was no future of a tolerable life for their children. Even if they were being educated in the Bolshevised schools to work for the Soviets, they were haunted by the fear that inevitably they would be replaced by children of what were considered to be the *real* proletariat.

Instead of a classless society, the new class of reds was persecuting the defenceless classes, even as Czarist Black Hundreds hounded the revolutionists under the *ancien regime*. It is not to be wondered at since the Russian Revolution has revealed its true character to the world, that people, wherever they are faced with the ultimate choice of Communism or Fascism, prefer the latter with its perverted principle of national or racial unity as against the internecine class war of Communism. Even if Capitalists and bondholders may be altogether ruthless and reactionary as a class, they are aware that if the working class is destroyed, their capital is worthless. It took the Russian Revolution to teach the working people of the world that if they destroy the technical engineering brains of industry they will be helpless.

Evidently the failure of the social experiment of the Russian Revolution inspired its principals to establish the Soviet as a sacrosanct state with an infallible government. The bigoted disciples of Marx transferred their heritage of faith from the domain of religion to that of social science and soon became a universal menace. For all of mankind has had experience of divinity and infallibility in religion, sometimes, with catastrophic consequences. And the Communists, under the pretense of modernism and progressivism, were pushing the world backwards beyond the divine rights of kings to the mysticism of dictatorship and infallibility in political and social science. Expertly mixing the ingredients of orthodoxy and heterodoxy, they appealed directly to the primitive religious instincts of the masses in the vast field of modern industry, which, more than any, requires expanding scientific research and free intellectual enquiry. Yet, strangely enough, it was the intellectuals and intelligentsia of the world and not the masses who were fooled and stampeded by Communist tactics.

The Negro intellectuals of the colleges and the National Negro Congress have merely consistently followed the lead of their white half brothers—with a difference, however. While many of their outstanding white colleagues wisely ran to save themselves when the Communists ripped off their masks and flashed daggers, the Negroes stood emotionally fixed like the boy on the burning deck.

The intellectual, discovered in error, is as vicious as a tiger. And in this the Negro intellectual is like any other. He fights the popular movements of his people because he knows that they are right and he is wrong. He is aware that the avenues normally open to Negroes are limited and that Negroes are faced with making a choice. They may choose to allow an unscrupulous white faction such as the Communists to exploit them. Or extreme nationalists may prefer to learn from the Indians and obtain "Negro Reservations." Then, there is the possibility of intensive culture of the Negro communities, eventually to become more effective in the national life.

The aggregated community idea of Negro life is expressed in the great pioneer effort of Booker T. Washington in the Tuskegee Institute. By his special work among his people, Booker T. Washington made Tuskegee a model for the nation in vocational training. From the confines of Tuskegee he reached out to stir the world. And he drew the world to visit and learn from Tuskegee. In his time rulers and statesmen and educators delighted to honor him. His has been the most constructive mind among Negroes since Emancipation. Yet there was nothing startlingly new in the plan of Booker T. Washington. He followed the ancient classic way of all peoples who work together for self preservation and advancement. It was the way of the Anglo-Saxon pioneers who won America from the Indians. It is the way of all European groups that have settled in America.

Booker T. Washington was bitterly opposed by that northern group of Negroes who saw the specter of Segregation in his efforts to create a model Negro institution. Their most militant mouthpiece was the Massachusetts-born and Harvard- and-Heidelberg educated William Ewart Burghardt

DuBois for twenty-five years the foremost animator of the National Association for the Advancement of Colored People. Dr. DuBois created consternation among the intellectuals of his group in 1935, when he resigned from the National Association and declared himself a partisan of the Booker T. Washington plan of facing the future of the Negro in America. Immediately he was tagged as a Segregationist by a formidable array of opponents, and his ripe experience of over twenty-five years of research and journalistic work is rarely publicized for the enlightenment of the group.

In building up the National Negro Congress, the Communists have shied clear of the classic personality of Booker T. Washington. They chose instead the vibrant romantic figure of the great Negro leader of the Abolitionist period, Frederick Douglass. Yet Frederick Douglass was so opposed to Communism that he became estranged from those white abolitionists who were partisans of Communist theories. Present-day Communists also ignore one of the most interesting items in the career of Frederick Douglass, the occasion of his forfeiting his enormous influence among Negroes by taking as his second wife a white woman. There was hostility among some of his white admirers, but the greatest intolerance was on the side of the Negro group.

The idea of the constructive development of Negro communities commercially, politically and culturally, should be actively prosecuted, in spite of intellectual opposition. The Negro minority has been compelled of necessity to create its own preachers and teachers, doctors and lawyers. If these were proportionately complemented by police officers, sheriffs and judges, principals of schools, landlords and businessmen, etc., the Negro community, instead of remaining un-American, would take on the social aspect of its white counterpart. Undoubtedly this would result in the easing of the tension of the race problem and Negroes would begin to regard themselves more as one other American minority. At present, in overwhelming majority, they see the world divided as white humanity against colored humanity. Most of their social difficulties, the setbacks in the struggle for existence, even congenial handicaps, are attributed to white malevolence. A perusal of the Negro Press attests this. It is a dismal, negative lamentation of prejudicial discriminations of the white world against the colored.

Negroes are irritated by the attitude of white police; they complain of the unfairness and apparently contemptuous demeanor of white judges. If there were more Negro than white police in colored communities, if there were a proportionate number of Negro judges, clerks of court and other officials, the feeling of the colored people towards American justice might undergo a salutary change. They would not always think in terms of white justice and colored victims. They would soon discover that Negro officials, like white ones all belong to a special pattern. The Negro masses would have the proper respect for the official and educated members of their group, which is so generally lacking under the present set-up. The whites would have a more balanced appreciation of the Negro group and its talents.

The Communist approach to the Negro is doomed to failure. By its ardent proselytizing it has militated against the normal development of friendly relations between the colored and white people. People do not want interracial friendships thrust down their throats like a purge. But by their aggressive and tactless tactics the Communists have only succeeded in stirring up resentment among intelligent Negroes. Some of the latter have reacted like people who cut loose from restraint after experiencing a formidable exaltation at a missionary revival campaign.

There is no short cut to Utopia, if Utopia is realizable. Russian Communism has not resolved the problem of minority groups. Indeed it has served overwhelmingly to aggravate it. In Russia I met Armenian, Ukrainian, Lettish, Esthonian and Jewish intellectuals who were preoccupied with the future adjustment of each particular group. If national and racial problems were automatically eliminated by the establishment of a Communist State, the Soviet government need not have discovered the necessity of founding the autonomous colony of Birobidjan for the Jews. And it is not to the credit of Communist Russia that Palestine should have attracted more Russian Jews than any other type.

Russia has a great lesson to teach. And Negroes might learn from it just what they should not do. They can learn enough at least to save themselves from becoming the black butt of Communism.

Books by Claude McKay

available in paperbound editions
from Harcourt Brace Jovanovich, Inc.

BANJO, HB 185

HARLEM: NEGRO METROPOLIS, HB 224

A LONG WAY FROM HOME (AUTOBIOGRAPHY), HB 172

SELECTED POEMS OF CLAUDE MCKAY, HB 161